the CERTAINTY TRAP

Can Christians and Muslims afford the luxury of fundamentalism?

the CERTAINTY TRAP

Can Christians and Muslims afford the luxury of fundamentalism?

BILL MUSK

WILLIAM CAREY LIBRARY

The Certainty Trap: Can Christians and Muslims afford the luxury of fundamentalism?

Cover: Hugh Pinder
Typesetting: Mark Harvey

Published by William Carey Library
1605 E. Elizabeth Street, Pasadena, California 91104
www.missionbooks.org

William Carey Library is a ministry of the
U.S. Center for World Mission, Pasadena, California
www.uscwm.org

Printed in the United States of America.

Library of Congress Cataloging-in-Publication Data

Musk, Bill A.
The certainty trap : can Christians and Muslims afford the luxury of fundamentalism? / Bill A. Musk.
p. cm.
Includes bibliographical references and index.
ISBN 978-0-87808-519-4
1. Missions to Muslims. 2. Christianity and other religions--Islam. 3. Islam--Relations--Christianity. 4. Religious fundamentalism. I. Title.
BV2625.M86 2007
297.2'72--dc22

2007027354

by the same author

THE UNSEEN FACE OF ISLAM
HOLY WAR
TOUCHING THE SOUL OF ISLAM
KISSING COUSINS?

Contents

Figures		ix
Preface		xiii

A certain belief

Chapter One	"Fighting" means fighting, for heaven's sake!	3
Chapter Two	This is the way the world ends!	20

Questioning certainty

Chapter Three	Sorry, I didn't really mean that!	37
Chapter Four	Here's what that really means!	60
Chapter Five	It makes sense if you take into account . . .	78
Chapter Six	Relying on a text	109
Chapter Seven	Securing a holy Bible?	128
Chapter Eight	Ascertaining a holy Qur'ân?	142
Chapter Nine	The clear and the not-so-clear	154
Chapter Ten	The genius of genealogies	164

Certain believing amid uncertainty

Chapter Eleven	Answering the Islamists	175
Chapter Twelve	Beware the uncertainty trap!	193
Chapter Thirteen	Escaping the certainty trap!	210
Chapter Fourteen	A straight path less certain?	220

Appendices

1. Transliteration	239
2. An Introductory Bibliography	241
3. Glossary	246
4. Index	253

List of Figures

1	Faraj's argument concerning *jihâd*	8
2	The "Verse of the Sword"	12
3	Falwell on "Facing our National Sins"	24
4	Examples of reference to *tanzîl* or "sending down" in the Qur'ân	38
5	Abrogated verses in the Qur'ân according to al-Suyûtî	39
6	Shâh Walî Allâh's list of abrogated verses	41
7	Abrogated verses promoting tolerance	58
8	"Law" as referenced in the Bible	61
9	Tâhâ's view of Meccan versus Medinan *tanzîl*	72
10	Exegetes of the Qur'ân	79
11	"The Satanic verses"	96
12	Masoretic Text versus Samaritan Pentateuch, Septuagint and New Testament	110
13	Ending of Job 42 in Masoretic Text and Septuagint	111
14	Mark 1:1	120
15	Terms used by the Synoptics to convey Jesus' divinity	121
16	The Old Testament	130
17	Protestant and Roman Catholic terminology	133
18	Geographical foci of New Testament texts	135
19	Eusebius' categorisation of books available for inclusion in the New Testament	137
20	Apocryphal New Testament books	138
21	Significant writings of the Apostolic Fathers	139
22	Significant codices of the Qur'ân consulted by Zaid ibn Thâbit	147
23	Chronological revelations concerning interest/usury	162
24	The genealogies of Jesus according to Matthew and Luke	165
25	The Egyptian Supreme Court's decision on Abû Zaid's "apostasy"	182
26	Esack's hermeneutical keys for a theology of liberation	188
27	George Marsden on the history of fundamentalism in the USA	194
28	John Hick on Cantwell Smith	202
29	Dogma: yes, but . . .	209
30	Revelation as portrayed in Islam and Christianity	213

But then I sigh; and, with a piece of scripture,
Tell them that God bids us do good for evil:
And thus I clothe my naked villainy
With old odd ends stolen out of holy writ;
And seem a saint, when most I play the devil.

Gloucester in *King Richard III*, act 1, scene 3

There is
no innocent interpretation,
no innocent interpreter,
no innocent text.

David Tracy in *Plurality and Ambiguity: Hermeneutics, Religion, Hope*,
SCM Press Ltd.: London (1988), p 79

Preface

A BOMBSHELL FOR MANY!

The motivation for producing this book is strongly personal. In the summer of 2005 I was enjoying a sabbatical from my daily work as a vicar in a busy parish in southwest London. I spent the first week of my sabbatical travelling daily to the British Library near King's Cross station in London in order to read some books on the rather academic subject of "hermeneutics".[1] On the Thursday morning, I found myself being turned away from Brixton underground station because of a reported "power surge" on the system. I returned home to a telephone call from one of my married daughters who filled me in on what was reputedly going on in London. My daughter was very concerned for her husband who had that morning travelled during the rush hour to Russell Square. Happily, he managed to get in touch with her later in the day to let her know he was safe – though he had heard the explosion on the number 30 bus, just a few minutes after he had arrived at his destination.

In front of my television on that awful Thursday – the seventh of July, or 7/7 as it came to be nicknamed – I wept many times. During the day, it gradually became clear that the London underground system had been shut down because of a coordinated bomb attack. How could the victims and witnesses of such carnage ever be retrieved to faith in any kind of sovereign and good God? Later, as the Islamist claims for the atrocities were made public through the worldwide web, I cried again. How can people of any faith come to such an evil expression of their understanding of God's will? How, now, can tolerance-loving Westerners view their Muslim neighbours with anything but suspicion? I groaned, also, because I felt that Prime Minister Tony Blair was sadly wrong in his initial words from the G8 summit at Gleneagles – you cannot simply declare that perpetrators of such acts are not true Muslims. For the reality is that they are – or at least, they themselves make a strong case for being so. Indeed, in their own view, they see themselves as the truest

[1] The interpretation, especially, of Scripture.

Muslims. True to what? True to what has been revealed to them. As far as the Islamists are concerned, it is other Muslims who are aberrant, other Muslims who are not true Muslims. The Islamists are so sure about their case, they loudly announce, because it is clearly supported within their scripture – within the Qur'ân. The Qur'ân is the primary motivator and justifier of their extreme actions. Its verses fill their minds. Its commands become their duty to fulfil. The Qur'ân comprises the "sword" in the hands of the Islamists.

This book is in large part an examination of the Qur'ân and the kind of authority it holds for all Muslims. In appealing to the Qur'ân, the Islamists make it considerably difficult, if not risky, for other Muslims to question or oppose them. For what if the Islamists are right? What if the Qur'ân actually says what they are saying? The Islamists, we might well conclude, have sprung the certainty trap!

THE QUR'ÂN: PROVIDER OF CERTAINTY

Herein lies the difficulty today for the worldwide Muslim community. With regard to its scripture, the Muslim community has traditionally been literalist, "fundamentalist" even. It takes the qur'ânic revelation to be literally God's word, in God's language, unerringly conveyed to humankind through Prophet Muḥammad. A typical summary of this process is given in Ghulam Sarwar's *Islam: Beliefs and Teachings*:

> Each and every word of the *Qur'ân* was recorded as soon as it was revealed by Allah to the prophet through angel *Jibrâ'îl*. The Prophet's Secretary, *Zaid Bin Thâbit*, used to record them exactly as the Prophet told him . . . [After the Prophet's death] A committee was formed under *Zaid Bin Thâbit* to gather the scattered material of the *Qur'ân* into one volume . . . Copies were prepared [of that complete text] and they were checked with the original. Standard copies were then sent to different parts of the Islamic State.[2]

Muslims, moreover, are convinced that the text in their hands, ever since its initial revealing, is an accurate record of the original

[2] Ghulam Sarwar, *Islam, Beliefs and Teachings*, The Muslim Educational Trust: London (1987), pp 34–35. For a detailed description of the processes of Qur'ân compilation and a questioning of that description, see Chapter 3 of Bill Musk, *Kissing Cousins?* Monarch Books: Oxford (2005), pp 84–117. In several respects the burden of this book takes up the questions raised at the conclusion of that chapter about scripted texts being the bearers of revelation.

recitation made by Prophet Muḥammad. What they recite today comprises absolutely the text as sent down from heaven to earth through Prophet Muḥammad at the beginning of the seventh century AD:

> No other book in the world can match the *Qur'ân* in respect of its recording and preservation. The astonishing fact about this book of Allah is that it has remained unchanged even to a dot over the last fourteen hundred years . . . The *Qur'ân* exists today in its original form unaltered and undistorted . . . No variation of text can be found in it.[3]

As a consequence, the Qur'ân became, and remains, the greatest authority for law-making, for the determination of morality and for the formulating of belief for *all* Muslims. All Muslims believe that the Qur'ân comprises, in itself, the word of God.

In a strong sense, then, the majority of Muslims in today's world function within what might be called a "hermeneutic of certainty". They may know precisely what God wants because they retain the record of what he has revealed concerning his will. Islam comprises a call to all of them to submit (the word *islâm* in Arabic means "submission") to that will. Muslims are required to be "submitted" persons. A concern for their guardianship of the original recitation (*qur'ân* means "recitation" in Arabic) leads Muslims especially to honour those who memorise its 114 suras by heart. Recitation is only permitted in Arabic, the language of the Qur'ân, even for non-Arabic speakers. Copies of the Qur'ân are treated with great respect, never placed on the floor, often wrapped in cloth and specially looked after. Those who know the data of revelation are accorded great authority over peoples' lives, because they are the ones who pronounce the pronouncements of the Qur'ân. Muslims are certain in their faith because of their certainty about the Qur'ân.[4] They are literalists about God's word to them. Theirs is, as we have suggested, a hermeneutic of certainty.

[3] *Ibid.*, p 33.

[4] One might reasonably argue that such "certainty" about the Qur'ân only came to be applied to a literalist or fixed reading of the text in the thirteenth century. As Tahir Abbas recounts, at that time – with the end of Muslim rule in Spain – the ulema or religious scholars reduced the concept of *'ilm* from "all knowledge" to "religious knowledge" and limited the idea of *ijma'* from meaning "consensus of the community" to just that of the ulema themselves. The gates of *ijtihâd*, or independent reasoning, were tightly shut. As a result, "the interpretation of the Qur'an was frozen in history. It lost its dynamism; this transformed society from an open to a closed one." Tahir Abbas, "British South Asian Muslims: before and after September 11," in Tahir Abbas (ed.), *Muslim Britain: Communities under Pressure*, Zed Books: London (2005), p 7.

Now the Islamists – the Muslim fundamentalists – have changed everything! How are ordinary Muslims to react to loud and constant declarations (by the Islamists) of a greater faithfulness on their part to the strictures of God's word? Isn't aspiration to such greater faithfulness supposed to be every Muslim's vocation? The majority Muslim community finds itself today between a rock and a hard place.

On the one hand, the majority Muslim community shares with other (non-Muslim) communities a total incomprehension of how young Muslims – male or female – might find it within themselves to strap a shrapnel bomb to their bodies and blow themselves up in a crowded queue in Baghdad, or inside a packed restaurant in Tel Aviv, or on a commuter bus in Tavistock Square. Such extremism and violence is abhorred. After the London bombings, the Muslim Council of Britain quickly declared that "religious precepts cannot be used to justify such crimes, which are completely contrary to our teaching and practice".[5] The majority of Muslims in the United Kingdom and around the world genuinely believe and live as though Islam is primarily a religion about peaceful living. Imam Abdul Jalil Sajid, chairman of the Muslim Council for Religious and Racial Harmony UK, contends that "No school of Islam allows the targeting of civilians or the killing of innocents. Indiscriminate, senseless and targeted killing has no justification in Islam".[6] I need to emphasise this kind of Muslim voice, in the light of my concentration throughout this book on the claims of contemporary Islamists who justify to themselves, from the Qur'ân and other sources, the use of instruments of terror for achieving their goals. There are Muslim fundamentalists (in the sense that most ordinary, orthodox Muslims are "fundamentalist" or at least "literalist" in their view of the Qur'ân), and even some avowed Islamists, who are neither militant in their stance nor supportive of terror. The whole of this paragraph comprises "on the one hand".

On the other hand, the majority Muslim community finds itself upstaged by the radical Islamists' claim to be more authentically Islamic. The radical Islamists shout that theirs is a greater faithfulness to the revelation given via Prophet Muḥammad. Contrary to

[5] As quoted by Ziauddin Sardar in his article "The Struggle for Islam's Soul" in *New Statesman* (18 July 2005), p 10.

[6] *Ibid.*, p 10.

Imam Sajid's claim, such Islamists evidently *are* using Islamic sources to justify their violent actions. They claim to be faithful emulators of how the Prophet worked out his faith within the theocratic state built by him in Medina. They contend that they are being literally true to the demands of God as revealed in the Qur'ân. As Dr Ghayasuddin Siddiqui, director of the Muslim Institute, is bold enough to admit: "The terrorists are using Islamic sources to justify their actions. How can one then say it has nothing to do with Islam?"[7]

My suggestion in this book is that perhaps some "good" might be retrieved from the horror of what has occurred at the hands of violent Islamists in New York, Beslan, Madrid and London. That "good" would find expression in a loosening of the common Muslim hermeneutic of certainty. Perhaps the over-the-top manifestation of "obedience to God's word" of radical Muslim extremists might help provoke other Muslims to rethink their hermeneutic of certainty. Are there other ways in which the Qur'ân might be read and revered? Could it become a different kind of "sword" in the hands of contemporary Muslims?

In a previous book[8] I have explored why some Muslims become fundamentalists. Here, I propose to consider what the current resurgence of militant Islamism (Islamic fundamentalism) might come to mean for orthodox Muslims in their view of the Qur'ân. Islamism has thrived on Muslims' concern for "certainty." Can that concern come in for some interrogation? My contention is that the impact of people like the four or eight or more London suicide-bombers will prove to be far greater on contemporary non-fundamentalist Muslims than upon any non-Muslim onlookers.

QUESTIONING CERTAINTY

It is not just the Qur'ân that is under examination in the following chapters. And it is not just a sense of needing to make some response to the events of 7/7 out of my experience of living amongst Muslims in the Middle East that makes this book about Islam intensely personal. Rethinking a hermeneutic of certainty has been part of my own heritage as an evangelical Christian. I imbibed that hermeneutic as part of my experience of coming to living faith in

[7] *Ibid.*, p 10.

[8] See Bill Musk, *Holy War: Why some Muslims become fundamentalists*, Monarch: London, (2003).

Jesus Christ. I took it with me to the Middle East, where it was strongly challenged.

I am deeply grateful to those from a conservative evangelical (in those days "fundamentalist") background who led me to Christ and nurtured me in my newfound faith. Such people took the Bible very seriously and I learned to do so as well. I attended a lively, growing church in which a massive, central, raised pulpit, 45 minute sermons twice a Sunday, and lots of marked-up Bibles brought by church members into services each week, declared the seriousness with which "the Word of God" was taken. Hidden within that concern about "taking the Bible seriously", however, was a largely unstated but quite specific understanding of what doing that – taking the Bible seriously – might mean.

I learned as a new believer that "reading the text literally" and acknowledging the Bible as both "infallible" and "inerrant" were part and parcel of what a born-again believer in Christ does with conviction. It was not that easy, I must say, to put one's finger accurately on what those important words "infallible" or "inerrant" meant. Where might one draw the line between a "not misleading" (that is, infallible) and "not leading to error" (that is, inerrant) scripture as scripture *per se* – the Word of the living God – on the one hand, and, on the other hand, summaries of that Word which are in reality human interpretations of scripture? I'm thinking of ways in which a verse of the Bible is made to pronounce on a subject totally outside of any consideration of the context of that verse. I'm thinking of ways in which verses are lined up, like ammunition to a machine-gun, in order to be fired out at someone (often, in those days, Roman Catholics, Pentecostals or Charismatics) in proof-text fashion. "Reading the text literally" can easily become a pretext for blindly and falsely insisting that a literalist understanding of poetic or apocalyptic literature is the only way to be faithful to what the Bible says. Claims for the truth in a scientific sense of descriptions in Genesis concerning creation were part of the badge to be proudly worn by Bible-believing Christians.

Alongside such views went a sympathy for a dispensationalist reading of biblical history (how God orders different periods of salvation history) and a consequent conviction about God's role in current affairs – like the establishment of the state of Israel, or the role of the USSR in the world or the development of the European Economic Community (these were the 1970s!). Apocalyptic visions recorded in the Bible became the handmaid of a search through contemporary newspapers to discover how far along the road towards rapture or tribulation (depending on your millennialist view!) Christians and "the world" had reached. Respect for those who led me to Christ, plus a certain excitement about being so seemingly sure concerning what God's word (or, in my learned vocabulary, "God's Word") might mean and how the world might well end, allowed me to be content with – excited about – my inherited hermeneutic of certainty.

The bearer of such a Christian hermeneutic of certainty hears the Bible – all of it – as literally God's word and finds no problem in that hearing. I remember as a young Christian drawing battle plans on maps illustrating Joshua's advances into Canaan. It was an exciting exercise, seeing God's side beating up the enemy. The Jews had to win! I was viewing in the book of Joshua an early precursor to what God had recently done again during the Six Days War of 1967, within my own lifetime. Little Israel shaming all those powerful, hostile neighbours! It was only after living through months of Lebanon's bloody civil war in the 1970s that questions about bloodshed and violence and triumphalism and ethnic hatred raised a deeper interrogation in me about what I perceived the Bible to be recording so racingly.[9] I still accept that Joshua's military conquest happened, and that God was involved in the blood and horror of it happening. But my reading of it today is a lot more sober and I have questions of God as to what it all meant, or how he saw it. Was the concept of *hêrem* ("holy destruction") or the association of acts of annihilation with the holiness of *Yahweh* an accommodation that God made to the culture of that time? In what sense can it be said that God consecrates people or places to destruction? In what manner might it be suggested that the former inhabitants of the land "deserved" such severe judgment? Deuteronomy 20:17 ("Completely destroy them – the Hittites, Amorites, Canaanites, Perizzites, Hivites and Jebusites – as the Lord your God has commanded you") and equivalent verses elsewhere in the Old Testament comprise a genre of "holy war" text that coloured the process by which the conquest of Canaan, especially, took place. The Qur'ân is not the first scripture to come up with holy war verses.

[9] For a full and uncomfortable record of the Lebanese civil war of 1975–1990 and its larger context see Robert Fisk, *Pity the Nation: Lebanon at War*, Oxford University Press: Oxford (2001).

Yes – I understand that *Yahweh* had been incredibly patient over many generations with the faithless inhabitants of that land. Yes – I understand that *Yahweh* was equally ruthless about removing the people of Israel from the land when they in turn proved unwilling to live within it in obedience to him. And yes – I understand, and tremble, that our creator is also our judge. He does only what is truly right. Nevertheless, after my experience of Lebanon in 1975, I find great difficulty in contemplating these texts that speak of God as willing what appear to be the equivalent of modern "ethnic cleansings". I trust this God, but I don't understand him!

In the mission organisation of which I was a part in my first years of living in the Middle East, decisions about authority, finances, mission strategy, lifestyle choices, spirituality were all reputedly made on the basis of "what the Bible says" – yet gradually my wife and I became aware of the frail human mix in that process. Was appeal to Scripture being used by authority figures to control team members or to cover up organisational or personal irresponsibility? How about my own superior attitude to my wife or other women – how much of that selfishness and pride was a lazy appropriation by me of an attitude expressed in (Old Testament) Jewish or (New Testament) Graeco-Roman norms? The man is the "head", it's in the Bible! Or is it? Or is that the only view expressed? Or is that simply an accommodation to certain cultural realities of biblical times whilst God tried to sort out other issues in the divine-human matrix?

Whilst living in the Middle East, I pursued some postgraduate studies within the University of South Africa, an academic institution based in Pretoria. My visit to UNISA to defend my dissertation and sit some final exams immersed me in a country where, still, the ruling race justified its (unjust) ordering of society by appealing to the Bible. Afrikaners looked back to the "Great Trek" of 1836 as their equivalent of Israel's "exodus" from Egypt. Their victory without loss of life over 10,000 Zulu warriors in a battle at Blood River two years into that trek was interpreted in terms of God's intervention on their behalf. God, they declared, had established a covenant with them. They, in response, established their own republic in which they would honour him. Black Africans were quickly identified as the "Canaanites" whose tenure in the land needed to be undermined and replaced. The National Party promoted a program of racial separateness in which "apartheid" and the realisation of "promised land" went hand in hand. Strong appeal was made, of course, to the Old Testament and the supposed "ordering" of the races developing from the sons of Noah.[10] The institutionalisation of racial discrimination through the apartheid laws from 1948 onwards found alleged biblical justification for its harsh processes. I visited Pretoria and Johannesburg in 1984. It would be another two years before the Dutch Reformed Church in South Africa finally came to state publicly that apartheid could not be accepted on Christian-ethical grounds.

Would such a history of racial discrimination – on Christian, religious or biblical grounds – ever have occurred, I wondered, if the New Testament had been a little more daring in its castigation of slavery? Apart from Paul's hints to Philemon about receiving back his converted, runaway slave Onesimus on equal terms as a "brother" in Christ, the apostle for the most part appears to challenge little the huge Roman-controlled institution of slavery. Slaves are to obey their masters, says Paul. Masters are to treat their slaves fairly, instructs the apostle. Indeed, it took nearly two millennia for enlightened Christian readers of Old and New Testaments to reach the conclusion that Paul's theological statement about there being "neither . . . slave nor free" in Christ (Galatians 3:28) actually meant that slavery was totally unjustified.

God's word (in both Old Testament and New) is conveyed within certain contexts. How much does it endorse, or temporarily accept, or strongly challenge those contexts? How can one acknowledge the Bible as authoritative and yet not fall into the trap of harnessing its endemic authority to allow verses from different contexts to justify beliefs or practices that, with deeper reflection, might not appear to be so justified?

Then there was the reality of discovering what it feels like to be a certain kind of Christian living as a minority amongst different kinds of Christians. I went to live and work in Lebanon, sure of my relationship with Christ as an evangelical, "born-again" believer. I expected to find some fellow-believers amongst other Protestant denominations in that land, whatever their background. I thought I knew, however, that Roman Catholic and Orthodox Christians were basically "non-biblical" and belonged to spiritually dead denominations. Certainty was sufficient – in this case for me as an evangelical Christian – until I came face to face with other certainties. Gradually,

[10] Two other significant Bible passages made much of in support of such an appeal were found in Deuteronomy 32:8 and Acts 17:26.

in the Middle East, I came to know deeply faithful Orthodox, Catholic and other Protestant brothers and sisters with different constructs of faith and life, based, reputedly, on the Bible. And that was just the Christians! I also met "good" Muslims who contrasted strongly with some "bad" mission leaders. If integrity is a measure of Christ-likeness, how do we evaluate the rotten "insider" and the "holy" outsider? I noticed that this seemed to be a theme that came up quite a lot in Jesus' dealings with his disciples![11] My hermeneutic of certainty was unravelling.

For many years, my family lived in Egypt while I worked with Egyptian Christians in mission and church-related ministry. Being immersed in a Muslim environment in which "certainty" was very much the common religious hermeneutic with regard to the Qur'ân helped me to reflect on ways in which my own (and many other Western Christians') perspective on the Bible was equally unwholesome. How mixed up in our perspective was a national or cultural sense of pride in which Arabs, or Muslims, find an assigned role as "the bad guys"? What kind of "certainty" might be valid, untainted by human, ethnocentric conditioning? And how might a sureness or confidence in God's word find expression in a manner that is not strongly culturally driven? Most of the missionaries and many of the Western Christian church plants that I came across in the Middle East tended to be strongly fundamentalist and (in my view) strongly prejudiced in their political outlook. There was no doubting such Christians' zeal or love or self-sacrifice, but the biblical hermeneutic by which they functioned did not really hold out much of a future – much gospel – for their audience. Arabs – Christian or Muslim – were seen as obstacles to God's plans for Israel in the last days before the second coming of Jesus Christ.

There is more! It is my strong suspicion, shared with many of my contemporaries – Christian and Muslim – that a Christian fundamentalist view undergirds, if it does not actually inform, current, dominant Western perspectives and policies in our groaning world. In its North American manifestations, especially, Christian fundamentalism plays a significant role on the world stage, justifying a "war on terror" that both inflames Islamism and makes ordinary

[11] See, for example, the vignette on "the good outside" and "the bad inside" in Mark 9:38–50, and the question left hanging over Jesus' disciples as they headed towards Jerusalem. Which would these friends of Jesus during his public ministry prove themselves to be when the arrests began: the "good" or the "bad"?

Muslims more resistant to hearing any "gospel" from Christian mouths. Any present day, Christian involvement in mission to Muslims that is non-understanding of this powerful undermining-from-within of its intentions is effectively working blind. Again I need to emphasise that not every North American "fundamentalist" necessarily agrees with those theologians and pastors who claim to speak on their behalf or who support the White House in its particular instigation of a global war against terror. The Christian fundamentalists discussed in chapter 2 of this book purport to represent many millions of American evangelical Christians. I recognise that there are many American evangelicals – fundamentalists even – who would label the likes of Hal Lindsey, Pat Robertson and Jerry Falwell as extremist.[12] At the same time, it does seem to me that – with or without overt, mass conviction and support – an extremist brand of North American fundamentalism does today find itself at the heart of endorsing what the United States of America is currently doing on the international scene. That endorsement is seen by most of the rest of the world as religiously motivated.

So, this book is personal. I am still a convinced evangelical. I believe my faith is related to a foundational certainty. Christianity is not at heart "pie in the sky." Both the textual history of the Bible and much of the story of those texts can be strongly interrogated. My Christian faith derives from a real Christ, a real cross, a real resurrection. I believe in a real Abraham, a real flood, and a real creation. I hope that I will continue to take the Bible very seriously. I believe that it does not mislead. I believe that it does not lead into error. It has been my practice for many years to read through the whole text each twelve months. I have tried to allow the Bible to inform my thinking and evaluating of my own and others' cultures and life experiences. Apologetics – at which most of us Christians are very bad – focuses the mind on what can or cannot be defended. The foundations of our faith are firm; there need be no doubt there. I remain convinced that the Bible is God's word, and God's word to us today. I want to promote some certainty!

[12] Defining such terms as "evangelical" and "fundamentalist" is a difficult issue. George Marsden comments, for example, that "today we can identify at least fourteen varieties of evangelicalism" in North America. In *Understanding Fundamentalism and Evangelicalism*, Eerdmans, Grand Rapids (1991), p 110. Some fundamentalists, of course – such as Bob Jones III – have condemned Falwell as only a "pseudofundamentalist" (*Ibid*, p 76)! My point about the likes of Jerry Falwell is that they have successfully projected their brand of fundamentalism towards the centres of American life, primarily through political action.

At the same time, I am aware that a blind, or dogmatic, literalist interpretation of the Bible can be more than just intellectually dishonest. It can also be unfaithful. None of us human beings – Christian or otherwise – has the whole truth sorted out. Too often, our strongest affirmations belie our deepest doubts. A Christian hermeneutic of certainty can easily provide a cover for the imposition upon others of personal (or cultural, or even political) will or mindset or control. How the Bible carries innate authority and how it is given authority in hearers' lives is a complex issue. I hope in the following chapters to come to some discernment of what might be an appropriate or faithful attitude to the Bible for a committed Christian to hold in today's complex world.

RESPONDING TO THE BOMBSHELL

These chapters, then, are addressed to many readers. They constitute a challenge to ordinary Muslims and ordinary Christians who operate, for whatever reason, within a surviving hermeneutic of certainty. They query where certainty might validly lie in texts purporting to constitute revelation from God. "Watch out", they warn, "for the certainty trap!" I am asking whether ordinary Muslims and ordinary Christians might increasingly become voices for a faithful but non-fundamentalist version of their own constituency's view of Scripture.

These chapters also comprise an appeal to all who despair of religion – of the kind of religious living that can find manifestation in the blowing up of innocent people or in the manipulation of the weak on the basis of "God's Word says so". Can the despairing and damaged be inspired to re-engage with a God who seeks to reveal himself to humankind? I am asking whether the disillusioned might allow that most Muslims and most Christians do not advocate the extreme fundamentalist perspectives of those currently at the "noisy end" of their respective faiths.

These chapters further form a provocation to those who operate only from a hermeneutic of suspicion. The normal stance of postmodern Westerners is one of suspicion of any proposition purporting to convey absolute truth. Knowledge is seen as relative, not absolute. Overarching meta-narratives are strongly distrusted. Some faith leaders, theologians indeed, contend that the only way of rescuing holy books from fundamentalists is by undermining or denying their "divine" aspect. I want to assert that holy books are "holy" – that is, beyond the purely human – and are designed to examine us as much as we might examine them. I believe, as a Christian, that God wants surely to speak to us through his word.

These chapters, finally, seek to encourage those who want to treat holy books seriously, but don't know how. Is there only one way that a scripture can be interpreted? Who might legitimately have a veto on interpretation? Can we ever say that "scripture" is the same as "the word of God"? If we can, what do we mean by that equation in the light of Scripture's own pointing to Jesus Christ as "Word" of God?

In this book we shall travel over delicate ground, for I am trying to do two contrasting things. On the one hand, I am trying to engender a question in those who are so certain of what the Qur'ân (especially) says. Can the Muslim majority come to view the authority of the Qur'ân in a way that is different from the recently received norm? Such a proposal constitutes, I guess, a challenge to contemporary Muslim theologians to rethink their attitude to the Qur'ân in the aftermath of 9/11 and 7/7. Some aspects of the manner in which the text of the Bible has been interrogated might provide some helpful models or precedents. On the other hand, I am endeavouring to suggest that the Bible (especially) does have an authority that needs to be heeded, though not in a "fundamentalist" sense. The voice of God is heard in or through scripture and it would be good for us to hear that voice today with increasing humility. This is, I know, a provocation to all of us who count ourselves believing Christians, subject to God's word. I want us all to hear God's voice – God's conversation with us – in that word more clearly.

We begin the body of this book by highlighting the "certainty trap". Within the faiths of both Islam and Christianity, "a certain belief" is proferred to, and in considerable manner accepted by, members of each faith community. We consider in depth the claim that Islamists make concerning their loyalty to the qur'ânic revelation (chapter 1). They state strongly that they are the more faithful followers of the revelation given by God to humankind via Prophet Muḥammad. Their rhetoric concerning *jihâd*, supremely, illustrates the delicate and difficult position in which non-Islamist Muslims now find themselves. Whose is the most accurate reading of what "holy war" means in Islam – the traditionalists' or the Islamists'? Christians (and Jews) are no strangers to this kind of debate, for "fundamentalism" is a phenomenon common in recent decades to all monotheistic faiths. The kind of self-examination that Muslims are potentially being led towards in this country and elsewhere needs to be mirrored by an equivalent self-questioning by those of us who, as Christians, especially in powerful Western nations, are partly responsible for the injustices of the world in which we live today. We look at the phenomenon of fundamentalism in Christianity and its contribution towards the messy state of international affairs in which we – and especially Muslims – currently find ourselves (chapter 2).

The major consideration of this book is with the questioning of certainty. We are strongly provoked to such consideration by the Islamist agenda. We will discover, however, that there are aspects of the historic, Islamic faith that offer the possibility of questioning a hermeneutic of certainty. We are also provoked to such consideration by the evident connection between fundamentalist Christianity and political outlook (especially in the United States of America) – a connection that serves to inflame Islamism on the world scene. We ask whether a hermeneutic of certainty is a faithful stance for Christians, any more than for Muslims.

We commence our interrogation of the "certainty trap" with a look at the nature of "abrogation" in holy texts (chapters 3 and 4). The Islamists declare forthrightly that certain verses of the Qur'ân are abrogated by other verses. They accumulate support through such a process for their interpretation of how, for example, Muslims should relate to non-Muslims. This is a sensitive area for any faith that is based upon scripted revelation. For Christianity, the apostle Paul speaks of Christ as constituting the "end" of the Law: we look at what abrogation might amount to within a Christian consideration of the Old Testament or the Law. We further evaluate the creative attempt of one Muslim theologian and political leader to re-engage the concept of abrogation in a manner that deliberately undermines the Islamist perspective.

How might one understand or respond to texts that are given in one context and yet are held as authoritative in different contexts? In chapters 5 and 6 we investigate the role of exegesis in giving understanding to God's word in changing circumstances. Some of those changing circumstances seem to occur as the revelation itself was actually being given or affirmed – in the cases of both Qur'ân and New Testament. Issues of interpretation are central in accessing and assessing what is presented as God's speaking to humankind.

What might be the relation between divine "giving" and human "receiving" as revelation is in process of occurring? The Qur'ân "developed" gradually over 23 years as it came to be the text received by the end of the process as one, "complete" book. What might we learn from the details of such gradual, earthly accumulation? Similarly, with the Bible – texts were gradually defined and gathered, essentially in Hebrew and Greek. How and why did such defining and gathering proceed to issue in the Old and New Testaments as we now know them? In chapters 7 and 8 we consider the matter of inspiration and trace the processes involved in the canonisation[13] of emerging scripture within both faiths.

Our final area of inquiry (chapters 9 and 10) concerns how a scripted revelation presents itself. What does it say it is for? How does it describe its own coming into being? How does it differentiate between simple-to-understand and not-so-simple-to-understand elements of its content? How might such differentiation find reasonable explanation? Such enquiry into the self-referential nature of Qur'ân and Bible takes us into the realm of theology. Can it stimulate in us all a theologising that is more dynamic than a purely literalist approach to sacred text would allow?

Having seriously questioned "certainty", we move to the delicate matter of offering a more nuanced suggestion as to how people of convinced faith might live "faithfully" in today's world. There are many contemporary Muslims who in reflecting on the nature of the Qur'ân and its interpretation have come up with conclusions very different from those of the Islamists. We consider some of such Muslims' propositions in chapter 11.

As I prepared and reflected upon the material investigated in this book, it became increasingly apparent that I was ignoring a large element of the context – secular humanist and post-Christian – that predominates in the contemporary, Western world. Many Westerners have had enough of religion, full stop! Richard Dawkins represents a popular voice for rationalism of an atheistic nature in British society today![14] Many theologians, from David Jenkins to John Spong, have sought to restate their views on the Bible in order

[13] Used in this book in the sense of a formal sanctioning of a text (biblical or qur'ânic) by the relevant religious authorities.

[14] See, for example, Richard Dawkins, *The God Delusion*, Bantam Press: London (2006).

to engage those enamoured by a hermeneutic of suspicion. In such restatement, the Bible becomes a quaint, context-limited, collection of stories reflecting the beliefs of primitive, credulous peoples. It does not connect with a post-modern, Western, "scientific" world. So, jettison the Bible! We spend chapter 12 suggesting that falling into the "uncertainty trap" is not a healthy option for convinced followers of God.

The final two chapters of this book make some suggestions for a Christian (chapter 13) and Muslim (chapter 14) escaping from the certainty trap. Somehow, people of real faith at the beginning of the third millennium need to find a way of living somewhere between a hermeneutic of certainty and a hermeneutic of suspicion. That median existence requires a willingness to thrive in a world where dogma (in its true meaning of "seeming to be the case") and doubt coexist as part of the framework of faith. I suggest that the story of Jesus – where "glory" or ultimate certainty comes via "shame" or huge uncertainty – offers a paradigm we would all do well to consider seriously.

As is clear from the outline just sketched, we shall consider parallels between Islam and Christianity throughout the pages that follow – all in an effort to throw up a suggestion as to how texts purporting to be from God might be perceived to carry authoritative weight in a non-fundamentalist sense. We will discover some empathy across the faith traditions!

At the same time, it will become clear through the following chapters that there needs to follow some other, significant fallout from the London bombings. A call, such as mine, for a radically different view of the Qur'ân on the part of Muslims needs to be balanced by an equally strong questioning of the value of the current, Western-initiated "war on terror", and the Christian underpinnings for its justification, especially in North American society. Is force of arms really the best way to undermine an Islamist ideology? Does it not rather play into the hands of such people? Since the overthrow of Saddam Hussein, however awful a tyrant he may have been, Iraq has become the breeding ground for neo-Kharijite, Islamist perspectives and the recruiting ground for suicide bombers. A Western ("Christian") programme of demonising and destroying the Islamist enemy only unveils the poverty endemic within a Christian fundamentalist-driven view of how this world works. That view needs to be rethought.

I do think there is room for suggesting that, hopefully, some "good" might arise out of the awful realities of 7/7. At a local level, many British Muslims and Christians are allowing very positive historic relationships to mature and guide them in their responses to the recent actions of Muslim terrorists in London. Others are tentatively exploring such open relationships. We live on the cusp of a dramatic shift in the willingness of Muslims to hear the Christian story, to examine a Christian gospel that eschews a wielding of the sword for religious or political ends. Previous, patient relationship and contemporary acts of solidarity have encouraged that possibility. I am a missions-oriented Christian at heart, and at the micro-level I am encouraged by the positive stories arising on the ground out of Christian overtures towards Muslims since 7/7. In my view – forgive the reiteration – the biggest threat to Muslims hearing the Christian gospel today, indeed, the largest precipitator of potential ghetto-isation in our society, comes not so much from Muslim terrorists as from a Western political insistence that its war on terror has nothing to do with inflaming Islamism. That insistence derives from a worldview – especially in its North American variety – that stems from a Christian fundamentalist base. I am convinced that the struggle for the soul of Christianity (especially in the United States of America) is as much a part of the global scene today as the struggle for the soul of Islam.

So this book ends with a proposition. I want to suggest that it is quite normal, quite faithful, for people of trust in God to live with uncertainty. Authority does not have to be neatly tied to human constructions of "truth". Alternatively stated, there *can* be room for doubt in certainty. We may be released from the certainty trap!

ACKNOWLEDGEMENTS

I am grateful to the Diocese of Southwark for arranging for me to attend a two-week clergy course at St George's House, Windsor Castle in January 2004. The subject of that course was "Secularisation – threat or promise?" In preparation for it I produced a paper in which I began to put my initial thoughts on this subject into coherent form. The same diocese also granted me a three-month sabbatical in the summer of 2005. Part of that sabbatical has been used to research, consider and write up my more considered thoughts on this subject in this slim volume. I have appreciated the resources made available at St Deiniol's Library at Hawarden where I stayed to do some of the writing and editing of this book. I am thankful for the graciousness of members of Holy Trinity & St Matthias, Tulse Hill for allowing me to leave them to it for the duration of my sabbatical. I am especially indebted to Daniel Frett and Silas Edmonds for their critiques of the developing text. My deepest thanks are due to my family for tiptoeing around me while I was shut in my study working on this material.

A certain belief

Chapter 1

"Fighting" means fighting, for heaven's sake!

AMERICAN, Russian, Spanish – and more recently British – minds have had to try and wrestle with the reality that some peoples' interpretation of a holy text leads them to terrorise others in unthinkable ways. Innocent civilians, including women and children – people of all faiths and none – are randomly targeted by suicidal hit-squads composed of young adult Muslims. The men forming those hit-squads evidently believe that they are doing what God is ordering them to do. Their actions are accompanied by spiritual preparation and initiated with prayer. The cry upon their lips as they die is "Allahu akbar!" or "God is great!" Their reward for killing the "unbelievers" will be to gain quick access to paradise, plus they will accrue honour as "martyrs" for the Islamic cause. How can Westerners of any variety ever come to appreciate that sort of mindset in the world of the twenty-first century?

If Westerners find the issue of Islamist terrorism an unnerving challenge to their understanding of what life might be about, a greater challenge, it seems to me, is the one that is put before contemporary *Muslims* by their fellow-Muslim extremists. How can today's orthodox Muslim community *not* appreciate the mindset of the Islamists? After all, it claims to derive from the Qur'ân. It claims to be based on the example of Prophet Muḥammad. It purports to have the support of famous Islamic theologians. It is evidently actioned by contemporary religious spokesmen – people knowing well the data of revelation – who give their consent or approval to violent forms of "holy war".

In other words, the actions and beliefs of contemporary Islamists constitute, I am convinced, the greatest challenge to the traditional hermeneutic of certainty within Islam. Why? Because those Islamists are saying: "Listen! Ours is the original, most faithful interpretation of the Qur'ân! Our interpretation is consistent with how Prophet Muḥammad himself lived out his 'submission' to God! We are the true Muslims here!"

GOD SAYS: "KILL THEM!"

The Islamists are nitpickers about holy text and are fired with an ideological vision. They repeatedly quote chapter and verse of the Qur'ân in order to justify their beliefs and actions.

What they are waging is *holy* war – that is the point. It is fighting that originates in the will of God. *Jihâd* comprises part of Muslim faithfulness in submission to God's will.

In order to appreciate where such Islamists are coming from, we need to recognise the importance within Islam of the concept of *ijtihâd*. The Arabic word literally means "exertion" and refers to a deduction on a legal or theological matter that is made by a *mujtahid* or knowledgeable theologian. How to work out what it means to be a Muslim in the world is the task of a *mujtahid*. The spectrum of opinion represented by the proponents of *ijtihâd* may range from the most liberal to the ultra-conservative.

Historically, within the development of Islam, there has consistently been an ultra-conservative stream of interpretation. It began with the Kharijîs, a purist sect who were responsible for the assassination of 'Alî, the fourth caliph (in AD 659). Their approach, which essentially saw all non-Kharijî Muslims as faithless or apostate and thus legitimate targets for attack, has influenced individuals and groups at different times. Kharijîs themselves led several rebellions during the 'Abbasid period (AD 749–1258). Their philosophy influenced Ibn Taymîyya (AD 1263–1328), a conservative theologian whose name we shall meet in the following paragraphs. The Wahhâbî sect, followers of Muḥammad ibn 'Abd al-Wahhâb (AD 1703–1787), are rooted in that tradition. The Wahhâbîs have entrenched themselves, of course, as the dominant voice in Saudi Arabian Islam. Deobandis, also, tend to have spawned reformist Muslims whose views veer towards the far right in their interpretation of what it means to be a faithful Muslim. The Deobandis take their name from a seminary founded in Deoband (a hundred miles north of Delhi in India) in AD 1867. The founders of this seminary rejected non-Islamic knowledge and established a reformist and scholarly tradition within Indian Islam in the nineteenth century. Out of Deobandi seminaries functioning in Pakistan in the late twentieth century came many of the foot soldiers for the Talibân armies within Afghanistan.

Sardar characterises this extremist stream of expression within historical Islam as having three main elements. Firstly, it is ahistoric – it focuses only on a utopia that exists outside time. Secondly, it is monolithic and unable to accommodate or live alongside any other Islamic perspective. Thirdly it is aggressively self-righteous, insistent upon imposing its own notion of what faithfulness means upon all others.[1] Abû Zaid (whom we shall meet more fully in chapter 11) summarises the aspirations – and tenor – of supporters of this stream of expression in the following manner:

> A variety of political Islamist groups, known as fundamentalists, see the jurist view of the Qur'an as the only true and valid understanding of Islam. It follows then that *sharî'a* law – human law derived largely from the foundational texts of Islam (the Qur'an and Prophetic Tradition) along with the consensus of earlier generations – must be implemented in an Islamic society. Throughout most of Islamic history, the jurists' understanding of religion has taken hold and often has been held in place by force.[2]

During the twentieth century, emerging initially as part of the general Muslim move towards finding a theological rationale for opposing dominating imperial powers, a renewed Islamist genre of *ijtihâd* developed alongside other Muslim perspectives. People in the tradition of Sayyid Abû'l-'Alâ' Mawdûdî and Sayyid Qutb came to produce theological perspectives that justified the use of force in fulfilment of a scriptural requirement for *jihâd*. The well-known slogan of the Muslim Brotherhood well expresses their motivation and priorities:

> Allah is our objective.
> The Messenger is our leader.
> The Qur'ân is our law.
> *Jihâd* is our way.
> Dying in the way of Allah is our highest hope.[3]

Ijtihâd, then, provides the permission and precedent for Islamists' contemporary reinterpreting of Islam's holy text. Often, as a result of such re-interpretative "exertion", a *fatwâ* or legal opinion comes to be made – declaring that it is right in God's eyes, for example, to target foreign tourists in Luxor and Sharm al-Sheikh, or to "kill

[1] Sardar (2005), *op. cit.*, pp 11–12.
[2] Nasr Abu Zaid with Esther R. Nelson, *Voice of an Exile: Reflections on Islam*, Praeger: Westport, Connecticut (2004), p 203.
[3] As quoted by Ziauddin Sardar in *Desperately Seeking Paradise*, Granta Books: London (2004), p 36.

Americans everywhere," or to capture school-children in Beslan, or to set a fiery cross ablaze in the heart of London's transportation system. The Islamists rely in their *ijtihâd* on the opinions of earlier, famous, radical theologians – people like Ibn Ḥanbal, founder of the conservative "Hanbalite" school of Islamic jurisprudence. They comprise a modern continuation of a radical and historical stream of qur'ânic interpretation within Islam. As such, they call into question previous and traditional understandings of what the Qur'ân says. Their pet subject, it would seem, is the concept of holy war or *jihâd*. What does *jihâd* really mean, they ask?

The Islamists' calling into question of traditional views (of *jihâd*, for example) must, surely, comprise a massive challenge to the supposed or assumed idea that the Qur'ân can only ever have one (historic) meaning. It wrong-foots those spokespersons for Islam who operate within a hermeneutic of certainty but who now find themselves accused of lacking certainty where, in the view of the Islamist, the Qur'ân gives such sureness. It makes it hard for most Muslims not to feel condemned for their own comparative lack of self-sacrificing commitment to the word given by God.

EGYPTIAN APOSTASY

Let me illustrate my "take" on the Islamists and scripture from the group involved in the assassination of President Anwar Sadat of Egypt in October, 1981. My family was living in Egypt during that period of Islamist anger with their national leader. Sadat's executioners were motivated by a relatively young ideologue, Muḥammad 'Abd al-Salâm Faraj. This intelligent man was a graduate in electrical engineering from Cairo University. In the late 1970s, while working in Alexandria, he was recruited to the Egyptian Islamist group called *al-Jihâd*. When the leaders of that group's cell in Alexandria were arrested, the cell fizzled out. Faraj, however, avoided arrest because he was not one of the cell's leaders. At some point Faraj moved back to Cairo where he obtained employment at the University of Cairo. Over the next year or so, he worked clandestinely with a couple of other men to bring together various Islamist cells to form a new *al-Jihâd* group.

During the summer of 1980, Faraj authored a pamphlet that would eventually be refuted, point by point, by none less than the

Mufti of Egypt. That refutation was printed in a national newspaper two months after Sadat's death. Faraj's pamphlet expresses the ideology behind the militancy of the men who saw Sadat as standing in the way of God's will for Egypt. As such, it illustrates the challenge that Islamism poses for orthodox Muslims concerning their view of the Qur'ân as comprising God's revelation to them.

The title of Faraj's work is *The Neglected Duty* (*Al-Farîḍa al-Ghâ'iba*).[4] It begins by quoting the Qur'ân:

> Has not the Time arrived for the Believers that their hearts in all humility should engage in the remembrance of Allah and of the Truth which has been revealed (to them), and that they should not become like those to whom was given Revelation aforetime, but long ages passed over them and their hearts grew hard? For many among them are rebellious transgressors. (Sura 57:16)

The "Neglected Duty" is, of course, *jihâd.* Faraj aims to stir his readership to an armed struggle against the rebellious transgressors in contemporary Egyptian society. Although President Sadat is never mentioned by name in the text of the pamphlet, it is obvious that his regime constitutes the current infidel or apostate state against which *jihâd* must be waged. Faraj's constant theme is that the contemporary "spiritual" health of Muslims in Egypt is far from what God would have it to be (see figure 1).

Those seeking to bring about a positive change in that state of health are going about it in the wrong way, claims Faraj in the opening section of his pamphlet. The benevolent societies, of which there are thousands in Egypt, may do a lot of good work in the short term but do they bring about the foundation of an Islamic state? The Ṣûfî movement may assist many Egyptian Muslims with growing in personal piety but by doing so they help too many Egyptians miss the wood for the trees: the common goal has to be, not more piety, but obedience to God's Word – bringing in the rule of God.

The Muslim Brotherhood (an avowedly Islamist group) and other reformists aim to achieve some change by getting involved in Egyptian politics and exerting pressure from within the party system. Faraj suggests that all political parties collaborate to some extent with the state within which they are active. Other radical

[4] Faraj's pamphlet might better be translated "*The Missing Precept*". An English translation of *Al-Farîḍa al-Ghâ'iba* is found in Johannes J. G. Jansen, *The Neglected Duty: The Creed of Sadat's Assassins and Islamic Resurgence in the Middle East*, MacMillan: New York (1986), pp 159–234.

Egyptian Muslims seek to proceed by infiltrating the government apparatus. Perhaps the author has in mind here Sheikh al-Sha'râwî, a popular religious leader with a strong TV following who climbed to being a Cabinet Minister in the late 1970s. An infiltrator, however, has still to show support of the status quo, and such support would naturally exclude him from being in a position to deny the status quo and inaugurate something totally different.

What about those fellow Islamists or reformists who withdraw from *jâhilî* society to form their own, faithful "groups of separation" that live apart from fellow Muslims, in caves or furnished apartments, in a "true" Islamic setting? Faraj's words here constitute a critical reference to fellow Islamists who took to withdrawing from Egyptian polity in the 1970s in order to live in communes within caves in the countryside or within furnished apartments on the edges of various cities. There they sought to live as "true" Muslims, away from a depraved or *jâhilî* society. Faraj asks how that kind of procedure can bring into reality an Islamic state.

Figure 1

Faraj's argument concerning *jihâd*

The neglected duty	*Jihâd* in the way of God
Introduction	God's guidance Islamic state required Contemporary Egypt Rulers in apostasy
Ibn Taymîyya's thesis	Then and now
Islamic groups in Egypt	Charitable associations Pietistic Muslims Political parties Infiltration of positions of power Non-violent *da'wah* Emigration (*hijra*) Education
God's methodology	Offensive *jihâd*
The nature of true *jihâd*	
Methodology for true *jihâd*	

Faraj looks round the contemporary Islamic scene in Egypt and declares that all existing routes to reform miss the essential method, authenticated by God himself and clearly declared within the Qur'ân. That method is *jihâd*. The only way to bring about an Islamic state is for a small minority of Muslims to become radically committed to *jihâd* in the sense of armed struggle. The qur'ânic promise is that if only the true Muslims will take the initiative and obey God's command to *jihâd*, then as they open fire on the unbelievers God himself will intervene on their behalf and change everything:

> Fight them, and Allah will punish them by your hands, cover them with shame, help you (to victory) over them, heal the breasts of Believers . . . (Sura 9:14)

The establishment of an Islamic state on earth is clearly God's intention. Therefore it is God who is responsible for working out the details of how that establishment comes about as the true Muslims begin to obey him by fighting for it. Faraj was promoting a faith project.

Faraj also deals in detail with military tactics, explaining the methodology for fighting as it is advocated in the Qur'ân and by prophetic example (in the *sunna* of the Prophet, recorded in the *ḥadîth* literature). After all, the faith-fighting has to be done in the prescribed manner in order for God to lend to it his authority. Authorised tactics include: the use of deception; the infiltrating of the ranks of the foe; the acceptability of killing women and children en route to routing the main enemy; and the allowance for destroying the material and natural heritage of the enemy. In other words, tactics of terror are specifically allowed or authorised by appeal to the records of what Prophet Muḥammad said or did or approved.

This bleakly stated point about tactics of terror against "innocents" may be illustrated by looking at one of Faraj's supporting arguments. In his pamphlet, he includes a reference to al-Nawawî's commentary on a *ḥadîth*[5] recorded by both al-Bukhârî[6] and Muslim[7] in their chapters on the duty of *jihâd*. The transmitted tradition, quoted here from al-Bukhârî, declares:

[5] *Ḥadîth* (singular) or "prophetic tradition" referring to an account of some word or act of Prophet Muḥammad. The *aḥadîth* (plural) constitute the most significant, written authority for Muslims after the Qur'ân.

[6] To be found in Muḥammad bin Ismâîl bin al-Mughîrah al-Bukhârî, *al-Ṣaḥîḥ*, trans. Muhammad Muhsin Khan, Kazi Publications: Chicago (1976–1979), vol 4, book 52, chap 146, trad 256, pp 158–159.

[7] To be found in Abû'l-Ḥasan Muslim Ibn al-Ḥajjâj, *al-Jâmi'al-Ṣaḥîḥ*, trans. 'Abdul Ḥamîd Ṣiddîqî, Sh. Muhammad Ashraf: Lahore (1976), vol 3, book 17, chap 712, trads 4321–4323, pp 946–947.

> Narrated Aṣ-Ṣa'b bin Jaththâmah: The Prophet passed by me at a place called Al-Abwâ' or Waddân, and was asked whether it was permissible to attack the pagan warriors at night with the probability of exposing their women and children to danger. The Prophet replied, "They (i.e. women and children) are from them (i.e. pagans)".

Al-Nawawî's comment on this *ḥadîth*, as recorded by Faraj, announces:

> The apostle of God – God's Peace be upon Him – was asked to give an opinion about the children of the polytheists who were 'attacked at night' and some of their women and children were killed, whereupon He said: 'They are part of their fathers,' that is, there is no objection to it because the rules applying to their fathers pertain to them as well, in inheritance, marriage, retaliation, blood-money, and other things.[8]

This means, concludes Faraj, ". . . when they do not do it on purpose without need for it (it is allowed to kill these dependents)".[9] So, in Faraj's view, it is permissible, in some circumstances, to kill dependents, just as it is allowed, in some circumstances, to destroy the "trees of the infidels" (that is their property – things like buildings or trains or buses), because such killing or destruction is all for the sake of the "greater good". In Faraj's argument, the "greater good" comprises bringing in the rule of God – the establishment of an Islamic state. The espousal of violence, in Faraj's appeal to Qur'ân and *ḥadîth*, is made the test of whether contemporary Muslims are serious about their faith. If they are, as true Islamists they will determine to fight (their part of the bargain) and God will miraculously do the rest.

The heart of Faraj's pamphlet focuses on two sources: the Qur'ân and the writings of an orthodox Muslim theologian named Ibn Taymîyya. We will not look in depth at Faraj's detailed discussion concerning Ibn Taymîyya, though we need to note that the former theologian is quoted by Faraj on nearly every page of his text. The significance of such extensive quotation is simple. It provides a legal precedent for Faraj's current objective – the calling of Muslims to wage war on Muslims. In his own day, Ibn Taymîyya came up with theological justification for supporting the waging of war by Muslim Mamluks on Muslim Mongols. The basis of Ibn Taymîyya's argu-

[8] Jansen *op. cit.*, p 217.
[9] *Ibid.*, p 217.

ment was that the Mongols were apostate Muslims and therefore needed to suffer the penalty applying to apostasy. Every group of Muslims that transgresses Islamic law should be combated, even though they continue to profess Islam. Faraj declares that Ibn Taymîyya's legal opinion (*fatwâ*) concerning the Mongols authorises a similar dealing with Egypt's contemporary "Mongol" ruler, the unnamed Anwar Sadat.

We do need to note in detail Faraj's appeal to the Qur'ân in support of his provocative views. He especially focuses[10] on a famous abrogating[11] verse (Sura 9:5), popularly known as the "Verse of the Sword" (we shall look in more depth at the important issue of abrogation in chapter 3):

> "But when the forbidden months are past, then fight and slay the Pagans wherever ye find them, and seize them, beleaguer them, and lie in wait for them in every stratagem (of war); but if they repent, and establish regular prayers and practise regular charity, then open the way for them: for Allah is Oft-forgiving, Most Merciful."

Actually, in his quoting of this verse, Faraj finishes his quotation at the words ". . . stratagem (of war)". Ibn Kathîr[12] exegetes[13] the words "seize them, beleaguer them, and lie in wait for them in every stratagem" as meaning:

> . . . do not wait until you find them. Rather, seek and besiege them in their areas and forts, gather intelligence about them in the various roads and fairways so that what is made wide looks ever smaller to them. This way, they will have no choice, but to die or embrace Islam.

Faraj quotes former commentators on the Qur'ân to demonstrate the abrogating force of this radical verse. His quotations are summarised in figure 2.

Weighty opinion is thus brought to bear concerning the significance of the "Verse of the Sword". It is a powerful verse, not only for the number of previous verses that it cancels, but for the complete change of attitude it brings in terms of how a Muslim might perceive non-Muslims.

[10] *Ibid.*, pp 195–196.

[11] "Abrogation" refers to a cancelling out or replacement of one verse by another.

[12] The *Tafsîr* of Ibn Kathîr is available on the internet at http://www.tafsir.com. His commentary as quoted here may be found at Sura 9: "This is the Ayah of the Sword."

[13] From "exegesis", or exposition of Scripture.

Figure 2

The "Verse of the Sword"

Name of commentator	Comment as quoted by Faraj
Ibn Kathîr quoting al-Ḍaḥḥâk ibn Muzâḥim	"It cancelled every treaty between the Prophet – God's Peace be upon Him – and any infidel, and every contract and every term."
Al-ʿÛfî quoting Ibn ʿAbbâs	"No contract nor covenant of protection was left to a single infidel since [this] dissolution [of treaty obligations] was revealed."
Muḥammad ibn Aḥmad ibn Muḥammad ibn Juzayy al-Kalbî in *Tafsîr al-Tashîl li-ʿUlûm al-Tanzîl*	"The abrogation of the command to be at peace with the infidels, to forgive them, to be [passively] exposed to them and to endure their insults preceded here the command to fight them. This makes it superfluous to repeat the abrogation of the command to live in peace with the infidels at each Qur'anic passage [where this is relevant]. [Such a command to live in peace with them] is found in 114 verses in 54 surahs. This is all abrogated by His word: 'Slay the polytheists wherever ye find them' (Qur'ân 9:5) and 'Fighting is prescribed for you' (Qur'ân 2:216)."
Al-Ḥusayn ibn Faḍl	"This is the verse of the sword. It abrogates every verse in the Qur'ân in which suffering the insults of the enemy is mentioned."
Imâm Abû ʿAbdallâh Muḥammad ibn Ḥazm in *Al-Nâsikh wa'l-Mansûkh*	"In 114 verses in 48 surahs everything is abrogated by the Word of God – Exalted and Majestic He is –: 'Slay the polytheists wherever ye find them' (Qur'ân 9:5)"
Imâm Abû al-Qâsim Hibbat Allâh ibn Salâmah	". . . it abrogates 114 verses from the Qur'ân and then the end of it abrogates the beginning of it, because the verse ends with: 'If they repent and establish the Prayer and pay the Zakât, then set them free'."

Faraj goes on to quote two theologians in support of the contention that the abrogating "Verse of the Sword" was itself abrogated by Sura 47:4:

> Therefore, when ye meet the Unbelievers (in fight), smite at their necks; At length, when ye have thoroughly subdued them, bind a bond firmly (on

> them): thereafter (is the time for) either generosity or ransom: Until the war lays down its burdens. Thus (are ye commanded): but if it had been Allah's Will, He could certainly have exacted retribution from them (Himself); but (He lets you fight) in order to test you, some with others. But those who are slain in the Way of Allah, – He will never let their deeds be lost.

Ibn Kathîr suggests that the clause "smite their necks" means "when you fight against them, cut them down totally with your swords", while the clause "when ye have thoroughly subdued them" means "when you have killed and utterly destroyed them."[14] The two theologians quoted by Faraj – al-Suddî and al-Ḍaḥḥâk – declare that "this verse is harsher on the infidels than the Verse of the Sword."[15]

The end result of all the abrogation is that, quite clearly, fighting is made obligatory. Faraj's point is that "fighting" means fighting – *jihâd* means the sword. You cannot interpret these abrogating verses in any way other than in the sense of physical combat. His conclusion is simply and forcefully put. When God made the duty of fasting obligatory, he (God) announced: "Fasting is prescribed to you" (Sura 2:183). Similarly, with regard to the duty of *jihâd*, God declared: "Fighting is prescribed for you" (Sura 2:216). Thus, says Faraj, "the [real character of this] duty is clearly spelled out in the text of the Qur'ân: It is fighting, which means confrontation and blood".[16] Ibn Kathîr draws the same conclusion in his commentary:

> In this Ayah, Allah made it obligatory for the Muslims to fight in *jihâd* against the evil of the enemy who transgresses against Islam. Az-Zuhri said, "Jihad is required from every person, whether he actually joins the fighting or remains behind. Whoever remains behind is required to give support, if support is warranted; to provide aid, if aid is needed; and to march forth, if he is commanded to do so. If he is not needed, then he remains behind".[17]

Ibn Kathîr quotes a *ḥadîth* from Abû Hurayra that supports his exegesis of this verse:

[14] Ibn Kathîr, *op. cit.*, Sura 47: "The Command to strike the Enemies' Necks, tighten their bonds, and then free Them either by an Act of Grace or for a Ransom."

[15] Jansen, *op. cit.*, p 196.

[16] *Ibid.*, p 199.

[17] Ibn Kathîr, *op. cit.*, Sura 2: "Jihad is made Obligatory."

> He who has died, and not fought for the faith, nor said in his heart, "Would to God I was a champion and killed in the road of God", has died a kind of hypocrite.[18]

In the minds of such commentators on the Qur'ân, "fighting" means fighting, for heaven's sake! We are informed, moreover, that, according to other *ḥadîth*, this is a fighting that will continue until the last hour, or until the day of resurrection.[19]

THE OBLIGATION OF *JIHÂD*

Islamists like Faraj (and commentators like Ibn Kathîr) have no patience with a view of the concept of *jihâd* that is anything less than what they believe to be the qur'ânic perspective. They dismiss talk of a "greater" and "lesser" *jihâd*, the "greater" referring to a spiritualised equivalent of striving for God, the "lesser" to physical fighting.[20] In their view, the interpretation of *jihâd* as a so-called spiritual striving against the world, the flesh and the devil is an irrelevancy. It is physical fighting that God has in view in the Verse of the Sword, they insist. They find justification for their perspective in the exegesis of early Qur'ân interpreters and in the deliberations of former

[18] To be found in Muḥammad ibn 'Abd Allâh (trans. A. N. Matthews), *Mishcàt-ul-Masábìh. A Collection of the Most Authentic Traditions Regarding the Actions and Sayings of Muhammed*, Hindoostanee Press: Calcutta (1809), vol 2, book 17, chap 1, part 1, p 239.

[19] For example, in *ibid.*, vol 2, book 17, chap 1, part 2, p 240: "Îmrân ibn Ḥuṣayn: 'A class of my sects will always fight for the word of religion, and will overcome their enemies, until Dajjal shall fight with the last of them'."

[20] Humayan Ansari summarises some of those other concepts of *jihâd* which the Islamists dismiss: "Some Muslim scholars have privileged *al-jihad al-akbar* (higher *jihad* or the struggle against one's own desires and temptations) over *al-jihad al-asghar* (lesser *jihad* or armed fighting in the path of Islam), while many classical jurists certainly felt that the Prophet considered the greater endeavour to be 'the struggle against one's self', of which *jihad bil qalam* (struggle against ignorance through knowledge) and *jihad bil nafs* (struggle against one's own destructive tendencies) were a part." In "Attitudes to Jihad, Martyrdom and Terrorism among British Muslims", in Tahir Abbas (ed.), *op. cit.*, p 147. See also 'Ali B. Uthmân Al-Jullâbî Al-Hujwîrî (trans. Reynold A. Nicholson), *Kashf al-Mahjub of Al Hujwiri*, Luzac: London (1976) where al-Hujwîrî sets out his "Discourse on the Mortification of the Lower Soul." The discourse begins with the following assertion: "God has said: 'Those who strive to the utmost (*jâhadû*) for Our sake, We will guide them into Our ways' (Kor xxix, 69). And the Prophet said: 'The (*mujâhid*) is he who struggles with all his might against himself (*jâhada nafsahu*) for God's sake.' And he also said: 'We have returned from the lesser war (*al-jihâd al-asghar*) to the greater war (*al-jihâd al-akbar*).' On being asked, 'What is the greater war?' he replied, 'It is the struggle against one's self' (*mujâhadat al-nafs*). Thus the apostle adjudged the mortification of the lower soul to be superior to the Holy War against unbelievers, because the former is more painful." In *ibid.*, pp 200–201. The word *jihâd* itself derives from *jahada* meaning "to exert," "to struggle" or "to strive". See the helpful article by Douglas E. Streusand, "What Does Jihad Mean?" in Middle East Quarterly (1997), vol 4, no 3.

theologians, like Ibn Taymîyya. They can be assured that they are not, then, acting as "innovators" (a "bad" word in Islam) but as reformers, calling believers back to faithfulness.

The detailed meaning of text and context in the Qur'ân is the crucial *sine qua non* in their many pages of exegesis and justification. In essence, for modern militant Islamists, *jihâd* is identified as the divinely given means of challenging oppression and establishing the rule of Islam. Most of the Islamic world knows of the Islamists' exegetical deliberations. Most of the rest of the world now knows some of the consequences of their view of what the Qur'ân says.

As such, the Islamists may be seen as shifting the hermeneutic of certainty in a hitherto unprecedented way. They ride on the allowance for *ijtihâd*, serve up their interpretation of *jihâd* as a return to the literal meaning of the qur'ânic text, and come up with an ideology and plan of action that takes their fellow-believers by surprise. It is an ideology and plan of action that is hard to stand up to without appearing considerably unfaithful as a Muslim.

After the assassination of President Anwar Sadat, various "involved parties" stood trial in the Egyptian Supreme Court. Among the defendants was a blind sheikh named Omar Abdul Rahman. The transcript of the final court session, during which the Egyptian attorney general questioned Sheikh Omar, reads as a humiliation of the attorney general at the hands of a cogent sheikh. The blind religious leader argued consistently from what he saw as the proper Islamic perspective, peppering his responses to the attorney general with stabs of sarcasm:[21]

ATTORNEY GENERAL: Jihad is not killing. This is not Islam's teaching. Jihad is a spiritual fight against evil, poverty, sickness and sin. Killing is only from the devil.

SHEIKH RAHMAN: From where does the attorney general come up with this understanding? Are there verses in the Quran that I don't know about that say that jihad is a spiritual fight against evil, poverty, sickness and sin? Perhaps there is new inspiration from Allah that our attorney general received recently and the rest of the Muslims do not yet know.

ATTORNEY GENERAL: Declaring that our Islamic society is heathen, infidels or renegades is an insult to our merciful Allah, his commands and his law.

[21] Quoted from the fuller account of the transcript as given in Mark A. Gabriel, *Islam and Terrorism*, Charisma House: Lake Mary, Florida (2002), pp 159–161. Mark Gabriel (assumed name) is a former professor of Islamic history at al-Azhar university, Egypt.

SHEIKH RAHMAN:	Which commands and laws are you talking about? The ones that compromised adultery, gambling and alcohol? Is this not our merciful Allah's command? Mr. Attorney General, your commands and laws are from the devil.
ATTORNEY GENERAL:	If any Muslim society confesses that Allah is the only God and Muḥammad is his prophet, no one has the right to accuse them of being infidels.
SHEIKH RAHMAN:	What you say is not the real truth. Someone can confess that Allah is God and Muḥammad is his prophet, but he can do something against his confession, and this takes him outside of Islam.
ATTORNEY GENERAL:	President Al-Sadat was a great man who sacrificed his life for the love of Allah and the love of his country.
SHEIKH RAHMAN:	Do you know how this man sacrificed his life for the love of his country? He is the same man who declared that all religions are equal. He made the infidels and the grandchildren of "monkeys and pigs" equal to the Muslims . . .

The court acquitted Sheikh Omar.

DEALING WITH ISLAMISM

The political authorities in Egypt and elsewhere have tended to view the Islamists as a security problem rather than as an ideological threat. Arrests and repression become the answer to Islamism in such circumstances. That answer, however, often serves to inflame the Islamists and to secure more people to their perspective. Violence begets violence, on both sides. Just look at Algeria and the cycle of harsh governmental action against the Islamists answered by the Islamists' indulgence in multiple assassinations throughout the country.

Muslim religious authorities in the West, as a consequence, sound increasingly unconvincing to their non-Muslim compatriots when they protest that Islam is a religion of "peace". Their protestation finds little backing in terms of reality on the ground in many Muslim nations. They find it hard to point to a wide, public debate within Islam about what "Islam" means. How does "Islam" equate to "peace"? How does Muḥammad's leadership in Medina equate to "peace"? Such delicate questions remain largely unaddressed, especially in the public domain. Rather, the "fundamentalists" are executed, imprisoned, silenced. Or else they are forced to flee overseas, to claim asylum in countries such as the United Kingdom. Eventually, some confused, young, indigenous, British Muslims have found themselves recruited by such asylum-seekers to the Islamist perspective and persuaded to act as foot-soldiers in its cause. Hence the violence of 7/7.

The lack of proper debate about what a hermeneutic of certainty might mean comes back to haunt the worldwide Muslim community, and especially those who adamantly refuse to engage meaningfully with the Islamist issue.

Since the arrest of a British shoe-bomber on a plane to America, the deaths of British suicide bombers in Israel, and the murderous suicides of British Islamist foot-soldiers in London, some elements of the British government and some Islamic authorities within the United Kingdom *have* begun to approach the Islamist issue as an ideological matter. They are each talking about disillusioned, non-integrated Muslim youths who feel alienated both from traditional Muslim immigrant communities and from the contemporary Western secular humanist world. Such youths provide prime targets for recruitment by envisioned and envisioning Islamists. However, for British Muslim leaders to be enabled freely to pursue alternative views of what Islam might mean – as a religion of "peace" – there needs to be proposed some new permission for responsibly critiquing the Qur'ân. Why? Simply because the sacred text itself appears to make most sense when read as supporting, proposing even, a sense of holy warring that is physical and prolonged. How is the Prophet's own life to be properly emulated if *jihâd* is emasculated of its physical sense? Prophet Muḥammad many times rode into battle to conquer with a sword. In the years following his death, the sword was used to "pacify" the rebellious Arab tribes. "Wielding the sword" – that reality is involved in the historic meaning of *jihâd*. Even for those who propose a difference between a "greater" and a "lesser" *jihâd* with an emphasis on the former as involving spiritual discipline, the other kind of *jihâd* – the "lesser", physical variety – still remains in the background as an admitted possibility.

A process of *ijtihâd* that allows contemporary Islamists to propose their reconstruction of Islamic theologising must surely be made to permit the possibility of other hermeneutical shifts in Muslim approaches to the Qur'ân. Who is going to apply a form of textual or historical criticism to the Qur'ân in a way equivalent to what

Christians have done with the Bible, setting it in its context, subjecting it to linguistic, exegetical and theological scrutiny? Historically, a few Muslims living in the West – theologians of the ilk of Fazlur Rahman – have dared to interrogate the historic and orthodox interpretations of the qur'ânic text. Today, the journalist Irshad Manji – self-styled Islamic "refusenik" and author of *The Trouble with Islam* – typifies Muslims in the West who have used their relative freedom to excuse a different approach to Qur'ân appreciation.[22] Manji's liberal view, however, remains very much a minority one. Muslims like Manji (and Muslim theologians like Rahman before her), moreover, speak out their different approaches at their own risk. They can find themselves under threat for their public avowal of a different genre of Islam – an avowal only possible because it is made from within Western nations such as the United States of America, where both Rahman and Manji have resided.

It also has to be recognised that many moderate Muslims, for all their hatred of terrorism, have some sympathy with the Islamists' perspective. Islam is equivalent to "peace" only when people are brought to appropriate submission to God. That is the burden of the second half of the Verse of the Sword:

> ". . . but if they repent, and establish regular prayers and practise regular charity, then open the way for them: for Allah is Oft-forgiving, Most Merciful." (Sura 9:5b)

"Peace" is dependent upon submission. The question is: "How is submission to be brought about?" Can the process be only irenic? Such a view looks suspiciously unfaithful or innovative. How can you ignore what the text meant in Muḥammad's day (physical fighting) and still come up with a vision of the Qur'ân as authoritative for today?

There are further difficulties. It is a fact that the Islamists' diagnosis of the ills of the modern world resonates strongly with many ordinary Muslims, whatever their particular interpretation of the meaning of *jihâd*. Many Muslims feel frustrated that Muslim nations and people still seem subject to the national self-interest of the Western "Christian" giant – the United States of America – with many international issues involving Muslims being "solved" only in the sense of their being accommodated to America's will. Again,

[22] Irshad Manji, *The Trouble with Islam*, Mainstream Publishing: Edinburgh (2004).

how might the Muslim (silent) majority answer the strong appeal by the Islamists to Qur'ân and tradition (*ḥadîth*) when it is left to the Islamists especially to give voice to the general Muslim anger at current injustices in the world? The Islamists have, in a very real sense, occupied the moral high ground, and it is difficult for their co-religionists to publicly stand against them.

The subtle but strong undermining of orthodox Islamic perspectives by the Islamists over the past 100 years cannot, I think, be denied. It has been firmly and widely promoted by the sermons and orations of serious students of the Qur'ân – knowledgeable Muslim leaders in the lineage of Mawdûdî, al-Banna, Qutb, Khomeini and al-Turâbî. Most of such ideologues suffered grievously in their respective situations for their faithfulness to a literalist reading of the Qur'ân. Their sufferings lend a disproportionate authority to their pronouncements on behalf of God.

The Islamists, in their insistent appeal to Qur'ân and *ḥadîth*, have perhaps brought the contemporary worldwide Muslim community a challenge that will prove far more powerful than the many, awful bombs that their suicide foot-soldiers have delivered. The Islamists' claim to faithfulness to the original expression of Islam undermines the understandings of Islam that have traditionally been handed down as "orthodox". What seemed to be certain can be so no longer, for the Islamists have posited a more faithful and literal obedience to what was originally given. One wonders about the long-term implications of the Islamists' powerful exegesis for the traditional hermeneutic of certainty within Islam. Is it possible for Muslims to remain so sure about what the Qur'ân reveals once the Islamists have finished with them?

Chapter 2

This is the way the world ends!

IMAGINE noisy, cosmopolitan Jerusalem! Imagine Pastor Cohen, North American church leader and tour guide to Christian pilgrims who have come with him to see how God is fulfilling prophecy in the holy land within their own lifetime. Imagine Victoria Clark, English visitor and friend of the leaders of some of the ancient churches in Jerusalem, somewhat cynical hearer of Cohen's Palm Pilot summary of what the Bible says:

> Pastor Cohen is hurrying on – tap, tap, tapping – in search of Daniel, chapter nine. "You want an end days prophecy," he says slowly, peering at his scrolling screen. "Here we are! 'Seventy weeks of years are decreed concerning your people and your holy city . . . and at the end there shall be war; desolations are decreed.' That'll be the Battle of Armageddon . . . then there's what happens when God finds that only a small part of his chosen people has recognized Jesus as the messiah. Here we go – verses eight and nine – 'two thirds shall be cut off and perish and one third shall be left alive'."
>
> Pastor Cohen and his sort are assisting Jewish immigration to Israel in the belief that the majority of Jews who then fail to recognize Jesus as their messiah will perish – along with secular agnostics, Muslims, Buddhists and Hindus and all other non-Christians. I wonder if Israelis are aware that an energetic section of the Christian Church has cast them as expendable extras in a second great Holocaust aimed at hastening Jesus' return to earth.
>
> Pastor Cohen seems oblivious to my unease at his eager contemplation of the approaching apocalypse. Feeling secure among the automatically saved, I imagine, he races on – tap, tap, tap – "Now here's a more direct reference to Christ's second coming: 'On that day his feet shall stand on the Mount of Olives . . . and the mount of Olives shall be split in two from east to west.' There's a geographical fault line there already, so that's got to happen."
>
> "But what if what we've got here," I interject, "is not a foolproof forecast but some tribal history mixed with myth and ancient propaganda?"
>
> Switching off his Palm Pilot at last and leaning back in his chair he pauses. A practised pastor, he slows his tempo and softens his tone. "Look, I don't claim to understand 99 per cent of what's in the Bible. That's not the point. The point is that I believe every single word of it's the true word of God."[1]

[1] Victoria Clark, *Holy Fire: The Battle for Christ's Tomb*, Macmillan: London (2005), pp138–139.

OTHER CERTAINTIES

The current, or perhaps more accurately, emerging struggle for the soul of Islam that has been provoked by the rise of the modern Islamists is a phenomenon by no means unique to the religion of Islam. Other faiths, also, have experienced, and continue to undergo, a battle for what they might mean in their human expressions.

Gilles Kepel, in his book *The Revenge of God*,[2] argues forcefully for the existence of a frightening trend in contemporary times. He charts the resurgence of religious belief of a fundamentalist genre in the late twentieth century within the faiths of Islam, Christianity and Judaism. Against a background of disillusionment with political ideologies and secular utopias, he discerns a widespread renewal of a provocative kind of religious belief. That renewal has proceeded "from above" and "from below" in those areas of the world where monotheistic faiths constitute part of the background of the people concerned.

The renewal that occurs "from above" arrives in the form of a cornering of state power. That state power is then utilised to promote the fundamentalists' ends. Examples of this are discerned in the Islamic Revolution promoted by Imam Khomeini within Iran (for Islam), or in the role of Menachim Begin's Likud Party in establishing Jewish settlements in occupied territory after 1977 (for Judaism), or in the mobilisation of fundamentalist Christians in the United States that led to the successful elections of Ronald Reagan and George W. Bush as presidents who would re-Christianise America (for Christianity).

The renewal that works "from below" is less tangible in one sense, but more widespread. The Judaising/Islamising of the Israeli/Palestinian conflict constitutes one manifestation. The groundswell of religiously-motivated approaches to the condemning of abortion or the teaching of creationism in the United States constitutes another. The two forms of renewal – from above and from below – are vitally linked.

Perhaps most disturbing in Kepel's commentary on religious fundamentalism, as it finds recent expression within Judaism,

[2] Gilles Kepel, *The Revenge of God: The Resurgence of Islam, Christianity and Judaism in the Modern World* (trans. Alan Braley), Polity Press: Cambridge (1994).

Christianity and Islam, is the role that violence plays at its heart. Violence of a verbal, political or military nature is common to proponents of fundamentalism within all three religious communities.

"CHRISTIAN" AMERICA

From the perspective of Muslim (and other) onlookers, contemporary America is a "Christian" nation. Its international policies reflect, in their eyes, a specifically Christian or religious motive. Such a conclusion is surely understandable, if not completely justified. Dating from the 1970s, that religious motivation became increasingly admitted by many prominent Americans and promoted as unselfconsciously fundamentalist.

Jimmy Carter, "born-again" American President, drew support from the evangelical right in his successful election bid in 1976. So much so that *Newsweek* forthrightly declared 1976 the "Year of the Evangelicals".[3] With Ronald Reagan's election as President in 1980, American, Christian fundamentalist movements – such as Jerry Falwell's Moral Majority, launched in 1979 – grew rapidly in public profile and political clout. Indeed, the fundamentalist groups of the "New Christian Right" claimed the credit for Reagan's successes in both 1980 and 1984. These consecutive political achievements carried the image of an end-of-century success equivalent to the establishing of Prohibition, a society-altering phenomenon that was legally executed in 1919 and which lasted until 1933. That former achievement had shown "the power of a conservative, rigorist Protestant ethic in the American social system", as Kepel puts it.[4]

Now, at the end of the twentieth century, a new band of evangelicals was coming to ascendancy within the American church scene and was flexing its social and political muscles. Tony Campolo, contemporary American evangelical leader and author, describes its arrival:

> Evangelicalism is on a roll. Mainline denominations have been sidelined as evangelicalism has grown in size and significance across the American scene. Fundamentalism, which most sociologists predicted would fade into oblivion by the beginning of the twenty-first century, has done just

[3] Noted by George M. Marsden in *Fundamentalism and American Culture*, Oxford University Press: Oxford (2006), p 242.

[4] Kepel, *op. cit.*, p 107.

> the opposite. Reclothed under the more respected label of *evangelicalism*, fundamentalist Christianity has shown surprising signs of vitality and gained dominance over American church life.[5]

The newly arrived fundamentalist Christians came out of the churches into the political limelight with a strong social conscience. They proved compassionate for the homeless within America and for the hungry in different countries of the world. They organised themselves, as we have seen, into a powerful lobby affecting American politics. The major aim of this New Christian Right in putting modern, "Christian" leaders in the White House was primarily focused around altering legislation on contemporary, critical social issues within American society: abortion, homosexuality, pornography, humanism, and the fractured family (see figure 3).[6]

A conviction about what was wrong with America and a passion to put things right – on the domestic scene – drove the move to reclaim the socio-political world for God. Falwell expressed for many Americans precisely that conviction and that passion:

> As a pastor and as a parent I am calling my fellow American citizens to unite in a moral crusade for righteousness in our generation. It is time to call America back to her moral roots. It is time to call America back to God. We need a revival of righteous living based on a proper confession of sin and repentance of heart if we are to remain the land of the free and the home of the brave! I am convinced that God is calling millions of Americans in the so-often silent majority to join in the moral-majority crusade to turn America around in our lifetime.[7]

Moral Majority was disbanded by Falwell in 1990 but was soon replaced by the Christian Coalition, a political action group led by Pat Robertson, founder of the Christian Broadcasting Network (CBN). Pat Robertson had made an unsuccessful bid for the presidency itself in 1988. In the wake of that unsuccessful bid, he used his large network of campaign workers to promote the growth of the Christian Coalition. The stated goals of the Christian Coalition were to take control of the Republican Party and to elect Christian candidates to public office. Christian Coalition was managed by Ralph Reed, former president of the Young Republicans, who set about shifting the focus of Christian politics away from Washington

[5] Tony Campolo, *Speaking My Mind*, W Publishing Group: Nashville (2004), p 11.

[6] These five issues were identified by Jerry Falwell in his Action Programme. See Jerry Falwell, *Listen, America!* Doubleday: New York (1980), pp 252–254.

[7] *Ibid.*, p 266.

Figure 3

Falwell on "Facing our National Sins"

Sin of . . .	Falwell's comment
Abortion	In 1973, nine men, by a majority vote, declared that it was legitimate to kill unborn children. The U.S. Supreme Court, in a decision known as *Rowe vs. Wade*, granted women an absolute right to abortion on demand during the first two trimesters of pregnancy and an almost unqualified right to abortion in the last trimester.
Homosexuality	In 1979, the National Civil Rights Act would give [Falwell wrote as the legislation was being debated in Congress] homosexuals the same benefits as the 1964 Civil Rights Act, meaning that they could not be discriminated against by any employing body because of "sexual preference".
Pornography	Currently a $4 billion per annum industry. In 1973 it was decided by a divided U.S. Supreme Court in the case *Miller vs. California* that communities must decide what constitutes obscenity.
Humanism	The contemporary philosophy that glorifies man as man, apart from God. Rampant, especially, in the world of education.
Fractured family	Skyrocketing divorce rate and the development of alternative lifestyles.

DC to thousands of communities across the United States. Local chapters of the Christian Coalition inspired and trained candidates to run for school boards, state assemblies and Republican Party leadership. The organisation claimed credit in 1994, during the congressional elections, for ensuring that the majority of the nation's evangelical Protestants identified themselves as Republicans. Voter guides were issued through church services, advising Christians about policies in favour of which they should vote during the coming elections. In process was a re-Christianisation of American society from above. It was a potent process, as Kepel suggests:

> Among all the movements of religious reaffirmation that have appeared on the world political scene since the mid-1970s, the American Evangelists and Fundamentalists hold a position both singular and central.[8]

[8] Kepel, *op. cit.*, p 136.

"READING" THE BIBLE

"A fundamentalist is an evangelical who is angry about something." George Marsden's catchy summary well depicts the motor force behind the emergence of the Religious Right into the political limelight within the United States of America during the last three decades of the twentieth century.[9] Fueling that anger and informing that (laudable) concern for the moral state of their nation went a particular perspective on the Bible and a distinctive view as to how the Bible should be received or interpreted. The masses of the New Christian Right, upon whom leaders like Falwell called, mostly comprised Protestant Christians brought up on the dispensationalism written into the *Scofield Reference Bible* (first published in 1909) and popularly exegeted in Hal Lindsey's *The Late Great Planet Earth* (first published in 1970).[10]

Dispensationalists claim that we are currently experiencing the closing period of church history prior to the Second Coming of Jesus Christ. They name it the "Laodicean" period, and its presence marks the end of the "dispensation of grace", the dispensation in which they believe all humanity is now living. Soon to arrive will be the "dispensation of the kingdom", inaugurated by Christ's return to reign over the earth for a thousand years.[11] Christ's return at such a point is thus labelled "premillennial" or "prior to the thousand years". All dispensationalists, plus many non-dispensationalists, are premillennial in their view of the end-times.[12] Before the glorious return and reign – or *parousia*[13] – of Jesus Christ, however, a period

[9] Marsden (1991) *op. cit.*, p 1. Marsden's more precise definition of an American fundamentalist is "an evangelical who is militant in opposition to liberal theology in the churches or to changes in cultural values or mores, such as those associated with 'secular humanism'." In *ibid.*, p 1.

[10] Lindsey's book, though never on the *New York Times* "best-seller" list, was the best-selling book in America during the 1970s. See Marsden (1991), *op.cit.*, p 77.

[11] Revelation 20:1–6 provides the primary source text for this conviction.

[12] The seed-thought of evangelical, premillennial doctrine most likely originated with a Roman Catholic. In 1827, Edward Irving published his translation of a treatise in Spanish, written by a Chilean Jesuit naming himself Juan Josafat Ben-Ezra, entitled *The Coming of Messiah in Glory and Majesty* (L.B. Seeley & Son: London). The thrust of the treatise was that the present age would close with the second advent of Jesus Christ, which would therefore precede the millennium. See David W. Bebbington, *The Dominance of Evangelicalism*, Inter-Varsity Press: Leicester (2005), p 179.

[13] The Greek word *parousia* carries the connotation "appearance and subsequent presence with".

of great upheaval and suffering lies in store for the inhabitants of this world. Seven years of painful grief – or "Great Tribulation" – are expected to unfold on earth.[14] There are differences of opinion as to whether Christians will remain on earth and share in the time of tribulation or whether they will be raptured out of the world so that only unbelievers and apostate Christians will be "left behind".[15] The latter opinion, technically known as the "pre-tribulational rapture" view of premillenial dispensationalism, is currently the view most widely held by dispensationalists in the United States of America.[16] After the years of tribulation are expended, the thousand-year reign of Christ on earth will begin.

"Something like that!" I'm tempted to quip at the end of this brief and inadequate description of some of the major eschatological convictions of contemporary Christian dispensationalists. The major point to be made, however, is quite clear. The emphases of the various premillennialist views on eschatology arise from a commonly held and distinctive hermeneutic:

> Evangelicals in general believed in accepting as true whatever the Bible taught, but the issue of how far the text was to be understood metaphorically was not agreed. The appeal to the literal sense became a watchword of the premillennial school.[17]

References in the Bible to eschatological events are to be taken as literally true, according to this hermeneutic. Perhaps not surprisingly, dispensationalists strongly disassociate themselves from Christians

[14] The idea of a "great tribulation" is derived from Jesus' words at Matthew 24:21 (and parallel texts). The belief that such a tribulation will last seven years in all is deduced from Daniel's prophecy of "seventy weeks" (Daniel 9:24–26), with each "week" representing 7 years. The last seven-year period is often divided into two 3½ year periods (after Daniel 9:27 and with reference to the "forty-two months" of Revelation 13:5).

[15] Hence the title of the *Left Behind* series by Tim LaHaye and Jerry B. Jenkins. The *Left Behind* series describe scenarios of the "rapture" of true believers in Christ and the ensuing chaos on earth for those left behind. Though the books are presented as fiction, readers find themselves being presented through them with the main tenets of dispensationalism. In the concerned words of Gershom Gorenberg: "The *Left Behind* books are giving millions of people an interpretive paradigm in which extreme views seem sensible. Propaganda in the guise of fiction, they demand our attention." Gershom Gorenberg, "Intolerance: The Bestseller." Review of *Left Behind* series, by Tim LaHaye and Jerry Jenkins, in *American Prospect* (23 September, 2002), pp 44–47.

[16] As hinted here, it needs to be noted that not all premillenialists are pre-tribulationists; some hold a "mid-tribulationist", some a "post-tribulationist", view with differently nuanced convictions concerning the relationship between the rapture to heaven of Christians then alive on earth and the *parousia* of Jesus Christ.

[17] Bebbington, *op. cit.*, pp 183–184.

and churches that they deem to be apostate. They also tend to be world-denying rather than world-affirming – after all, in their view the whole creation is about to go to the dogs:

> If there is any idea that such thinking is harmless, consider the fact that dispensationalist clergymen, such as Jerry Falwell, advised former president George H.W. Bush, as they did former president Ronald Reagan, to embrace a world-view in which America was deemed the instrument of God to raise up an army to fight against the demonic force of the Evil Empire. President Reagan was convinced that he was called to build up the military power of the United States so as to make its army the inevitable victor at Armageddon. Now there is growing evidence that President George W. Bush may be falling into this same kind of thinking as he talks about the need to destroy those nations that make up what he has called "the axis of evil".[18]

Apart from strong convictions about moral and ethical issues within American public life, and strong sympathy for a dispensationalist perspective on the times in which we live, the belief system of Hal Lindsey, Jerry Falwell and Pat Robertson – and an estimated 40+ million[19] American evangelical fundamentalists – finds an external focus in convictions, especially, about God and the Middle East. That external focus concentrates on the biblical land of Zion and the modern Zionist State of Israel. These two phenomena become equated in the Christian fundamentalist perspective. Marsden makes the pointed comment, concerning this melding of theology and geo-politics: "The one major area of practical politics where premillennialism is operative is policy towards the state of Israel".[20] In the attitudes and actions of successive American presidents, this externally focused aspect of Christian fundamentalism has found continuing expression at the end of the twentieth century and into the new millennium.

President Carter, for example, early admitted how his own Christian Zionist views tended to influence his policy decisions with regard to the Middle East. He saw the State of Israel as:

> a return at last, to the biblical land from which the Jews were driven so many hundreds of years ago . . . The establishment of the nation of Israel is the fulfilment of biblical prophecy and the very essence of its fulfilment.[21]

[18] Campolo, *op. cit.*, p 213.

[19] Falwell would claim to represent 70 million such constituents in 2002.

[20] Marsden (2006), *op. cit.*, p 249.

[21] Speech by President Jimmy Carter on 1 May 1978, *Department of State Bulletin*, vol 78, no 2015 (1978), p 4; quoted in Stephen Sizer, *Christian Zionism: Road-map to Armageddon?* Inter-Varsity Press: Leicester (2004), p 86.

During Carter's presidency, Franklin Littell and Christians Concerned for Israel[22] successfully lobbied both the Congress and the Administration, persuading them to withdraw a previous commitment to sell F-15s and other reconnaissance equipment to Saudi Arabia, a strong ally of the USA in those years. The same pressure group later mobilised Christian voices in Washington against the sale of AWACS planes to the Saudis, with equivalent success. Israel had to be seen to come first in terms of foreign policy focus.

President George H.W. Bush supported the famous "House Resolution 457" (in 1990) that called on the United Nations to repeal its Resolution 3379. UN Resolution 3379 had been endorsed by the General Assembly in 1975. It was intended to reprimand all forms of racism and discrimination on the part of UN member nations. Only the final few words of the 450-word resolution were directed towards Israel: "Zionism is a form of racism and discrimination." The House Resolution 457 declared, to the contrary: "Zionism is a national movement of the Jewish people for self-determination, a legitimate and moral aspiration characteristic of many national groups in the modern world."[23] US pressure to repeal UN Resolution 3379 finally produced the result desired by the Christian Zionists in 1991 when the world body uncharacteristically repealed one of its own resolutions.

President Ronald Reagan, influenced by dispensationalist evangelists such as Jerry Falwell and Pat Robertson, believed that one of his responsibilities was to promote a military build-up so that the USA would be ready for the battle of Armageddon. The President was quoted in the *Washington Post* as declaring to Tom Dine, director of the American Israel Public Affairs Committee:

> You know, I turn back to your ancient prophets in the Old Testament and signs foretelling Armageddon, and I find myself wondering if – if we're the generation that's going to see that come about. I don't know if you've noted any of those prophecies lately, but believe me, they certainly describe the times we're going through.[24]

[22] Franklin Littell established Christians Concerned for Israel shortly after the Six-Day War in June 1967. The aim of the organisation was to reactivate the pro-Israel spirit in the mainline Protestant churches.

[23] It was the National Christian Leadership Conference for Israel, an organisation organised by Franklin Littell and associated with Falwell's Moral Majority, that spearheaded the campaigning from 1985 onwards to repeal UN Resolution 3379.

[24] Ronnie Dugger, "Does Reagan Expect a Nuclear Armageddon?" in *Washington Post*, 18th April, 1984, C1. Quoted by Rammy M. Haija, "The Armageddon Lobby: Dispensationalist Christian Zionism and the Shaping of US Policy towards Israel-Palestine" in *Holy Land Studies*, vol. 5, no. 1 (2006), p 88.

In a *60 Minutes* interview in October 2002, during President George W. Bush's first term, Jerry Falwell stated: "I think now we can count on President Bush to do the right thing for Israel every time."[25] Falwell's comments came in the light of Bush's actions during April of that year when the President turned a blind eye to Israel's destroying of several West Bank cities. An article published in *Time* magazine at that time made the following, pointed claim:

> Today the most influential lobbying on behalf of Israel is being done by a group not usually seen as an ally of the largely Democratic Jewish community: Evangelical Christians.[26]

Falwell met with George W. Bush several times during his first term in office specifically to discuss the matter of US support of Israel. According to Falwell, the President's views on Israel were consistent with his own.

The Christian fundamentalists' interpretation of prophecy includes the conviction, as supplied by dispensationalist theologians, that Solomon's Temple must be rebuilt on Mount Zion before Christ returns. They believe, moreover, that a nuclear Armageddon is inevitable and will most likely occur in this generation's lifetime – with the result that the great planet earth will be transformed into the *late* great planet earth.

SUPPORTING GOD'S "CHOSEN" PEOPLE?

Ever since 1967, the Zionist State of Israel's connection with the New Christian Right in America has grown. After the infamous "Six Days War", the National Council of Churches in America called for an end to Israeli occupation of Arab lands. Israel was keen for alternative sympathisers within the United States and the Christian fundamentalists were beginning to come of age. Within a decade, Israel's links to Zionist Christians in the USA had been firmly put in place. At a gala dinner in New York City, hosted in 1979 by then Likud leader and Israeli Prime Minister Menahem Begin, Jerry Falwell and Billy Graham were both presented with the

[25] "Bob Simon Interviews Jerry Falwell", *60 Minutes*, CBS (6 October 2002), quoted in Haija, *op. cit.*, p 89.

[26] Romesh Ratnetsar, "The Right's New Crusade: Lobbying for Israel" in *Time* (6 May 2002), p 26, quoted in Haija, *op. cit.*, p 76.

Jabotinsky Centennial Medal.[27] The Jabotinsky medal is awarded by the State of Israel to a person who is considered a lifetime friend of the nation. The presentation of the two inaugural medals to Falwell and Graham acknowledged their long-time, staunch support of Israel. At the New York gala dinner, the Israel/Christian Zionist connection was publicly and lavishly formalised.

In 1980, Prime Minister Begin illegally annexed Arab East Jerusalem. Thirteen foreign embassies protested the annexation by shifting their residences from West Jerusalem to Tel Aviv. Israel's response included an invitation for the creation of a "Christian" Embassy in Jerusalem. The resulting International Christian Embassy became the organising force behind Christian charismatic gatherings in Jerusalem during the Feast of Tabernacles from 1982 onwards. In 1985, the Christian Zionist Congress was inaugurated in Jerusalem. Both Jews and Christians attended. At one meeting some Christians suggested that, not only should all Jews be encouraged to move to the State of Israel, but Israel should annex the West Bank. An Israeli Jewish man, referring to a recent Israeli poll, stated that a third of Israel's citizens would favour returning the West Bank to the Palestinians in exchange for peace. The spokesperson for the International Christian Embassy in Jerusalem angrily intervened, declaring, "We don't care what the Israelis vote! We care what God says, and God gave that land to the Jews!"[28] The resolution calling for an annexation of the West Bank was passed unanimously by the Christian voters at the session.

The origins, growth and connections of American fundamentalist Christians with the Zionist State of Israel were researched and published in 1986 by an American author, Grace Halsell. Her book, *Prophecy and Politics*, is subtitled "Militant Evangelists on the Road to Nuclear War." In this book Halsell relates her experience of pilgrimages to Israel with Jerry Falwell's organisation. She describes the "marriage of convenience" between the State of Israel and the New Christian Right.[29] Halsell closes her account with a chapter entitled

[27] The Jabotinsky Centennial Medal was named after Vladimir Jabotinsky, right-wing Zionist leader.

[28] Reported by Grace Halsell in *Prophecy and Politics: Militant Evangelists on the Road to Nuclear War*, Lawrence Hill & Company: Westport, Connecticut (1986).

[29] Donald Wagner uses stronger language than "marriage of convenience", suggesting that the leadership of the Israeli government deliberately exploited American Christian Zionist groups. He also notes that while Jewish groups in the USA and Israel strongly oppose any kind of religious alliance with the Christian Zionists, they have accepted a political alliance

"JerUSAlem: Mixing Politics and Religion" in which she cites the support given by an array of North American tele-evangelists and others to the conviction that Jerusalem belongs exclusively, by divine apportioning, to the Jews.[30] The book is a frightening analysis of a closed Christian mindset that believes that the world is doomed to a nuclear showdown in the valley of Jezreel. Born-again Christians need not worry about that showdown, however, because they will be raptured out of the way before the fireworks start:

> I heard Falwell sum up his reason why a nuclear Armageddon would not bother him. "You know why I'm not worried?" he said. "I ain't gonna be here."[31]

Halsell's book was translated into Arabic and distributed widely in Egypt in the late 1980s. It confirmed in the minds of Muslim readers that the theology of Christian Zionism is behind the "biased foreign policy" of the United States government in its approach to Middle Eastern affairs.[32]

In the identifying by the Christian fundamentalists of who the end-time "bad guys" are, a shift began to take place in the 1990s. With the collapse of the European Communist bloc and the undermining of Russia as a world power, Hal Lindsey, for example, began to re-classify the end-time enemies of Israel. What had been pinpointed by him in 1970 as "the Russian force" was expanded in 1997 to "the Russian-Muslim force".[33] Fundamentalist Christians are queuing up today to announce: "This is the way the world ends!"

with the movement because it provides another voice for Israeli interests within US policy. See Donald Wagner, *Anxious for Armageddon*, Herald Press: Scottsdale (1995).

[30] Robert Fisk highlights the continuation of such support in his summary of a full-page advertisement in the *New York Times* on 18 April 1997 that was signed by ten Christian "spiritual leaders", including Pat Robertson and Jerry Falwell. The advertisement reaffirmed belief in a "divine mandate" requiring that "Jerusalem must remain undivided as the eternal capital of the Jewish people." In Robert Fisk, *The Great War for Civilisation: The Conquest of the Middle East*, HarperCollins: London (2005), p 525.

[31] Grace Halsell, *op. cit.*, (1986), p 39. See also Stephen Sizer, *Christian Zionism: Road Map to Armageddon?* IVP: Leicester (2004). There are British equivalents to American Christian fundamentalism. David Pawson, for example, declares: "I see everywhere in the Bible prophecies of the restoration of a theocracy in Israel. We may ask, how could it happen in modern Israel, since it is a secular state? But God will resolve the problem . . . What will happen in the future is the spiritual return and restoration, and it is on its way. We Christian Zionists announce the Kingdom of Israel. One day everybody will see a spiritual Israel again." From his address given at the Christian Zionist Congress in Basle, August 1985 and quoted by Colin Chapman in *Whose Promised Land?* (Lion: Oxford (2002), p 278.

[32] Nabeel Jabbour, *The Rumbling Volcano: Islamic Fundamentalism in Egypt*, Mandate Press: Pasadena (1993), p 224.

[33] As recounted by Stephen Sizer in *op. cit.*, p 125. The references are to Hal Lindsey, *The Late Great Planet Earth*, Lakeland: London (1970), p 160, and Hal Lindsey, *Apocalypse Code*, Western Front: Palos Verdes (1997), p 153.

Of course, the post-9/11 response of strongly Christian-motivated political leaders to the agendas of the Islamists at an international level has arisen out of their "biblical" view of the world. They have defined an "axis of evil" and put in place a foreign policy designed to crush that evil before it ever again comes to American shores. Campolo describes the strong support for such a "just war" policy offered to those political leaders by the American, fundamentalist Christian community. In a *Larry King Live* television broadcast just before the commencement of the Iraq War, a Methodist bishop and a Roman Catholic priest spoke against war while two well-known television evangelists spoke in favour of it:

> Those two men stated in no uncertain terms that what was about to happen in Iraq was a fulfilment of biblical prophecy, and the evangelical community widely circulated their opinion. In the book of Revelation, we read about the Battle of Armageddon (Rev. 16) in which, in anticipation of Christ's rule over the world, the armies of God defeat the armies of Satan. Books supporting the belief that the coming war in Iraq was this battle appeared in Christian bookstores and a rash of radio preachers upheld the same message.[34]

The "war on terror" might truly be caricatured as the forces of one fundamentalist mindset trying to bomb into oblivion the forces of an opposing fundamentalist mindset. The scenario adds up to a nightmarish description of a potentially self-fulfilling prophecy.

FRUITS OF FUNDAMENTALISM

Kenneth Cragg incisively depicts the essence of "fundamentalism" as constituting a "cultural annexation of God".[35] By such ideological recasting of Bible or Qur'ân, God is "allowed" to work only in the propositionally permitted ways that human beings set up. Out of his study of the Christian variety of fundamentalism in America, Kepel concludes that:

> Ever since the mid-1970s Fundamentalists have steered the Evangelical movement (in the wider meaning of the term) towards the more 'conservative' parties, working for the election of Ronald Reagan in 1980 and 1984 . . . During this period there were again similarities to situations observable in Catholicism and in Islam.[36]

[34] Campolo, *op. cit.*, p 164.
[35] Kenneth Cragg, *Jesus and the Muslim: An Exploration*, George Allen & Unwin: London (1985), p 285.
[36] Kepel, *op. cit.*, p 138.

The "fundamentalist" dye colours most of our human hearts, for it is an expression of our egocentricity. Equivalent movements within Judaism, Buddhism and Hinduism to those described here concerning Islam and Protestant Christianity can quickly be identified. For those of us who purport to believe in the one God, we would control even him if we could. The Islamists, of course, strongly believe that God himself authors what they do. The Christian fundamentalists believe the same about God and themselves! Each constituency exercises a similar approach to decoding its holy scripture: it employs a literalist qur'ânic or biblical hermeneutic. Each constituency's members see themselves as remaining peculiarly "faithful" to their text. They see themselves, moreover, as alone shining out as those truly "faithful" to God among their fellow faith-members. And their equivalent goals? That the rest of mankind be forced to agree in the one divinely sanctioned view: "their" view!

Bombs planted on the commuter transportation system in London have caused huge collateral damage within British Muslim communities up and down the land. Within those communities the discovery that the perpetrators were *British* Muslims has caused great soul-searching. Some British Muslims are, of course, in denial. Many British Muslims feel very vulnerable, with considerable justification. Some, however, have reflected hard on 7/7 and recognise that Islamism is a *Muslim* problem, requiring a Muslim answer:

> So it just won't do to say that these people are "not Muslims", as the Muslim Council of Britain seems to suggest. We must acknowledge that the terrorists, and their neo-Kharijite tradition, are products of Islamic history. Only by recognising this brutal fact would we realise that the fight against terrorism is also an internal Muslim struggle within Islam. Indeed, it is a struggle for the very soul of Islam.[37]

It is my conviction that today in Britain, there are possibilities of non-fundamentalist Muslims questioning the nature of the "sword" in the hands of the Islamists. If Muslims would be moved by the Islamists to rethink their view of the "literalness" of the Qur'ân, there are some ready issues in the history of their faith's historic development that might contribute towards a healthy debate about what it means for God's word to be encapsulated in human speech.

To those ready issues we turn in the next section of this book. It is time to question certainty.

[37] Sardar, (2005), *op. cit.*, p 12.

Questioning certainty

Chapter 3

Sorry, I didn't really mean that!

THE Qur'ân is critical for Islamists. Their convictions about its demands upstage other Muslims simply because all Muslims see the revelation as being literally given by God. The Qur'ân comprises, absolutely, God's word to humankind. Although Prophet Muḥammad received and passed on the qur'ânic message in piecemeal manner, through thirteen years' residence at Mecca and ten years' residence at Medina, the whole body of revelation is seen by Muslims as being "sent down" by God. That divine action, with regard to the "giving" of the Qur'ân from above, elicits praise from Muslims' hearts and convinces them of its total trustworthiness.

"Sending down" or *tanzîl* describes a different view of revelation or inspiration from the biblical one. In the Islamic case, the human vehicle is not really engaged or involved in the formulating of the message. He is simply a vehicle for its recitation:

> The messenger (i.e. the angel bearing the message) is sent to the recipient of the Divine revelation, and the Divine message is delivered in words . . . The prophet's faculty of being spoken to by God is so highly developed that he receives the Divine messages, not only as ideas instilled into the mind or in the form of words uttered or heard under the influence of the Holy Spirit, but actually as Divine messages in words delivered through the Holy Spirit. In the terminology of Islâm this is called *waḥy matluww*, or *revelation that is recited*, and the Holy Qur'ân was from beginning to end delivered in this form to the Holy Prophet.[1]

God conveys the message through his Prophet who, as a result, finds himself in a state of inspiration. "Sending down" is at God's initiative and is carried out *via* (not in cooperation with) the human vehicle of revelation (see figure 4).

[1] Maulana Muhammad 'Ali, *The Religion of Islam*, National Publication & Printing House: Cairo (n.d.), p 22. It should be noticed that by reference to the "Holy Spirit" 'Ali means the angel Gabriel (see *ibid.* p 18). This is a standard Muslim understanding.

Figure 4

Examples of reference to *tanzîl* or "sending down" in the Qur'ân

We sent down the (Qur-ân) in Truth, and in Truth has it descended: and We sent thee but to give Glad Tidings and to warn (sinners). Sura 17:105	We have sent it down as an Arabic Qur-ân, in order that ye may learn wisdom. Sura 12:2	And this is a Book which We have sent down, bringing blessings, and confirming (the revelations) which came before it . . . Sura 6:92

Such a process appears to be tidy and self-protecting, but in reality there proved to be a problem when "revelation" proceeded in that fashion. Both in the ongoing process of conveying the Qur'ân via Prophet Muḥammad and with the later hindsight of commentators looking over the whole corpus of revelation, there proved to be places where the divine word appeared internally inconsistent – what was revealed at one point seemed to be contradicted by verses given at a later point in Muḥammad's life and leadership. The principle of "abrogation" came to be applied to such inconsistencies in order to explain them.

CHANGING GOD'S WORD?

By means of abrogation or cancellation, potentially contradictory passages of the Qur'ân find reconciliation. Normally, in this process, a later verse is said to replace a former verse. Verses that are abrogated are known as *mansûkh*; those doing the abrogating are referred to as *nâsikh*. The principle of abrogation finds strong qur'ânic support:

> None of Our revelations do We abrogate or cause to be forgotten, but We substitute something better or similar: Knowest thou not that Allah Hath power over all things? (Sura 2:106)

Some of the renowned commentators on the Qur'ân, such as al-Bayḍâwî and al-Zamakhsharî, insisted that abrogated verses should no longer be recited, while laws based upon them should be annulled. In some cases, it would seem, abrogated verses were removed from the text as part of the ongoing process of "sending

Figure 5

Abrogated verses in the Qur'ân according to al-Suyûtî

Subject of abrogation	**Abrogated verse *mansûkh***	**Abrogating verse *nâsikh***
facing the *qibla* (Mecca for Jerusalem)	2:115	2:144
retaliation (against person of equal rank to the one murdered, or against murderer only)	2:178	5:48
fast of Ramaḍân	2:183	2:187
expiation	2:184	2:185
the fear of God	3:102	64:16
jihâd	4:89	4:90
jihâd in sacred months (forbidden or allowed)	2:217	9:36
provision for widows	2:240	2:234
slaying enemies in sacred mosque	2:191	9:5
imprisonment of the adulteress	4:15	24:2
witnesses	5:109	65:2
jihâd with infidels	8:65	8:66
marriage of adulterers	24:3	24:32
the Prophet's wives	33:52	33:50
giving alms before assembling a council	58:13a	58:13b
payment to infidels for women taken in marriage	60:11	9:1
jihâd with infidels	9:39	9:91
the night prayer (how long)	73:2	73:20
permission to young children to enter a house	24:58	24:59
division of inheritance between males and females	4:7	4:11

down" via Prophet Muḥammad. In other cases, both the original abrogated text and the later abrogating text were retained and continue to be part of the Qur'ân. There is considerable discussion about which verses – abrogated and abrogating – remain within the Qur'ân.

Jalâlu'l-Dîn al-Suyûtî (AD 1445–1505) produced a list of twenty verses (remaining within the body of the Qur'ân) that were acknowledged by all commentaries at his disposal as having been abrogated during the lifetime of Prophet Muḥammad. In other words, while the process of "sending down" was still going on, it was made clear which verses were being replaced by new revelation. The list is produced as figure 5.

Shâh Walî Allâh (AD 1703–1762), by contrast, allowed only five abrogated verses.[2] Shâh Walî Allâh set out his principles of qur'ânic exegesis in a famous text (*al-Fawz al-Kabîr*) and classified the themes of the Qur'ân under five major subjects. He aimed at clarifying the Qur'ân for ordinary Muslims. Indeed, in line with that aim, he translated the Qur'ân into Persian. The critical verses that Shâh Walî Allâh deduced as abrogated/abrogating (along with their texts) are reproduced as figure 6.

We shall look later in this chapter at the intriguing case of a verse that is now missing from the Qur'ân – though referenced in the *ḥadîth* literature – that abrogates a verse that remains in the Qur'ân.

The phenomenon of abrogation or *naskh* is explained primarily, as we have noted, by reference to God's sovereignty (Sura 2:106). It finds rationalisation in the claim that abrogated verses were only intended to address temporary, specific situations.

ABROGATING WHICH WORD?

In more recent times, it has become the practice of some Muslim theologians to apply the concept of abrogation at least as much to the idea that a later revelation from God (such as the Qur'ân) abrogates a former revelation (such as the *Injîl* or Gospel) as to the idea that a later verse of the Qur'ân abrogates an earlier verse of that particular revelation from God. Maulana Muḥammad 'Ali, in *The Religion of Islam*, typifies this shift in the application of the concept of abrogation:

[2] Maulana Muhammad 'Ali, *op. cit.*, pp 41–42.

Figure 6

Shâh Walî Allâh's list of abrogated verses

Abrogated verse: *mansûkh*	**Abrogating verse: *nâsikh***
It is prescribed, when death approaches any of you, if he leave any goods that he make a bequest to parents and next of kin, according to reasonable usage; this is due from the Allah-fearing. (Sura 2:180)	Allah (thus) directs you as regards your children's (Inheritance): to the male, a portion equal to that of two females: if only daughters, two or more, their share is two-thirds of the inheritance; if only one, her share is a half. For parents, a sixth share of the inheritance to each, if the deceased left children; if no children, and the parents are the (only) heirs, the mother has a third; if the deceased left brothers (or sisters) the mother has a sixth. (The distribution in all cases is) after the payment of legacies and debts. Ye know not whether your parents or your children are nearest to you in benefit. These are settled portions ordained by Allah; and Allah is All-knowing, All-wise. (Sura 4:11)
Those of you who die and leave widows should bequeath for their widows a year's maintenance and residence; but if they leave (the residence), there is no blame on you for what they do with themselves, provided it is reasonable. And Allah is Exalted in Power, Wise. (Sura 2:240)	If any of you die and leave widows behind, they shall wait concerning themselves four months and ten days: When they have fulfilled their term, there is no blame on you if they dispose of themselves in a just and reasonable manner. And Allah is well acquainted with what ye do. (Sura 2:234)
O Prophet! rouse the Believers to the fight. If there are twenty amongst you, patient and persevering, they will vanquish two hundred: if a hundred, they will vanquish a thousand of the Unbelievers: for these are a people without understanding. (Sura 8:65)	For the present, Allah hath lightened your (task), for He knoweth that there is a weak spot in you: But (even so), if there are a hundred of you, patient and persevering, they will vanquish two hundred, and if a thousand, they will vanquish two thousand, with the leave of Allah: for Allah is with those who

Figure 6 (*cont.*)

Abrogated verse: *mansûkh*	**Abrogating verse: *nâsikh***
It is not lawful for thee (to marry more) women after this, nor to change them for (other) wives, even though their beauty attract thee, except any thy right hand should possess (as handmaidens): and Allah doth watch over all things. (Sura 33:52)	O Prophet! We have made lawful to thee thy wives to whom thou hast paid their dowers; and those whom thy right hand possesses out of the prisoners of war whom Allah has assigned to thee; and daughters of thy paternal uncles and aunts, and daughters of thy maternal uncles and aunts, who migrated (from Makka) with thee; and any believing woman who dedicates her soul to the Prophet if the Prophet wishes to wed her; – this only for thee, and not for the Believers (at large); We know what We have appointed for them as to their wives and the captives whom their right hands possess; – in order that there should be no difficulty for thee. And Allah is Oft-Forgiving, Most Merciful. (Sura 33:50)
O ye who believe! When ye consult the Messenger in private, spend something in charity before your private consultation. That will be best for you, and most conducive to purity (of conduct). But if ye find not (the wherewithal), Allah is Oft-Forgiving, Most Merciful.(Sura 58:12)	Is it that ye are afraid of spending sums in charity before your private consultation (with him)? If, then, ye do not so, and Allah forgives you, then (at least) establish regular prayer; practise regular charity; and obey Allah and His Messenger. And Allah is well-acquainted with all that ye do. (Sura 58:13)
O ye who believe! When ye consult the Messenger in private, spend something in charity before your private consultation. That will be best for you, and most conducive to purity (of conduct). But if ye find not (the wherewithal), Allah is Oft-Forgiving, Most Merciful. (Sura 58:12)	Is it that ye are afraid of spending sums in charity before your private consultation (with him)? If, then, ye do not so, and Allah forgives you, then (at least) establish regular prayer; practise regular charity; and obey Allah and His Messenger. And Allah is well-acquainted with all that ye do. (Sura 58:13)

That certain verses of the Qur'ân are abrogated by others is now an exploded theory. The two passages on which it was supposed to rest refer, really, to the abrogation, not of the passages of the Holy Qur'ân but, of the previous revelations whose place the Holy Qur'ân has taken.[3]

[3] Maulana Muhammad 'Ali, *op. cit.*, p 35.

'Ali goes on to deal specifically with the two passages or verses that he identifies as critical:

> When We substitute one revelation for another, – and Allah knows best what He reveals (in stages), – they say, "Thou art but a forger": but most of them understand not. (Sura 16:101)

> None of Our revelations do We abrogate or cause to be forgotten, but We substitute something better or similar: Knowest thou not that Allah Hath power over all things? (Sura 2:106)

Concerning the former passage (Sura 16:101), 'Ali identifies it as part of a Meccan revelation, that is, an early revelation. He argues that details of Islamic law were not revealed until Prophet Muḥammad resided in Medina and it is with regard to details of the law that the theory of abrogation came to be promoted. Consequently, a Meccan revelation would not speak of abrogation. Therefore, he suggests, the Meccan reference must be to the abrogation of previous divine messages that was brought about by the giving of the Qur'ân.

Concerning the latter passage (Sura 2:106), 'Ali argues that the context of this revelation is one in which Jews, or the followers of previous revelations, are being addressed. He also contends that the issue is not one of abrogation but of "causing to forget". Prophet Muḥammad did not forget any of the Qur'ân, but the Jews (in qur'ânic perspective) certainly did forget parts of the revelation sent down through Prophet Moses to *them*. Therefore, the Qur'ân was needed to take the place of that which was abrogated, that which had come to be forgotten by the Jews.

'Ali goes on to address each of the five cases of alleged abrogation allowed by Shâh Walî Allâh, arguing in each case why the principle of abrogation cannot be allowed to apply. He does not, however, deal specifically with the remaining sixteen of al-Suyûtî's twenty-one verses.

'Ali concludes that the principle on which the theory of abrogation is based is false, most fundamentally because it is contrary to the plain teaching of the Qur'ân. The Qur'ân elsewhere declares:

> Do they not consider the Qur'an (with care)? Had it been from other than Allah, they would surely have found therein much discrepancy. (Sura 4:82)

This verse, suggests 'Ali, clearly declares that no part of the Qur'ân is at variance with another part. If Muslim commentators would only meditate a bit more on the text – consider it "with care"

– they would discover its internal consistency. The concept of abrogation, in his view, is not needed.

In the *ḥadîth* literature, however, references to the process of abrogation are plainly delineated and strongly support the contention that the phenomenon relates internally to the text of the Qur'ân itself. The classic example, often employed to demonstrate the way abrogation proceeds, concerns the widow's bequest. The relevant qur'ânic verses are Sura 2:240 and Sura 2:234, with the latter being said to abrogate the former. These verses appear in the lists of both al-Suyûtî and Walî Allâh – the text is included in figure 6. Al-Bukhârî includes several *ḥadîth* concerning the process of abrogation apparent in these verses:

> Narrated Ibn Az-Zubair: I said to 'Uthman bin 'Affân (while he was collecting the Qur'ân) regarding the Verse: Those of you who die and leave wives . . . (2:240) "This Verse was abrogated by another Verse. So why should you write it? (Or leave it in the Qur'ân?)" 'Uthmân said, "O son of my brother! I will not shift anything of it from its place."[4]

Here the accepted fact of abrogation is baldly stated. Al-Bukhârî goes on to quote other traditions that explain the intent behind the abrogation. In those other traditions, however, it appears that the understanding of the application of abrogation in this instance proceeds in the opposite direction, with Sura 2:240 abrogating Sura 2:234:

> Narrated Mujâhid (regarding the Verse . . . 2:234). The widow, according to this Verse, was to spend this period of waiting with her husband's family, so Allâh revealed . . . Sura 2:240. So Allâh entitled the widow to be bequeathed extra maintenance for seven months and twenty nights, and that is the completion of one year. If she wished she could stay (in her husband's home) according to the will, and she could leave it if she wished, as Allâh says: ". . . without turning them out, but if they leave (the residence), there is no blame on you.' So the 'Idda (i.e. four months and ten days) is obligatory for her . . .[5]

Another oft-quoted example of the process of abrogation concerns the issue of drinking wine. Wine-drinking, along with gambling, was a fact of life in the early Muslim, Medinan community. At first the Qur'ân suggests that though such practices were significantly sinful, they also brought with them some benefits:

> They ask thee concerning wine and gambling. Say: "In them is great sin, and some profit, for men; but the sin is greater than the profit." They ask

[4] Recorded in al-Bukhârî, *al-Ṣaḥîḥ*, vol 6, book 60, chap 40, trad 53, p 40.
[5] Recorded in al-Bukhârî, *al-Ṣaḥîḥ*, vol 6, book 60, chap 40, trad 54, p 41.

> thee how much they are to spend; Say: "What is beyond your needs." Thus doth Allah Make clear to you His Signs: In order that ye may consider – (Sura 2:219).

Muslims were hereby warned that the ill effects outweighed the good effects in these habits. Those ill effects included the dishonour brought to God when Muslims came drunk to prayers:

> O ye who believe! Approach not prayers with a mind befogged, until ye can understand all that ye say, – nor in a state of ceremonial impurity (Except when travelling on the road), until after washing your whole body. If ye are ill, or on a journey, or one of you cometh from offices of nature, or ye have been in contact with women, and ye find no water, then take for yourselves clean sand or earth, and rub therewith your faces and hands. For Allah doth blot out sins and forgive again and again. (Sura 4:43)

A mind befogged, because intoxicated, is as undermining of prayer as ceremonial impurity, according to this revelation. It was not just prayer that was compromised by wine drinking. During the battle of Uhud, a number of Muslims were killed, some of whom had drunk alcohol on the morning of the conflict:

> Narrated Jâbir: Some people drank alcoholic beverages in the morning (of the day) of the Uhud battle and on the same day they were killed as martyrs, and that was before wine was prohibited.[6]

Eventually, during the later Medinan period, verses were revealed that defined intoxicants and gambling as abominations. Such indulgences were, from that point onwards, to be completely abandoned:

> O ye who believe! Intoxicants and gambling, (dedication of) stones, and (divination by) arrows, are an abomination, – of Satan's handwork: eschew such (abomination), that ye may prosper. Satan's plan is (but) to excite enmity and hatred between you, with intoxicants and gambling, and hinder you from the remembrance of Allah, and from prayer: will ye not then abstain? (Sura 5:90–91)

A *ḥadîth* fills out the context in which these verses of prohibition were sent down:

> Narrated Anas: The alcoholic drink which was spilled was Al-Faḍîkh. I used to offer alcoholic drinks to the people at the residence of Abû Ṭalḥa. Then the order of prohibiting alcoholic drinks was revealed, and the Prophet ordered somebody to announce that [Abû Ṭalḥa said to me, "Go out and see what this voice (this announcement) is." I went out and (on coming back) said, "This is somebody announcing that"] alcoholic

[6] Recorded in al-Bukhârî, *al-Ṣaḥîḥ*, vol 6, book 60, chap 108, trad 142, p 112.

> beverages have been prohibited. Abû Ṭalḥa said to me, "Go and spill it (i.e. the wine)," Then it (alcoholic drinks) was seen flowing through the streets of Medîna. At that time the wine was Al-Faḍîkh. The people said, "Some people (Muslims) were killed (during the battle of Uhud) while wine was in their stomachs." So Allâh revealed: – On those who believe and do good deeds there is no blame for what they ate (in the past). (5:93)[7]

The prohibition of drinking alcohol proceeded gradually, via the sending down of different verses that at first questioned its value, then condemned its interference with the ability to pray properly, and finally outlawed it altogether. With the outright outlawing of the drinking of alcohol, the Qur'ân makes clear that no blame attaches to those who had imbibed in the past, so long as they now live by this decree.

A process of abrogation allowed progress in revelation, illustrated here in the way in which it was determined that widows should be treated, and in the manner in which the drinking of alcoholic beverages came gradually to be abandoned.

A CHANGING, *DIVINE* WORD?

The "problem" of abrogation lies in two areas as far as hermeneutics, or interpretation, is concerned. Firstly, the Qur'ân specifically says on the one hand that "No change can there be in the Words of God" (Sura 10:64) and on the other hand that "We substitute one revelation for another" (Sura 16:101 – "We" delineates God speaking). This latter verse refers unambiguously to the substitution of texts within the Qur'ân itself in its use of the word *aya* for "revelation".[8] Such seeming contradictions in the Qur'ân have led to considerable debate by Muslim theologians. We shall investigate some aspects of that debate when we consider the question of whether the

[7] Recorded in al-Bukhârî, *al-Ṣaḥîḥ*, vol 6, book 60, chap 109, trad 144, p 113. The figures at the end of this *ḥadîth* refer to Sura 5:93. In Yusuf Ali's translation, the equivalent reference is Sura 5:96.

[8] In the Qur'ân, *aya* is used to refer to verses of the book itself and not, for example, to previous revelations such as the *Taurât* or *Injîl*. In those cases, the word *kitâb* or "book" is employed. Indeed, it was this claim that God had replaced some of the earlier verses/revelations of the Qur'ân that led Muḥammad's opponents to accuse him of being a forger. The accusation comes in the rest of Sura 16:101: "When We substitute one revelation for another, – and God knows best what He reveals (in stages), – they say, 'Thou art but a forger': but most of them understand not." Elsewhere, the Qur'ân makes clear that God may change or confirm whatever he chooses: "God doth blot out or confirm what He pleaseth: with Him is the Mother of the Book" (Sura 13:39).

Qur'ân is eternal or created. Could such debate come into vogue again in contemporary times?

Secondly, if the Qur'ân is an earthly copy of an eternally preserved "Word", why does it need to contain changes that only apply to its manifestation on earth? Could not the "correcting" verses have been substituted before sending down the ones that would need abrogating? Moreover, those parts of the Qur'ân that have been abrogated and removed from the Qur'ân – were they on the original heavenly tablet? If they were, then the Qur'ân as it emerged through "sending down" does not represent an exact replica of what appears on the heavenly tablet. If they were not, how did they come to be delivered at some point to Muḥammad as part of the heavenly text?

DEALING WITH ADULTERERS

The punishment prescribed in the Qur'ân for infidelity in marriage is one hundred lashes:

> The woman and the man guilty of adultery or fornication, – flog each of them with a hundred stripes: Let not compassion move you in their case, in a matter prescribed by Allah, if ye believe in Allah and the Last Day: and let a party of the Believers witness their punishment. (Sura 24:2)

This verse, however, is considered by Muslim commentators to be abrogated by a *ḥadîth* that refers to an unstated "Verse of Stoning" that was allegedly qur'ânic in origin.[9] The conviction that such a verse of stoning – as referred to in the *ḥadîth* – did originally occur in the body of the Qur'ân, arises from the claims of Caliph 'Umar (caliph, AD 634–644). Both al-Bukhârî and Muslim quote *ḥadîth* containing 'Umar's assertion about the original inclusion of the verse of stoning within the body of the Qur'ân:

> Allâh sent Muḥammad (may peace be upon him) with the Truth and revealed the Holy Book to him, and among what Allâh revealed, was the Verse of the Rajam (the stoning of a married person (male and female) who commits illegal sexual intercourse) and we did recite this Verse and understood and memorized it. Allâh's Apostle (may peace be upon him) did carry out the punishment of stoning and so did we after him. I am afraid that after a long time has passed, somebody will say, "By Allâh, we do not find the Verse of the Rajam in Allâh's Book", and thus they will go astray by leaving an obligation which Allâh has revealed. And the punishment of the

[9] There does exist a reference to a tradition in which the "Verse of Stoning" is cited. See below.

> Rajam is to be inflicted to any married person (male and female) who commits illegal sexual intercourse if the required evidence is available or there is conception or confession.[10]

> ʼAbdullah b. ʼAbbâs reported that ʻUmar b. Khaṭṭâb sat on the pulpit of Allah's Messenger (may peace be upon him) and said: Verily Allah sent Muḥammad (may peace be upon him) with truth and He sent down the Book upon him, and the verse of stoning was included in what was sent down to him. We recited it, retained it in our memory and understood it. Allah's Messenger (may peace be upon him) awarded the punishment of stoning to death (to the married adulterer and adulteress) and, after him, we also awarded the punishment of stoning. I am afraid that, with the lapse of time, the people (may forget it) and may say: We do not find the punishment of stoning in the Book of Allah, and thus go astray by abandoning this duty prescribed by Allah. Stoning is a duty laid down in Allah's book for married men and women who commit adultery when proof is established, or if there is pregnancy, or a confession.[11]

That such a verse of stoning did originally exist within the text of the Qur'ân is made the more likely by Ibn Ishâq's very early account of what happened during Caliph ʻUmar's last pilgrimage of his life. In Medina, according to Ibn Ishâq, the caliph climbed the pulpit in the mosque and declared:

> "I am about to say to you today something which God has willed that I should say and I do not know whether perhaps it is my last utterance. He who understands and he who heeds it let him take it with him whithersoever he goes; and as for him who fears that he will not heed it, he may not deny that I said it. God sent Muḥammad and sent down the scripture to him. Part of what he sent down was the passage on stoning; we read it, we were taught it, and we heeded it. The apostle stoned (adulterers) and we stoned them after him. I fear that in time to come men will say that they find no mention of stoning in God's book and thereby will go astray by neglecting an ordinance which God has sent down. Verily stoning in the book of God is a penalty laid on married men and women who commit adultery, if proof stands or pregnancy is clear or confession is made . . ."[12]

Ibn Ishâq's inclusion of this portion of Caliph ʻUmar's sermon in Medina confirms that the punishment of adultery by stoning within the jurisprudence of Islam derives from a very early tradition – much earlier, indeed, than the later collections of *ḥadîth*. Yet, the Qur'ân

[10] Recorded in al-Bukhârî, *al-Ṣaḥîḥ*, vol 8, book 82, chap 17, trad 817, pp 539–540.

[11] Recorded in Muslim, *al-Jâmiʻal-Ṣaḥîḥ*, vol 3, book 14, chap 681, trad 4194, p 912.

[12] The account of ʻUmar's sermon may be found in A. Guillaume, *The Life of Muhammad: A translation of Ibn Ishaq's Sirat Rasul Allah*, Oxford University Press: Oxford (1955), p 684. Ibn Ishâq was born in AH 85 and grew up in Medina; his is one of the earliest full-length biographies of Prophet Muḥammad.

itself only requires that adulterers be scourged. The puzzling discrepancy is even addressed in ʿUmar's sermon. ʿUmar declares that there used to be a qur'ânic verse that required stoning as punishment for adult men or women who committed adultery. Interestingly, in his sermon ʿUmar quotes the words of a second "vanished" verse, dealing with a different subject, that used to be part of the revelation and which the earliest of Muḥammad's companions used to recite. Again, this important tradition is included in both al-Bukhârî's collection of *ḥadîth* and in Ibn Ishâq's life of Muḥammad.

It is often claimed that the verse of stoning disappeared when the Qur'ân was compiled under the caliph ʿUthmân. If such a textual history is accurate, it provides a unique scenario in which reference to an abrogating verse, no longer to be found within the Qur'ân, is retained within the *ḥadîth* literature while the abrogated verse continues to remain within the Qur'ân. Does not such a textual history have some strong implications for a hermeneutic of certainty?

The surviving conviction concerning Prophet Muḥammad's personal treatment of adulterers, along with support for that conviction as expressed in the *ḥadîth* literature, resulted in a significant differentiation in the application of punishment for sexual infidelity. That differentiation has consistently informed *sharîʿa* law. Married people who commit adultery are to undergo "one hundred lashes and stoning to death" whereas unmarried people (who commit fornication) are to receive "one hundred lashes and exile for one year". In other words, the punishment for infidelity within marriage is determined by the *ḥadîth* material (through its reference to the verse of stoning), while the punishment for infidelity outside of marriage is clearly indicated in the body of the Qur'ân itself. ʿAbdul Siddîqî, in his translation of the *ḥadîth* material compiled by Muslim, makes the pertinent point about this correction or amplification of the qur'ânic text by the *ḥadîth*:

> Here is an example of an abrogation of Qur'ânic verses in which the words are abrogated whereas the ordinance has been conserved for all time to come in the Sharîʿah through the words of the Holy Prophet (may peace be upon him) such as his judgments in such cases of adultery. This also shows how closely the Qur'ân and the Sunnah are interlinked.[13]

From the very earliest expression of Islam within Medina in the years after the *hijra*, it is clear that Prophet Muḥammad insisted on the punishment of adulterers by stoning to death:

[13] See his comments in Muslim, *al-Jâmiʿal-Ṣaḥîḥ*, vol 3, book 14, chap 681, note 2155, p 912.

> Narrated Abû Hurayra and Zaid bin Khâlid al-Juhanî: A bedouin came and said, "O Allâh's Apostle! Judge between us according to Allâh's Book (Laws)." His opponent stood up and said, "He has said the truth, so judge between us according to Allâh's Laws." The bedouin said, "My son was a labourer for this man and committed illegal sexual intercourse with his wife. The people said to me, 'Your son is to be stoned to death,' so I ransomed my son for one hundred sheep and a slave girl. Then I asked the religious learned men and they said to me, 'Your son has to receive one hundred lashes plus one year of exile'." The Prophet (may peace be upon him) said, "I shall judge between you according to Allâh's Book (Laws)! As for the slave girl and the sheep, it shall be returned to you, and your son shall receive one hundred lashed and be exiled for one year. O you, Unais!" The Prophet addressed some man, "Go in the morning to the wife of this man and stone her to death." So Unais went to her the next morning and stoned her to death.[14]

Muslim includes many accounts of the application of this capital punishment to individuals who confessed their guilt to Prophet Muḥammad. The following example from his compilation of *ḥadîth* illustrates the point:

> Abû Hurayra reported that a person from amongst the Muslims came to Allah's Messenger (may peace be upon him) while he was in the mosque. He called him saying: Allah's Messenger, I have committed adultery. He (the Holy Prophet) turned away from him. He (again) came round facing him and said to him: Allah's Messenger, I have committed adultery. He (the Holy Prophet) turned away until he did that four times, and as he testified four times against his own self. Allah's Messenger (may peace be upon him) called him and said: Are you mad? He said: No. He (again) said: Are you married? He said: Yes. Thereupon Allah's Messenger (may peace be upon him) said: Take him and stone him.[15]

The derivation of the verse of stoning as it (allegedly) originally found a place in the qur'ânic corpus is enveloped in a tradition concerning an instance of confrontation between Prophet Muḥammad and some Jews in Medina. The following *ḥadîth* describes that instance. It appears in al-Bukhârî's compilation as part of an elucidation of Sura 2:146: "The people of the Book know this as they know their own sons; but some of them conceal the truth which they themselves know." Al-Bukhârî records:

> Narrated 'Abdullâh bin 'Umar (may Allah be pleased with him): The Jews came to Allâh's Apostle (may Allâh's blessings and peace be upon him)

[14] Recorded in al-Bukhârî, *al-Ṣaḥîḥ*, vol 9, book 89, chap 39, trad 303, p 232.
[15] Recorded in Muslim, *al-Jâmi' al-Ṣaḥîḥ*, vol 3, book 15, chap 682, trad 4196, p 913.

> and told him that a man and a woman from amongst them had committed illegal sexual intercourse. Allâh's Apostle (may Allâh's blessings and peace be upon him) said to them, "What do you find in the Torah (Old Testament) about the legal punishment of Ar-Rajm (stoning)?" They replied, (But) we announce their crime and lash them. 'Abdullâh bin Salâm said, "You are telling a lie; Torah contains the order of Rajm." They brought and opened the Torah and one of them placed his hand on the Verse of Rajm and read the verses preceding and following it. 'Abdullâh bin Salâm said to him, "Lift your hand." When he lifted his hand, the Verse of Rajm was written there. They said, "Muḥammad has told the truth; the Torah has the Verse of Rajm." The Prophet (may Allâh's blessings and peace be upon him) then gave the order that both of them should be stoned to death.[16]

There is considerable speculation as to whether Prophet Muḥammad, in authorising the punishment of stoning to death for acts of adultery, was affirming what he perceived to be God's word in the *Torah* on this matter.

There is further speculation concerning Sura *al-Aḥzâb* (Sura 33). The *ḥadîth* raise the question of whether this sura remains today as it was originally given. It is suggested that in its original form it included the missing verse of stoning:

> Zirr ibn Hubaish reported, "Ubayy ibn Ka'b said to me, 'What is the extent of Surat al-Aḥzâb?' I said, 'Seventy, or seventy-three verses.' He said, 'Yet it used to be equal to Surat al-Baqarah and in it we recited the verse of stoning.' I said, 'And what is the verse of stoning?' He replied, 'The fornicators among the married men (*ash-shaikh*) and married women (*ash-shaikhah*), stone them as an exemplary punishment from Allâh, and Allâh is Mighty and Wise'[17]

All such speculation by commentators on the Qur'ân bears implications for a "hermeneutic of certainty." It suggests that not all is transparent in traditional Muslim claims concerning the original content of the qur'ânic text. It raises questions about the process whereby an important verse of the Qur'ân appears to end up missing from the remembered text and appearing only (by reference) in the *ḥadîth*. The textual history of that verse in the *ḥadîth* seems to imply that Prophet Muḥammad in Medina still saw what he perceived to be the *Torah* as authentic and authoritative. He certainly based his juridical decisions in cases of adultery upon it. The

[16] Recorded in al-Bukhârî, *al-Ṣaḥîḥ*, vol 4, book 56, chap 25, trad 829, p 532–533.

[17] Al-Suyûtî, *al-Itqan fî Ulûm al-Qur'ân*, al-Maktabah al-Thaqâfiyah: Beirut (1973), p 124, as quoted in John Gilchrist *Jam' al-Qur'an: The Codification of the Qur'an Text*, TMFMT: Warley (1989), chap 4, "The Missing Passages of the Qur'an."

reference to the verse of stoning in the *ḥadîth* remained so strong that it was seen as abrogating the remaining qur'ânic reference to punishment for adultery.

A *ḥadîth* recorded by al-Bukhârî contains the words of another verse not found in the Qur'ân as it finally appeared. During Muḥammad's rulership in Medina, some of the tribes who had professed allegiance to him and who were residing close to the town appealed to him for help in facing their enemies. Prophet Muḥammad sent seventy of the *Anṣâr* who were, on arrival, duplicitously murdered by members of the tribes they had gone to assist:

> Then Allâh revealed to us a verse that was among the cancelled ones later on. It was: "We have met our Lord and He is pleased with us and has made us pleased."[18]

Here, the text of a verse once given but later abrogated is clearly preserved within the *ḥadîth* literature.

OTHER "MISSING" QUR'ÂNIC VERSES

Not surprisingly, reference to the verse of stoning appears in inter-Muslim controversies about *taḥrîf* or "distortions" in the Qur'ân. Sometimes, Shî'a Muslims are labelled as *kâfir* by Sunnî Muslims because *taḥrîf* traditions are said to exist in their texts. Those traditions mostly concern words or phrases that, it is claimed, the Shî'a have alleged were wrongfully cut out of verses of the Qur'ân. Abu Ameenah Bilal Philips, Jamaican-Canadian convert to Islam, has promulgated anti-Shî'a works produced by Sunnî polemicists who make such claims. Typical is the accusation that the Shî'as maintain that Sura 25:28 is supposed to have been amended by the Sunnîs to read "O would that I have not chosen such a one [instead of "the second"] as a friend". "The second" in the alleged original text would have referred to Abû Bakr and the implication is that that verse said that people would regret having followed Abû Bakr rather than 'Alî. Sura 3:110 is allegedly amended to read "You are the best of Imams" in the Shî'a records, substituting *imma* (imams) for *umma* (peoples). The verse "And we made 'Alî your in-law" is said to have been added by the Shî'as to Sura 94, whilst an alternative rendering of "people of the sacred shrine" is proposed in a Shî'a remake of

[18] Recorded in al-Bukhârî, *al-Ṣaḥîḥ*, vol 5, book 59, chap 27, trad 417, p 289.

Sura 33:33.[19] Sunnîs like Philips sometimes allege that Shî'as are convinced that several whole suras have disappeared from the Qur'ân. These suras are said to include one concerning 'Alî – known as "Sura al-Walaya" – and one comprising 41 verses concerning Muḥammad and 'Alî – called "Sura Nurayn" or "The Two Lights". Such allegations about missing suras are strenuously denied by most Shî'a scholars, who claim that they uphold the veracity of the received 'Uthmânic edition of the Qur'ân. The Shî'a do, however, interpret the Qur'ân in the light of their separate *ḥadîth* collections, a process that understandably invites hostile denunciation of their orthodoxy by some Sunnî Muslim theologians.

Shî'a responses to such accusations about their distorting the text of the Qur'ân via their *ḥadîth* literature often take the polemical line that within Sunnî tradition, also, there are elements of *taḥrîf*. They cite the *ḥadîth*, noted above, that quotes the sermon delivered by Caliph 'Umar during his last pilgrimage as leader of the Muslim community. In his sermon, the caliph plainly states: "Stoning is in the Book of God." They also quote a tradition from 'Âisha that would appear to support 'Umar's claims:

> When the verses *rajm* [stoning] and ayah *rezah kabir* descended, they were written on a piece of paper and kept under my pillow. Following the demise of Prophet Muḥammad a goat ate the piece of paper while we were mourning.[20]

Ibn Ḥazm al-Andalusi reputedly affirms this contention:

> The verses of stoning and breast feeding were in the possession of A'isha in a (Qur'anic) copy. When Muḥammad died and people became busy in the burial preparations, a domesticated animal entered in and ate it.[21]

As we have already indicated, Sura *al-Aḥzâb* (Sura 33) is often brought up in this disputation. There are some records of *ḥadîth* – not the most authentic, it has to be said – that include traditions in

[19] The *ḥadîth* collection of Muḥammad Baqîr ibn Muḥammad Taqi al-Majlisî (died AD 1699) is often held responsible for verbalising such alleged Shî'a accusations about the original text of the Qur'ân. Al-Majlisî produced *Bihâr al-Anwâr* or *Ocean of Light*, an encyclopaedic compilation of *ḥadîth* drawn from Sunnî as well as his own Shî'a sources, Dâr Ihya al-Nazâd al-'Arabî: Beirut (1983), 10 volumes. His compilation is, however, often criticised for not eliminating many weak traditions from its record.

[20] For example in the article "Sunnis & Tahreef (distortions) in Qur'an" as produced by the Answering-Ansar.org Project, p 1. This article can be found at http://www.answering-ansar.org/creed_of_shia_explained/en/chap3.php. The reference is to *Sunan Ibn Maja*, vol 2, p 39.

[21] Ibn Ḥazm, *op. cit.*, vol 8, part 2, pp 235–236.

which reliable individuals of the early Muslim community are said to have recalled a time when Sura 33 (*al-Aḥzâb*) was the same length as Sura 2 ("the Cow"). If that were true, Sura 33 would originally have included some 200 verses not found within it today. Significantly, this large, missing section is said to have contained verses commanding the death sentence for adulterers:

> Al-Muttaqi 'Ali bin Ḥusain al-Din in his book *Mukhtasar Kanz al-'Ummal* printed on the margin of Imam Aḥmad's *Musnad*, vol 2, page 2, in his *ḥadîth* about chapter 33, said that Ibn Mardawayh reported that Hudhayfah said: 'Umar said to me "How many verses are contained in the chapter of al-Aḥzâb?" I said, "72 or 73 verses." He said it was almost as long as the chapter of the Cow, which contains 287 verses, and in it there was the verse of stoning.[22]

Other disputants frequently refer to a *ḥadîth* deriving from 'Â'isha that mentions a different "missing verse" of the Qur'ân. This verse, that used to be recited by Muslims and which came to be abrogated, concerned the subject of suckling:

> 'Â'isha (Allah be pleased with her) reported that it had been revealed in the Holy Qur'ân that ten clear sucklings make the marriage unlawful, then it was abrogated (and substituted) by five sucklings and Allah's Apostle (may peace be upon him) died and it was before that time (found) in the Holy Qur'ân (and recited by the Muslims).[23]

This *ḥadîth* from 'Â'isha was widely reported. The verse quoted prohibited the marriage of two people who had been breastfed by the same woman at least ten times. The verse was later abrogated and another substituted for it, limiting the number of breastfeeding sessions to five. Neither verse, however, appears in the Qur'ân as it found final form.

The loss of whole suras is sometimes posited in the Shî'a-Sunnî debate with the Shî'as, in this case, accusing the Sunnîs of carelessness. Abû Mûsâ al-Ash'arî, a companion of Muḥammad and an early authority on the text of the Qur'ân, is reported as saying to the reciters of Basra:

> We used to recite a Sûra which resembled in length and severity to (Sûra) *Barâ'at* [Sura 2]. I have, however, forgotten it with the exception of this which I remember out of it: "If there were two valleys full of riches, for the son of Adam, he would long for a third valley, and nothing would fill

[22] In the article "Sunnis & Tahreef (distortions) in Qur'an", *op. cit.*, p 1.
[23] Recorded in Muslim, *al-Jâmi' al-Ṣaḥîḥ*, vol 2, book 8, chap 565, trad 3421, p 740.

> the stomach of the son of Adam but dust." And we used to recite a sûra which resembled one of the suras of *Musabbiḥât*, and I have forgotten it, but remember (this much) out of it: "O people who believe, why do you say that which you do not practise" (61:2) and "that is recorded in your necks as a witness (against you) and you would be asked about it on the Day of Resurrection" (17:13).[24]

The *Musabbiḥât* comprise those suras of the Qur'ân (57, 59, 61, 62 and 64) that begin with the words "*sabbaḥa*" or "*yusabbiḥu*", commencing a phrase that sings out: "Let everything that is in the heavens and the earth declare the praises and glory of God." As the *ḥadîth* recorded by Muslim indicates, the words of the first missing verse bring to mind Sura 61:2, while the words of the second verse are the same as Sura 17:13. The common defence of the integrity of the Qur'ân as it came to be finalised (for example by Sidîqî in his editorship of Muslim's *ḥadîth*) is that the words of such a recalled but no longer remaining sura have been abrogated in the process of "sending down", but that their meanings (even their precise wordings) have been preserved in other verses of the text.

The arguments between Sunnî and Shî'a polemicists expose differences of view about the detail of text – in terms of abrogated verses, alleged "missing" verses and the interpretation of verses. Such argumentation at the very least indicates that the hermeneutical issue is not necessarily as tidily settled as is often officially proposed.

SORTING OUT ABROGATION

My purpose in raising the question of abrogation (and associated "missing" verses) in this chapter is precisely that – to raise the question. Abrogation is a subject that has long been addressed by generations of Muslim scholars. Many lines of thought concerning it have been taken in legal and exegetical literature. From the earliest times until the present day, there has been discussion over which verses of the Qur'ân actually teach abrogation, plus what types of verse can be abrogated and which ones are abrogated (if the process is allowed). Theologians have differed in their view of how many verses abrogate or are abrogated (with a range from 5 to 248 verses[25]). Abrogation is

[24] Recorded in Muslim, *al-Jâmi'al-Ṣaḥîḥ*, vol 2, book 5, chap 391, trad 2286, p 501.

[25] Shâh Walî Allâh posits the lowest with 5 verses, while al-Farîsî suggests the highest, at 248 verses.

a subject that surfaces in inter-sectarian Muslim debate. It must surely be one of the elements of a more open debate amongst contemporary Muslims about the difficult matter of hermeneutics. In what sense can one say that the Qur'ân is authoritative when that authority appears to be undermined by a process of abrogation and verse replacement?

My point is that it is the Islamist agenda that most urgently provokes such questioning about the matter of abrogation and the nature of the authority of the Qur'ân. As we have seen in the case of Faraj from Egypt, the doctrine of abrogation features strongly in such Islamists' arguments for a literal interpretation of the concept of *jihâd*. In order for *jihâd* to be accepted as uncompromisingly literal or physical in its meaning, other verses of the Qur'ân that suggest a more gentle approach to non-Muslims need to be emasculated. Such emasculation proceeds by appealing to the process of abrogation. Strong support for the abrogating perspective is solicited from the *ḥadîth*. The result is a very heady mix of authoritative precedents commanding or supporting the use of violence in the execution of physical *jihâd*.

There are many verses of the Qur'ân that promote tolerance in religion, perhaps most famously Sura 2:256: "There is no compulsion in religion". Rafiqul-Haqq and Newton quote al-Nahas' summary of the different ways the doctrine of abrogation came to be applied to this verse:

> The scholars differed concerning Q. 2:256. Some said: "It has been abrogated for the Prophet compelled the Arabs to embrace Islam and fought them and did not accept any alternative but their surrender to Islam. The abrogating verse is Q. 9:73 'O Prophet, struggle with the unbelievers and hypocrites, and be thou harsh with them.' Mohammad asked Allah the permission to fight them and it was granted." Other scholars said Q. 2:256 has not been abrogated, but it had a special application. It was revealed concerning the people of the Book; they cannot be compelled to embrace Islam if they pay the Jizia (that is head tax on free non-Muslims under Muslim rule). It is only the idol worshippers who are compelled to embrace Islam and upon them Q. 9:73 applies. This is the opinion of Ibn 'Abbas which is the best opinion due to the authenticity of its chain of authority.[26]

[26] Al-Nahas, *Al-Nâsikh w'al-Mansûkh*, p 80. Also Ibn Ḥazm al-Andalusi, *Al-Nâsikh wa'l-Mansûkh*, Dar al-Kutub al-'Almaya: Beirut (1986), p 42. Quoted in M Rafiqul-Haqq and P. Newton, "Tolerance in Islam" (1996), posted on the internet at http://debate.domini.org/newton/tolerance.html, p 1.

If the application of the principle of abrogation to Sura 2:256 is capable of carrying some differentiation as to who might be put at risk by its cancellation, other processes of abrogation are far more clear cut (see figure 7). Ibn Ḥazm al-Andalusi, author of *al-Nâsikh w'al-Mansûkh*, is a clear proponent of Faraj's contention (see chapter 1) that 114 verses of the Qur'ân were all abrogated by one correcting verse.[27] Those abrogated verses spoke about tolerance in Islam while the abrogating verse comprises, of course, the infamous "Verse of the Sword" (Sura 9:5). Some of the "tolerance" verses, said to be abrogated by the verse of the sword, are included in figure 7. Such abrogation occurred, in Ibn Ḥazm's contention, before the death of Prophet Muḥammad.

The treatment of the verse of the sword within the *ḥadîth* literature is used to complement this appropriation of the doctrine of abrogation. Al-Bukhârî passes on the following tradition in a chapter dealing with Sura 9:5:

> Narrated Ibn 'Umar: Allâh's Apostle said: "I have been ordered (by Allâh) to fight against the people until they testify that none has the right to be worshipped but Allâh and that Muḥammad is Allâh's Apostle, and offer the prayers and give the obligatory charity, so if they perform all that then they save their lives and property from me except for Islâmic laws, and then their reckoning (accounts) will be done by Allâh."[28]

Elsewhere, the promise of paradise to those Muslims who die in such fighting is affirmed. In his "Book of *Jihâd*", al-Bukhârî offers a chapter entitled "Paradise is under the blades of swords". He passes on the testimony of al-Mughîra bin Shu'ba concerning the meaning behind God's promise in Sura 9:111 that Muslims who are involved in *jihâd* and who die will find themselves in paradise:

> Our Prophet told us about the message of our Lord that ". . . whoever amongst us is killed will go to Paradise" ÉUmar asked the Prophet, "Is it not true that our men who are killed will go to Paradise and their's (i.e. those of the Pagan's) will go to the (Hell) fire?" The Prophet said, "Yes."[29]

My contention is that contemporary Muslim scholars and leaders have to address the issue of abrogation as part of their response to the Islamists' agenda. It will not be good enough to simply dismiss

[27] Ibn Ḥazm al-Andalusi, *Al-Nâsikh wa'l-Mansûkh*, pp 12–18. Quoted in M Rafiqul-Haqq and P. Newton, "Tolerance in Islam" (1996), *op. cit.*, p 2.

[28] Recorded in al-Bukhârî, *al-Ṣaḥîḥ*, vol 1, book 2, chap 17, trad 24, pp 25–26.

[29] Recorded in al-Bukhârî, *al-Ṣaḥîḥ*, vol 4, book 52, chap 22, trad 72, p 55.

Figure 7

Abrogated verses promoting tolerance

<table>
<tr><th>Abrogated verses</th><th>Abrogating verse</th></tr>
<tr><td>Those who believe (in the Qur'an), and those who follow the Jewish (scriptures), and the Christians and the Sabians, – any who believe in Allah and the Last Day, and work righteousness, shall have their reward with their Lord; on them shall be no fear, nor shall they grieve. (Sura 2:62)</td><td rowspan="2">If anyone desires a religion other than Islam (submission to Allah), never will it be accepted of him; and in the Hereafter He will be in the ranks of those who have lost (All spiritual good). (Sura 3:85)</td></tr>
<tr><td>Those who believe (in the Qur'an), those who follow the Jewish (scriptures), and the Sabians and the Christians, – any who believe in Allah and the Last Day, and work righteousness, – on them shall be no fear, nor shall they grieve. (Sura 5:69)</td></tr>
<tr><td>We created not the heavens, the earth, and all between them, but for just ends. And the Hour is surely coming (when this will be manifest). So overlook (any human faults) with gracious forgiveness. (Sura 15:85)</td><td rowspan="4">But when the forbidden months are past, then fight and slay the Pagans wherever ye find them, and seize them, beleaguer them, and lie in wait for them in every stratagem (of war); but if they repent, and establish regular prayers and practise regular charity, then open the way for them: for Allah is Oft-forgiving, Most Merciful. (Sura 9:5)</td></tr>
<tr><td>And remember We took a covenant from the Children of Israel (to this effect): Worship none but Allah; treat with kindness your parents and kindred, and orphans and those in need; speak fair to the people; be steadfast in prayer; and practise regular charity. Then did ye turn back, except a few among you, and ye backslide (even now). (Sura 2:83)</td></tr>
<tr><td>If it had been thy Lord's will, they would all have believed, – all who are on earth! Wilt thou then compel mankind, against their will, to believe! (Sura 10:99)</td></tr>
<tr><td>To you be your Way, and to me mine. (Sura 109:6)</td></tr>
</table>

the practice of applying abrogation principles to verses within the Qur'ân and insisting that they actually apply to the Qur'ân's replacing of former revelations. Traditional methods for interpreting the Qur'ân must be subject to careful and reasoned evaluation. There needs to be a careful critique of the Islamic sources that appear so strongly to support the conviction and practice of extremists like Faraj.

Asma Barlas calls for just such evaluation and critique. She exemplifies someone from a moderate, orthodox Muslim background who is working to restate her respect for the Qur'ân in terms of what she perceives as its egalitarianism – thus undermining the claims of Islamists or misogynists to be truly qur'ânic:

> I believe that extremist interpretations of the Quran constitute misreadings of it and that the best way to challenge interpretive (*sic*) extremism is to rethink our methodologies for interpreting Islam. For too long, we have taken as canonical methods and readings that do an injustice to the Qur'an's own egalitarianism and that continue to provide extremists, misogynists, and vigilantes the ideological fuel necessary for their violence.[30]

Asma Barlas was one of the first women to join Pakistan's foreign service. She was fired by Zia-ul-Haq when she dared to criticise his presidency. She eventually had to seek political asylum in the United States of America. From there she has pursued her concern with the politics of meaning and the construction of religious knowledge in Islam. Barlas' concern really needs to become a broader issue of investigation within mainstream Islam.

[30] Asma Barlas, "Jihad = Holy War = Terrorism: The politics of conflation and denial". In *American Journal of Islamic Social Sciences* (2003), vol 20, number 1, p 60.

Chapter 4

Here's what that really means!

CHRISTIANITY is no stranger to the sensitive issue of abrogation. Indeed, central to the Christian view of the Bible is a conviction about the New Testament, or elements of it, as in some way abrogating the Old Testament, or elements of it.

In Romans 10:4, the apostle Paul dramatically declares: "Christ is the end of the law." The apostle's theme is abrogation. The question as to the manner in which Christ constitutes the end of the law has been one of considerable theological debate. Wider themes, such as the relationships between gospel and ten commandments (Decalogue), "grace" and "works", New Testament and Old Testament, have all been considered in such debate. In the paragraphs following, we shall look at some of the characteristics of this theological discussion and illustrate it in terms of Jesus' claim to be "Lord of the Sabbath".

Paul announced that the law was abrogated. It was ended or replaced by Christ. Yet Paul still used the law as a reference point for fellow-Christians in helping them to measure their Christlikeness (or lack of it!). He invokes the Law when writing to the Christians in Corinth, reminding them that the Law upholds the principle of someone in ministry being permitted to receive remuneration from that ministry (1 Corinthians 9:8–9). He appeals to the Law as supporting his contention that women should not speak in public meetings (1 Corinthians 14:34). To the Ephesian Christians, he suggests that the Law backs up his command that children should obey their parents in the Lord (Ephesians 6:2–3). For the most part, however, Paul sees the Law as being radically sidelined by Christ.

Part of the issue in the apostle's declaration of abrogation concerns what precisely is meant by Paul when he refers to "the law". In the Bible, the term can indicate radically different entities (see figure 8).

Figure 8

"Law" as referenced in the Bible

"Law" as . . .	Text
The Decalogue, given via Moses	The Lord said to Moses, "Come up to me on the mountain and stay here, and I will give you the tablets of stone, with the law and commands I have written for their instruction." (Exodus 24:12)
The whole of Old Testament	[Jesus speaking] "Or haven't you read in the Law that on the Sabbath the priests in the temple desecrate the day and yet are innocent?" (Matthew 12:5)
A taxation regulation in Egypt	So Joseph established it as a law concerning land in Egypt – still in force today – that a fifth of the produce belongs to Pharaoh. (Genesis 47:26)
Imperial edicts of the Medes and Persians	Then the men went as a group to the king and said to him, "Remember, O king, that according to the law of the Medes and Persians no decree or edict that the king issues can be changed." (Daniel 6:15)

Sometimes, Christian theologians have differentiated three elements of the "law" in the sense of the commandments of God as given via Moses on Mount Sinai. Those elements comprise ceremonial law, civil law, and moral law. The *Westminster Confession*,[1] for example, posits such a threefold division of the law:

I. God gave to Adam a law, as a covenant of works, by which He bound him and all his posterity to personal, entire, exact, and perpetual obedience . . .

II. This law, after his fall, continued to be a perfect rule of righteousness; and, as such, was delivered by God upon mount Sinai, in ten commandments . . .

[1] The *Westminster Confession of Faith*, Chapter 19: "Of the Law of God". The Westminster Confession was drawn up in AD 1643 by the Assembly of Divines to which was entrusted the task of organising the new "Establishment" in Scotland. In 1689, when Episcopacy was abolished in the church of Scotland, the confession became the official formulary of that (Presbyterian) Church. The text quoted here is from the second edition (AD 1647). The whole of the *Confession* may be found in Philip Schaff, *The Creeds of Christendom with a History and Critical Notes*, vol 3: "The Evangelical Protestant Creeds, with Translations", Harper: New York (1882), pp 600–675. Chapter 19 may be found on pp 640–643.

> III. Beside this law, commonly called moral, God was pleased to give to the people of Israel, as a Church under age, ceremonial laws, . . . partly of worship, . . . and partly holding forth divers instructions of moral duties . . .
> IV. To them also, as a body politic, he gave sundry judicial laws . . .

From such a differentiation, it is claimed, one might easily see how ceremonial law can be considered to be abrogated – the whole cultus of sacrifice involving the Levitical priesthood, for example, was clearly done away by Christ's sacrifice on the cross (Hebrews 10). Civil (or judicial) law, again, may well find itself over-ruled by the new approach that Christ brings – no longer "eye for eye and tooth for tooth" but a forgiving of one's enemies (Matthew 5:38–48). It is the moral law, especially as summarised in the Ten Commandments – so this argument by differentiation goes – that remains consistent throughout Old *and* New Testament periods. One might argue here that Paul himself takes for granted what the *Torah* has to declare in the moral sphere. He certainly believes, for example, that the gospel establishes rather than subverts the Decalogue:

> The commandments, "Do not commit adultery," "Do not murder," "Do not steal," "Do not covet," and whatever other commandment there may be, are summed up in this one rule: "Love your neighbour as yourself." Love does no harm to its neighbour. Therefore love is the fulfilment of the law. (Romans 13:9–10)

Jesus himself, inasmuch as he sometimes affirms the priority of one passage of the *Torah* or the Prophets over another, consistently argues that ceremonial or civil regulations were always subordinate to material concerned with moral matters. Think of his words to the Pharisees about the lawfulness of a man divorcing his wife:

> "It was because your hearts were hard that Moses wrote you this law," Jesus replied. "But at the beginning of creation God 'made them male and female.' 'For this reason a man will leave his father and mother and be united to his wife, and the two will become one flesh.' So they are no longer two, but one. Therefore what God has joined together, let man not separate." (Mark 10:5–9)

The weakness with such a theological concept of "selective abrogation" has been the difficulty of differentiating various kinds of law. Where does moral law end and ceremonial law begin? Where might civil law equate with moral law? It would appear that, at different times or in alternative theologies, various ceremonial or civil laws have been given the status of unchanging moral laws. Conversely, laws that have historically been viewed as moral have variously come to be reclassified as merely civil or ceremonial regulations of a bygone age. In some respects, it seems to me, such reclassifying dynamics lie at the heart of current Christian debate concerning the matter of homosexuality. For some contemporary Christians, the unacceptability of sexually active, homosexual relationships (whether conducted within an exclusive and faithful relationship or not) constitutes part of the unchanging moral law. For others, the matter has come to be restricted to an element in the civil law. From that standpoint, the condemnation of homosexuality in the Old Testament seems mostly to proceed from situations involving male shrine prostitutes, or to be argued against in the context of concern for the propagation of children. In the first case, the issue had mainly to do with the worship of idols. In the second case, the issue was about progeny for the tribes – heterosexual sexual relationships during a woman's monthly period were equally banned because they could not contribute to the production of progeny and the growth of the clan or tribe.

At the same time, some laws – even of the Decalogue itself – find multiple classification. The Sabbath regulation guides humankind's moral relationship to God but also determines the ceremonial and civil questions of how that moral relationship is to find expression. The prohibition against theft is a horizontal or civil ordinance yet it also has to do with humankind's moral relationship to God – is a person content with what God has given?

The weakness in arguing for abrogation by definition of what "law" might mean in differing circumstances leads to an impasse – different interpretations of the categorisation of "law" eventuate in alternative convictions as to what in the Decalogue or the Old Testament might be considered abrogated.

THE LAW'S PURPOSE

Another approach to the matter of abrogation has revolved around discussion concerning the overriding purpose of God in giving the law. Does the "law" reflect, in essence, the will of God for how human beings are to relate to him, to one another and to the created world? If the answer to this question is "yes", then clearly the "problem" about law-keeping has to do with humankind's attitude to God. After the "Fall" described in Genesis 3, doing God's will became an alien proposition to humankind. The law was sent to hedge humankind in, to limit our self-willedness, to be a kind of old-fashioned schoolteacher that would bring humanity, in desperation, to Christ. In Christ, humankind would find freedom from this regime and would be equipped to live the requirements of the law from within, as it were – by the Spirit.

Is the law, in essence, an accommodation, a "second best", in God's eyes, something that he wished he could do without but something that became necessary to try and stop the riot of self-willed humanity in its rush away from fellowship with himself? If that is the case, then reintegration with God through Christ might be said to reintroduce humankind to a pre-Fall relationship with God – one in which the quality of fellowship is spoken of in terms of partaking in the divine nature itself! Law – any law – in that scenario becomes irrelevant, unnecessary, unfaithful even. In Christ, there is no difference between the will of God and the will of redeemed humankind. Law is nowhere to be found on the agenda, but rather "freedom".

SPECIAL SABBATH?

This delicate question of the abrogation of Old Testament "law" by New Testament "Christ" finds particular poignancy in the matter of Sabbath-keeping. In each of the Synoptic Gospels, Jesus declares that "the Son of Man is Lord of the Sabbath" (Matthew 12:8; Mark 2:28; Luke 6:5). It is obviously, therefore, a very significant contention! The context of Jesus' declaration is an argument initiated by the Pharisees. These religious leaders were criticising Jesus for allowing his disciples to pick heads of corn, rub them in their hands and eat the kernels. Their criticism was not about *what* Jesus was permitting his disciples to do. After all the law (as in Deuteronomy 23:25: "If you enter your neighbour's grainfield, you may pick kernels with your hands . . .") allowed people to eat what they wished as they walked through a cornfield. The Pharisees' objection was about timing. It was a Sabbath day, and to their way of thinking, what the disciples of Jesus were doing amounted to a violation of the sacred rest-day. Jesus is described in each of the Synoptic

Gospels as defending his disciples and himself – after all, he was the real target of the Pharisees' angry criticism! He declares that, as Son of Man, he is "Lord of the Sabbath."

What does Jesus mean by this declaration? Does he mean that, as Son of Man – as God even – he is exempt? Is he claiming to be outside the law, above it, beyond it? Certainly, there has to be a sense in which God is perceived as beyond the law. God's righteousness is a quality personal to himself. It does not derive from the fact that he conforms to the law as revealed at Sinai. In that sense, surely, Jesus also has to be considered as truly beyond the law, as "Lord of the law" in effect.

The burden of incarnation, however, suggests that while the Christ may well have been beyond the law – "equal with God" in the words of Paul's hymn-quotation in Philippians 2:5 – he willingly placed himself under the law – "under law" (Galatians 4:4) – for the sake of humankind. He freely put himself in our place. In other words, part of Jesus' purpose in coming was to live in perfect obedience under the law. In the cornfield incident, by this incarnational perspective, Jesus was not excusing himself from perfect obedience to the law's requirement of Sabbath rest.

A far more radical conclusion might be drawn from this significant incident in Jesus' ministry as it is recorded in all three Synoptic Gospels. Perhaps Jesus was here suggesting that, with Messiah's arrival on earth, the Sabbath law as representative of the law as a whole (ceremonial, civil *and* moral), was no longer forceful because in him it found fulfilment. Law was abrogated in the sense of being perfectly lived out, perfectly displaced. Certainly inasmuch as the Sabbath law was part of the ceremonial law of the Old Testament, it constituted part of that "shadow of things that were to come" (Colossians 2:17). Jesus did indeed speak of a time when ceremonial law or historical precedent would give way to something much richer – a worshipping that was neither on this (Jerusalem) or that (Gerazim) mountain, nor in this (Jewish) nor that (Samaritan) tradition, but "in spirit and in truth" (John 4:23). Yet, Jesus' strong and consistent message to his followers is that he has not come to replace so much as to fulfil: "Do not think that I have come to abolish the law or the prophets; I have not come to abolish them but to fulfil them" (Matthew 5:17). It would be hard to find any indication in the New Testament that Jesus intended to set aside the law, including the Sabbath law. The Gospel-writer Luke, for example, records four disputes about the Sabbath in which Jesus was involved.[2] In each case, Jesus is portrayed as acting in accordance with the law. There is, on the other hand, plenty of evidence that Jesus saw himself as fulfilling the law. Jesus' "golden rule" of Matthew 7:12 is presented as constituting in essence "the law and the prophets". In his encounter with the rich young man who wanted to know what he should do to inherit eternal life, Jesus told him to "keep the commandments", going on to enumerate five of them (Matthew 19:16–19). When Jesus challenged his enemies to prove him guilty of sin (John 8:46), they could come up with no evidence, not even the transgression of ceremonial law. In his own use of Scripture (as we have seen with regard to divorce in Mark 10) Jesus happily upholds the priority of one passage of the *Torah* over another. My point is that the Old Testament texts were argued, not abandoned – and argued in the light of his own coming as Messiah. It would seem clear that neither Jesus' incarnation nor the commencement of his public ministry necessitated or involved or announced the dismantling of Sinaitic law.

So what did Jesus mean by his claim that he was "Lord of the Sabbath"? Perhaps, the major thrust of Jesus' claim is that he alone – the original instigator of this and other laws – was best positioned to explain, by living out, the true purpose of the Sabbath law, and to demonstrate thereby what true obedience to its spirit might look like. His explanation and demonstration comes, in this instance, in several ways. He begins by appealing to 1 Samuel 21:1–6. One wonders about the charged atmosphere in which his "defence" is delivered – "Have you never read . . .?" he begins! How well do his opponents know the text they are claiming to be defending? Jesus reminds his hearers that David *and his companions* (an emphatic phrase in the Greek), fleeing from Saul, were not condemned when they ate consecrated bread normally reserved for the priests (Matthew 12:3–4). They were hungry and in need. Such need gave David the right to commandeer bread for his followers from whatever source. Jesus' disciples, on campaign with him, have an equal right to commandeer grain to sustain them. Jesus also points out that there is a sense in which the priests themselves "violated" every Sabbath in that they had to work at their assigned duties in the temple on that rest-day – yet without condemnation (Matthew 12:5).

[2] The relevant passages are to be found in Luke 6:1–5; 6:6–11; 13:10–17 and 14:1–6.

Jesus declared that the overriding principle should be that the Sabbath was "made for man, not man for the Sabbath" (Mark 2:27). Hence, according to Jesus, the religious ritualism that the Pharisees had developed around the concept of "Sabbath" should never pre-empt the meeting of human need. Jesus quite clearly insisted that, contrary to Pharisaic thinking, it was lawful to do good on the Sabbath (Matthew 12:12; Mark 3:4; Luke 6:9). At the same time, it is likely that the action of taking grain constituted a sort of civil disobedience over the politics of food in Palestine.[3]

Jesus' exposition of Old Testament scripture suggested that a selfless, self-giving love for God and neighbour had been intended to permeate and give substance to the detail of law-keeping in Israel. The Pharisees represented a view of the law that promoted it only as a means of serving themselves, of elevating themselves, of making themselves righteous – even of feeding themselves. That perspective absolutely denied the spirit of the law as it found fulfilment in Jesus' embodiment of it:

> Our Lord came into conflict with the Pharisees not because He was opposed to the written word of the Law, to which both He and they appealed, but because in His judgment, the formalism and casuistry[[4]] of the legal system which the Pharisees had superimposed upon the Law rendered them insensitive to the living word of God . . . What roused his antagonism were such things as the casuistry which justified the practice of Corban; the false deduction that the command to love one's neighbour implied that one should hate one's enemies; the limiting of the divine prohibition of murder and adultery to the specific acts of murder and adultery; the assumption that the only oaths which need be taken seriously were those made by the actual use of the divine name; and the extension of the exception clause in the law of divorce so as to permit divorce "for any cause" whatever.[5]

LAW OR LIFE?

Jesus upheld the law by fulfilling its *intentions* perfectly. In so doing, he "fulfilled" in the sense of "transcending" rather than in the sense of "successfully keeping" the law. This distinction is well illustrated

[3] See Ched Myers' argument about this further dimension in *Binding the Strong Man: A Political Reading of Mark's Story of Jesus*, Orbis: New York (1988), pp 160–161.

[4] Getting around what conscience might dictate.

[5] Randolph Vincent Greenwood Tasker, *The Old Testament in the New Testament*, SCM: London (1946), p 32.

in the words Jesus speaks to the man with leprosy, as Matthew records them: "Then Jesus said to him, 'See that you don't tell anyone. But go, show yourself to the priest and offer the gift Moses commanded, as a testimony to them'." (Matthew 8:4) The cured man's obedience to the law of Moses is to serve as a testimony or announcement that the man has been healed:

> Thus the law of Moses itself is being used to testify to who Jesus is. In other words, in this context the supreme function of the gift Moses commanded (Lev 14:10–18) is not as a guilt offering but as a witness to Jesus. In his very act of submission to the law, Jesus makes the law point to himself.[6]

The law of Moses, we might say, looks forward to its own fulfilment. It is freighted with a prophetic sense, expecting an embodiment of itself that transcends itself. In Jesus Christ such fulfilling embodiment finds disclosure:

> As much as it is true that Jesus obeyed the law of Moses, his claims insisted that he stood over it – as its fulfilment (Matt. 5:17), as the Lord of the Sabbath (12:8), as the one to whom the law witnesses (8:4).[7]

Only Jesus, then, lived fully the will of his heavenly Father. The irony for our argument here is that in so doing, Jesus effectively sidelined or displaced or, indeed, abrogated the law, for it is his life, his Spirit, that produces what the law in itself could never produce. Christ is, indeed, the end of the law! Perhaps we might say that Jesus lived by the law incidentally in a sense – simply by living in a manner true to himself. His life illustrates what the law is trying to commend but can never, of itself, bring about. How might others come to share in such a kind of living in unity with God's will? Well, not by trying to keep the law but by participation in Jesus' death and resurrection.

By this reading, the entire Sinaitic law, including the Ten Commandments, was effectively abrogated at Christ's death. The Sinaitic expression of the will of God – though obviously not the will of the Father itself – was removed at Calvary. The code – moral, civil, ceremonial – that had sought to hem in and keep separate an Old Testament people for God, was cancelled at the cross. With Christ's death and resurrection came into existence a new opportu-

[6] Donald A. Carson, *When Jesus Confronts the World*, Inter-Varsity Press: Leicester (1987), p 23.
[7] *Ibid.*, p 24.

nity for Jews and Gentiles to enjoy fulfilling the spirit of the law – doing the will of the Father – from within as it were.

As a result, the church today chooses to use the Ten Commandments in its self-expression, not because the Sinaitic code by which they were mediated to humankind is still operative, but because those commandments continue to provide a broad and lasting summary of what conforming to God's will might mean. They provide that summary because they find fulfilment in the manner in which Jesus lived out the spirit behind them. The law's moral imperative, especially, indicates what "living by the Spirit of God" might look like on earth. If we obey Jesus' word, if we live Jesus' life, then the Ten Commandments will find expression in our lives. Such a motivation-from-within undermines the temptation to domesticate the law – a temptation to which the Pharisees of Jesus' day evidently succumbed. Instead, it expects of Jesus' followers a righteousness – produced by the Spirit – of the kind towards which the law essentially points.[8]

In Paul's terminology, the *Torah* no longer retains the religious importance it once owned. It is unable to bring anyone to salvation: "You who are trying to be justified by law have been alienated from Christ; you have fallen away from grace," he warns (Galatians 5:4). Christians do fulfil at least the moral concerns of the Law, but not because they are actually aiming to do that. Similarly with the ceremonial aspects of the Law. Paul accepts the theological or religious value of those ceremonies – they function as a type or foreshadowing of what will be completely fulfilled in Christ. So Paul is keen to use "ceremonial" language in writing to the Romans about the point of Jesus' crucifixion: "God presented him as a sacrifice of atonement, through faith in his blood" (Romans 3:25). He uses an image built upon the ritual of tabernacle and temple. But Paul will not let such ceremonial law be normative for the behaviour of believers in Christ:

> When Peter came to Antioch, I opposed him to his face, because he was in the wrong. Before certain men came from James, he used to eat with the Gentiles. But when they arrived, he began to draw back and separate himself from the Gentiles because he was afraid of those who belonged to the

[8] See Donald A. Carson's discussion of Matthew's presentation of Jesus' view of the law in his exposition of Matthew 5:17–20 in *The Expositor's Bible Commentary with the New International Version: Matthew Chapters 1 through 12*, Zondervan: Grand Rapids (1995), pp 142–147.

> circumcision group. The other Jews joined him in his hypocrisy, so that by their hypocrisy even Barnabas was led astray. When I saw that they were not acting in line with the truth of the gospel, I said to Peter in front of them all, "You are a Jew, yet you live like a Gentile and not like a Jew. How is it, then, that you force Gentiles to follow Jewish customs?" (Galatians 2:11–14)

> You are observing special days and months and seasons and years! (Galatians 4:10)

> Mark my words! I, Paul, tell you that if you let yourselves be circumcised, Christ will be of no value to you at all. Again I declare to every man who lets himself be circumcised that he is obligated to obey the whole law. (Galatians 5:2–3)

At the same time, Paul is willing for Jewish believers in Messiah to continue themselves to maintain distinctive Jewish practices – though only as long as there is no inference that those practices are part of the requirement for salvation. They may be continued as part of the culture of walking with God in a renewed, "Jewish" faith-expression.

As John Goldingay rightly suggests, Paul will not allow obedience to the *Torah* to be a salvation issue after the death and resurrection of Messiah. He will, however, allow or in some instances encourage obedience to the *Torah* as an expression of Christian discipleship. And he does use elements of the *Torah* (such as parts of the ceremonial or ritual law) as a theological resource.[9]

CHRISTIANS AND THE "LAW"

Perhaps, now, we might more clearly perceive why different groups of Christians choose to hold to different constellations of guidelines or "laws" in terms of what they say might or might not be pleasing to God. In the first instance, those constellations depend very much upon what is construed to be a more temporary "ceremonial" or "civil" expression of God's will, as opposed to an acclaimed first-order, immutable "moral" law that would require obedience in all circumstances. For some Christians, the "Sabbath law", as part of the Decalogue, represents just such a part of God's unchanging

[9] John Goldingay, *Models for Interpretation of Scripture*, Eerdmans: Grand Rapids (1995), p 103.

moral law. Seventh Day Adventists maintain an obedience to this law as part of their chosen or willed obedience to God in Christ:

> This Sabbath precept was placed in the midst of the moral law, or Ten Commandments, which were given by God to man. The law enunciated principles that are eternal and that, in their application to this earth, are based upon the abiding relationships of man to God and man to man . . .
>
> Seventh Day Adventists do not rely upon the Sabbath keeping as a *means* of salvation or of winning merit before God. We are saved by grace alone. Hence our Sabbath observance, as also our loyalty to every other command of God, is an expression of our love for our Creator and Redeemer.[10]

In the second instance, those constellations depend upon which aspects of Old Testament moral, civil or ceremonial law might be judged to constitute a faithful and contemporary expression of seeking to fulfil God's pleasure. Here, differences will emerge on matters like the use of alcohol by Christians, the measure of welcome and freedom afforded to certain groups of people (such as slaves or immigrants), the acceptance of lifestyles that differ from "traditional" biblical mores yet claim to reflect a wholesome fulfilment of the obligation to love God and neighbour.

In the third instance, we might accept that all of us Christians, freed from the demands of the law, all too easily seek to replace that liberty with shackles created for ourselves and others simply because we are not yet very whole in Christ. Is that not how, in New Testament times, the "Judaisers" used God's word in the Old Testament to tie legalistic strings to the gospel? Is that not why a wonderful church father like Chrysostomos still insisted on demonising the Jewish people, or why Calvin could apply capital punishment to eliminate a person whom he saw as heretical in his beliefs? Is it not why the historic papacy too often became embroiled in power politics and the processes of domination? From matters of financial stewardship to the "proper" way to worship, to definitions of what it means to be the church in the world – so much of the time these matters are made into litmus tests for determining who might be considered an insider or an outsider. They turn us Christians into legalists. We forget that the God whose will we are seeking to obey is in himself good. He is in himself love.

[10] Seventh Day Adventists Answer Questions on Doctrine, Review and Herald: Washington DC (1957), pp 150, 153 respectively. The italics are original. See T.H. Jemison, Christian Beliefs: Fundamental Biblical Teachings for Seventh-day Adventist College Courses, Pacific Press: Mountain View, California (1959). Part 8 of Jemison's book deals in detail with Seventh Day Adventist convictions concerning the Sabbath (pp 277–308).

The issue of abrogation has been a major facet of Christian debate concerning the kind of authority that applies to Old and New Testaments. It is closely linked to differing views of continuity or discontinuity as regards the "law" given by God at Sinai, or more generally in the Old Testament. One might, incidentally, make the observation that the concept of abrogation as applied to the Qur'ân tends to lead Muslims to "war", while its equivalent in the biblical tradition should lead Christians to "peace".

A BOLD QUESTIONING

An equivalent debate has been tentatively initiated within Islam. The hinge event in this debate is the *hijra*.[11] The Islamists have argued strongly that the period after *hijra* marks the apotheosis of Prophet Muḥammad's life and ministry. In Medina, the prophet turned statesman and under his emirship, law came to be defined and expressed. The Islamists look back to the Medinan years as illustrative of what it means to live truly by the will of God. Such a view has begun to be challenged by some Muslims.

Figure 9

Tâhâ's view of Meccan versus Medinan *tanzîl*[12]

Meccan *tanzîl*	**Medinan *tanzîl***
The stage of *al-islâm*	The stage of *al-imân*
Emphasis on prostration (e.g. Sura 96:19)	Emphasis on law
Equality of the sexes (e.g. Sura 84:10)	Higher position of males in society (e.g. Sura 4:34)
Monogamy preferred (e.g. Sura 4:3 with 4:129)	Polygamy allowed (e.g. Sura 4:34)
Abolition of slavery (e.g. Sura 16:75)	Admission of slavery (e.g. Sura 5:89)
Insistence on non-compulsive means of spreading Islam (e.g. Sura 16:125)	Introduction of concept of *jihâd* (e.g. Sura 9:5)

[11] "Migration": the date of Muḥammad's flight from Mecca on the fourth day of the first month of AD 622.

[12] "Sending down": the Islamic concept of how revelation proceeds from God to humankind.

A Ṣûfî scholar from Sudan, Maḥmûd Muḥammad Tâhâ (died AD 1985) argued for a radically different interpretation of the principle of abrogation.[13] His conviction was that the Meccan verses should take precedence over the Medinan verses. What comprised the word of God "sent down" in Mecca should be honoured above the word of God "sent down" in Medina. This was because the Meccan *tanzîl*, in his view, reflected the original, unadulterated word of God, whereas the Medinan *tanzîl* showed an adaptation of the original message to the exigencies of Medinan society (see figure 9).

Tâhâ characterised the Meccan verses as fundamentally open and liberating, whilst the Medinan verses he typified as specific and restrictive. Whilst the Prophet was in Mecca, Islam was presented in terms of freedom of choice with each individual having personal responsibility for making that choice. Tâhâ pinned this thesis on the following genre of verses from the Qur'ân:

> Invite (all) to the Way of thy Lord with wisdom and beautiful preaching; and argue with them in ways that are best and most gracious: for thy Lord knoweth best, who have strayed from His Path, and who receive guidance. (Sura 16:125)
>
> Say, "The truth is from your Lord": Let him who will believe, and let him who will, reject (it): for the wrong-doers We have prepared a Fire whose (smoke and flames), like the walls and roof of a tent, will hem them in: if they implore relief they will be granted water like melted brass, that will scald their faces, how dreadful the drink! How uncomfortable a couch to recline on! (Sura 18:29)

Perhaps the equality of all people, irrespective of their sex or religious belief, would have been established if such qur'ânic texts had been made the basis of the relevant *sharî'a* law. In the event, suggests Tâhâ, the Quraysh showed themselves unable to receive and live by such a revelation, even conspiring to kill Prophet Muḥammad. So the offer of freedom and responsibility was withdrawn. The twin concepts of compulsion and guardianship were imposed once Muḥammad had successfully migrated to Medina. There at Medina, also, the various verses explaining different levels of *jihâd* to defend and promote Islam were revealed, as were verses that discriminated against non-Muslims and women:

[13] The most significant of Tâhâ's writings is available in English as Mahmoud Mohamed Taha, *The Second Message of Islam* (trans. Abdullahi Ahmed An-Na'Im), Syracuse University Press: Syracuse, New York (1986).

> Fight those who believe not in Allah nor the Last Day, nor hold that forbidden which hath been forbidden by Allah and His Messenger, nor acknowledge the religion of Truth, (even if they are) of the People of the Book, until they pay the Jizya with willing submission, and feel themselves subdued. (Sura 9:29)

> Men are the protectors and maintainers of women, because Allah has given the one more (strength) than the other, and because they support them from their means. Therefore the righteous women are devoutly obedient, and guard in (the husband's) absence what Allah would have them guard. As to those women on whose part ye fear disloyalty and ill-conduct, admonish them (first), (Next), refuse to share their beds, (And last) beat them (lightly); but if they return to obedience, seek not against them Means (of annoyance): For Allah is Most High, great (above you all). (Sura 4:34)

Tâhâ suggested that the Prophet Muḥammad had no choice but to confirm the necessity of building *sharî'a* law on the material revealed whilst he was living in Medina. Over the following 300 years, the Muslim jurists gradually rationalised *sharî'a* law by systematising and categorising various crimes. Such a process involved the comparison of earlier texts from the time of Muḥammad's living in Mecca with those emanating from his stay in Medina. Any principles from Meccan days that appeared to be inconsistent with those from Medinan days were argued to have been repealed or abrogated. The verses on which the former principles were built – the Meccan material – remained within the text of the Qur'ân and reference to their outworking remained within the *ḥadîth* literature. They tended to carry the weight of ethical standards but had little authority in law.

Tâhâ proposed a different tack. He maintained that the shift from Meccan *tanzîl* to Medinan *tanzîl* was made because in the actual circumstances of Muḥammad's time – both external factors and the internal capabilities of Muslims – the Meccan principles could not yet be implemented in all their openness. They were, however, the ideal and the more original. The abrogation of the Meccan verses was, in his view, a temporary suspension. "Abrogation" or *naskh*, in his view, really constituted a postponement rather than a conclusive repeal. An appropriate context in the future would allow them to be clearly valid for implementation and enforcement.

Tâhâ suggested to his contemporary Sudanese that now was the time for Muslims to reverse the shift from Meccan to Medinan ethos. Now was the time to leave the Medinan, restrictive interpretation of Islam and move forward to fulfilling the liberating Meccan ideal. That ideal promoted the development of complete liberty and equality for all human beings regardless of sex, religion or faith. Tâhâ's thinking on this sensitive issue arose out of detention in prison under the British and a rigorous program of prayer, fasting and meditation. He felt that his vision for the future of Islam was God-given.

A VITAL LEGACY?

In terms of political reform, Tâhâ proposed to shift certain aspects of Islamic law from their foundation on Medinan texts to a reliance upon Meccan texts. "What is morally persuasive" would become the rationale for jurisprudence, rather than an appeal to a body of inherited law that had developed out of a need to work with unenlightened, second-best believers in their Medinan experience of Islam.

In the 1950s, the Republican Party in Sudan (co-founded in 1945 by Tâhâ) redirected its mandate towards propagating this more liberal interpretation of Islam. Over succeeding years, the Republican Party was outmanoeuvred by President Nimeiri in his drive to impose traditional *sharî'a* law on the nation. Eventually Tâhâ and other Republican Party leaders were arrested in 1983 and held in prison while Nimeiri introduced his laws. On their release in December 1984, Tâhâ and his fellow leaders started to campaign for the repeal of those laws. They were quickly rearrested and in January 1985, Tâhâ was condemned to death for apostasy. He was executed by hanging on 18 January, 1985. Tâhâ's view of "abrogation" cost him his life.

Tâhâ's creative theologising, however unpopular with those bent on imposing an Islamist agenda upon the political process within Sudan in the 1980s, seems to me to comprise a positive model for Muslims wishing today to respond to the proposal of contemporary Muslim extremists that theirs is the true fulfilment of what the Qur'ân commands. Tâhâ's perspective carries integrity as a Muslim perspective, based upon the whole text of the Qur'ân, not denying the flavour of what he calls the Medinan *tanzîl*, and arising out of prayerful meditation and suffering.

Tâhâ's contribution, as a result, avoids the "denial" aspect of many modern, Western Muslims' attempts to redeem Islam in their own eyes and before a hostile Western world. Typical in such attempts is the claim, for example, that in Prophet Muḥammad's lifetime only a defensive interpretation of *jihâd* was made:

> All those who believe or proclaim that Islam was spread on dint of sword – that it was only sword that was utilized, their notion is completely erroneous. Because, so long as people lived in Mecca they were not permitted to go for Jihad (Holy War) and the Muslims never raised the sword in Mecca. Even though they had been subjected to different types of tortures they kept patience.[14]

This author's motive is a conciliatory and positive one, and what he says is true as far as it goes. It is true that Islam was not spread only by the sword. It is true that, in the Meccan years, *jihâd* was not even mentioned in the qur'ânic verses sent down then. The author, however, fails to deal honestly with Prophet Muḥammad's rulership in Medina:

> All the wars that took place in the life of the Holy Prophet were fought in self-defence. Those wars were not at all based on offence. And the Prophet of God (PBUH) had not adopted any offensive practice. This happened all through his life. If you go through the history, you will find all the wars defensive, which were fought in defence of Islam.[15]

This claim is simply not true, and it undermines the goal of the author to try and explain away the activities of contemporary Islamic extremists as irrational and unfaithful. Instead of confessing the truth of Prophet Muḥammad's strong use of the sword, the author chooses instead to blame Aḥmad ibn Taymîyya for introducing the element of terrorism into Islam, and condemns 'Abd al-Wahhâb for building on that interpretation. The author thus seeks to uphold the perspective on relationships with peoples of other faiths that is evidenced in the Meccan verses of the Qur'ân – a worthy and generous gesture – but he does so by a process of denial concerning what the Medinan verses declare about *jihâd*, and what Islamic tradition reveals about Prophet Muḥammad's own application of the call to holy war. The perspective proposed by Tâhâ, in strong contrast, admits the reality of Medinan Islam, admits the supremacy of the "Verse of the Sword" in all its abrogating power, admits the use of coercion by Prophet Muḥammad – but

[14] Maulana Kazmi, *Roots of Terrorism*. This text has been sent to me by the author via email, in unpublished format. The quotation appears in "Chapter One: Who are the Originators of Terroriam in Islam?"
[15] *Ibid.*

argues from a qur'ânic perspective that a "better way" is proposed within that holy text.

Tâhâ modelled a radically different way of receiving the divine Word, of reading it. We need, now, to consider some of the factors involved in a human appreciation of a given – divinely given – text.

Chapter 5

It makes sense if you take into account . . .

THE purpose of this chapter is to illustrate that there is a delicate balance between text and context in at least the receiving of the qur'ânic revelation, if not in the giving of it. A divine "word" is sent down to produce certain results on earth. Prophet Muḥammad is its human mouthpiece. His message to others, like the people of the Quraysh – the tribe to which Muḥammad belonged – derives from what God speaks through him. How do those "others," like the Quraysh, hear what is recited? Well – from within a context surely. When the divine word comes down, it is not communicated into a vacuum, but within specific situations. As a consequence, it often appears that the "recitation" is connected with what is going on in the life of Prophet Muḥammad – in his relationship with the Quraysh for example. As we have noted, over a period of 23 years, the word sent down provokes, or comes across as being provoked by, affairs in the life of Prophet Muḥammad.

How might different generations of Muslims hear that extended delivery? And how might they comprehend it? Only, surely, if the hearer at the time or the reader at a later date is given to understand the context of the original acts of revelation. Islam knows a strong exegetical tradition. Producers of *tafsîr* (or exegesis) sought to explain the relationship between text and original context. Some of the most significant authors of *tafsîr* (out of thousands) are listed in figure 10.

In this chapter, we shall consider three suras in the context of their being "sent down". The lovely sura of Yusuf or Joseph (Sura 12) illustrates how an understanding of the context of the giving of a particular revelation is needed in order fully to appreciate it. The sura also raises the possibility that there might have been more than one way in which it was recited by the Prophet. The infamous "Satanic verses" incident (Sura 53) raises the interesting conundrum of how an eternal word might find itself subject to devilish intervention in the process of its being conveyed to earth. The sura dealing

Figure 10

Exegetes of the Qur'ân

Name	Date	Title of work
ʿAbdullah Ibn ʿAbbâs	d. AD 687?	
Muḥammad ibn-Jarîr al-Ṭabarî	d. AD 923	*Jâmiʿal Bayân fî Tafsîr al-Qur'ân*
al-Zamakhsharî	d. AD 1143	*al-Kashshâf ʿan Haqâ'iq al-Tanzîl*
Fakhr al-Dîn al-Râzî	d. AD 1210	*Mafâtih al-Ghayb (al-Tafsîr al-Kabîr)*
Abû ʿAbdullah Muḥammad al-Qurtubi	d. AD 1273	*al-Jamiʿlî-Ahkam al-Qur'ân*
al-Bayḍâwî	d. AD 1286	*Anwâr al-Tanzîl wa Asrâr al-Ta'wîl*
ʿImad al-Dîn ibn Kathîr	d. AD 1372	*Tafsîr ibn Kathîr*
Jalâl al-Dîn al-Suyûtî	d. AD 1505	*Tafsîr al-Jalâlayn*
Maḥmûd al-Alûsî	d. AD 1854	*Rûh al-Maʿan fî Tafsîr al-Qur'ân al-ʿAzîm wa'l-Sâb al-Mathâni*

with Prophet Muḥammad's night journey to heaven (Sura 17) provokes questions about how the Qur'ân is supposed to be heard: is it describing, in this sura, a literal ascent of the prophet to heaven or something else?

JOSEPH IN THE QUR'ÂN

The patriarch Yusuf or Joseph receives the most comprehensive treatment of any of the biblical prophets in the Qur'ân. The sura that contains this treatment (sura 12) constitutes the longest continuous narrative in the Qur'ân. It is obviously, therefore, a very significant accounting. The story itself is carried in the telling by a mixture of report and dialogue. The narrator is interrupted by seventeen different speaking parts. Of those parts, Jacob and Joseph are named but most of the characters remain unnamed – people like the water-drawer or the Witness or the two fellow-prisoners (the butler and the baker). At first reading, it is difficult to understand the point of the story, for some of the "voices" are not easily distinguished. If the sura is treated as a narrative play, divided by acts with scenes, it becomes much easier to follow. That is how it is reproduced in the following pages.[1]

According to traditional Muslim scholarship this sura (sura 12) is late Meccan, dating from the last period of Prophet Muḥammad's preaching in Mecca. It was a time of strong opposition, both to Muḥammad's message and to him personally. Verses 1, 2, 3 and 7 are considered differently, however. They are perceived as being Medinan, deriving from a slightly later period after Muḥammad had left Mecca and become established in Medina. They became part of the revelation later than the majority of verses in this sura. Thus, when this sura was first recited by the Prophet, it evidently began at verse 4 with Joseph addressing his father. As the story progresses, there are glosses on it (within the text) that come in direct words of commentary by God himself. Then, outside the story as it were, the added, Medinan verses provide a later, overarching summary of the point of the story. It is as if God wants to draw out – through both kinds of divine comment – significant lessons from Joseph's experience in order to encourage Muḥammad in his equivalent difficulties.

Act 1

Scene 1 (vv 4–6). Joseph recounts his dream to his father.

Behold! Joseph said to his father: "O my father! I did see eleven stars and the sun and the moon: I saw them prostrate themselves to me!" Said (the father): "My (dear) little son! Relate not thy vision to thy brothers, lest they concoct a plot against thee: for Satan is to man an avowed enemy! Thus will thy Lord choose thee and teach thee the interpretation of stories (and events) and perfect His favour to thee and to the posterity of Jacob – even as He perfected it to thy fathers Abraham and Isaac aforetime! For Allah is full of knowledge and wisdom."

Scene 2 (vv 8–10). The brothers concoct their plot against Joseph.

They said: "Truly Joseph and his brother are loved more by our father than we: But we are a goodly body! Really our father is obviously wandering (in his mind)! Slay ye Joseph or cast him out to some (unknown) land, so that the favour of your father may be given to you alone: (there will be time enough) for you to be righteous after that!" Said one of them: "Slay not Joseph, but if ye must do something, throw him down to the bottom of the well: he will be picked up by some caravan of travellers."

[1] This dramatic presentation of the story of Joseph is based upon that provided by A.H. Johns in his article "The Quranic presentation of the Joseph story". In G.R. Hawting & Abdul-Kader A. Shareef (eds.), *Approaches to the Qur'ân*, Routledge: London (1993), pp 37–70.

Scene 3 (vv 11–14). The brothers persuade Jacob to let Joseph go with them.

They said: "O our father! Why dost thou not trust us with Joseph, – seeing we are indeed his sincere well-wishers? Send him with us tomorrow to enjoy himself and play, and we shall take every care of him." (Jacob) said: "Really it saddens me that ye should take him away: I fear lest the wolf should devour him while ye attend not to him." They said: "If the wolf were to devour him while we are (so large) a party, then should we indeed (first) have perished ourselves!"

Scene 4 (v 15a). Joseph is deposited in the well.

So they did take him away, and they all agreed to throw him down to the bottom of the well:

Divine interjection (v 15b).

and We put into his heart (this Message): "Of a surety thou shalt (one day) tell them the truth of this their affair while they know (thee) not."

Scene 5 (vv 16–18). The brothers return to Jacob without Joseph but with a story.

Then they came to their father in the early part of the night, weeping. They said: "O our father! We went racing with one another, and left Joseph with our things; and the wolf devoured him . . . But thou wilt never believe us even though we tell the truth." They stained his shirt with false blood. He said: "Nay, but your minds have made up a tale (that may pass) with you, (for me) patience is most fitting: Against that which ye assert, it is Allah (alone) whose help can be sought."

Act 2

Scene 1 (vv 19–20). Joseph found in the well and sold to travellers.

Then there came a caravan of travellers: they sent their water-carrier (for water), and he let down his bucket (into the well) . . . He said: "Ah there! Good news! Here is a (fine) young man!" So they concealed him as a treasure! But Allah knoweth well all that they do! The (Brethren) sold him for a miserable price, for a few dirhams counted out: in such low estimation did they hold him!

Scene 2 (v 21a). The governor of Egypt (al-'Azîz) addresses his wife.

The man in Egypt who bought him, said to his wife: "Make his stay (among us) honourable: may be he will bring us much good, or we shall adopt him as a son."

Divine interjection (vv 21b–22).

Thus did We establish Joseph in the land, that We might teach him the interpretation of stories (and events). And Allah hath full power and control over His affairs; but most among mankind know it not. When Joseph attained his full manhood, We gave him power and knowledge: thus do We reward those who do right.

Act 3

Scene 1 (v 23). The governor's wife (Zulaykha) attempts to seduce Joseph.

But she in whose house he was, sought to seduce him from his (true) self: she fastened the doors, and said: "Now come, thou (dear one)!" He said: "Allah forbid! Truly (thy husband) is my lord! He made my sojourn agreeable! Truly to no good come those who do wrong!"

Divine interjection (v 24).

And (with passion) did she desire him, and he would have desired her, but that he saw the evidence of his Lord: thus (did We order) that We might turn away from him (all) evil and shameful deeds: for he was one of Our servants, sincere and purified.

Scene 2 (vv 25–29). Zulaykha face to face with al-'Azîz.

So they both raced each other to the door, and she tore his shirt from the back: they both found her lord near the door. She said: "What is the (fitting) punishment for one who formed an evil design against thy wife, but prison or a grievous chastisement?" He said: "It was she that sought to seduce me – from my (true) self." And one of her household saw (this) and bore witness, (thus): "If it be that his shirt is rent from the front, then is her tale true, and he is a liar! But if it be that his shirt is torn from the back, then is she the liar, and he is telling the truth!" So when he saw his shirt, – that it was torn at the back, – (her husband) said: "Behold! It is a snare of you women! Truly, mighty is your snare! O Joseph, pass this over! (O wife), ask forgiveness for thy sin, for truly thou hast been at fault!"

Scene 3 (v 30). Women of the city gossiping.

Ladies said in the city: "The wife of the (great) 'Aziz is seeking to seduce her slave from his (true) self: Truly hath he inspired her with violent love: we see she is evidently going astray."

Scene 4 (vv 31–32). Zulaykha shows Joseph to the women of the city.

When she heard of their malicious talk, she sent for them and prepared a banquet for them: she gave each of them a knife: and she said (to Joseph), "Come out before them." When they saw him, they did extol him, and (in their amazement) cut their hands: they said, "Allah preserve us! No mortal is this! This is none other than a noble angel!" She said: "There before you is the man about whom ye did blame me! I did seek to seduce him from his (true) self but he did firmly save himself guiltless! . . . and now, if he doth not my bidding, he shall certainly be cast into prison, and (what is more) be of the company of the vilest!"

Act 4

Scene 1 (vv 33–42). Joseph in prison and two fellow-prisoners.

He said: "O my Lord! The prison is more to my liking than that to which they invite me: Unless Thou turn away their snare from me, I should (in my youthful folly) feel inclined towards them and join the ranks of the ignorant." So his Lord hearkened to him (in his prayer), and turned away from him their snare: Verily He heareth and knoweth (all things). Then it occurred to the men, after they had seen the signs, (that it was best) to imprison him for a time. Now with him there came into the prison two young men. Said one of them: "I see myself (in a dream) pressing wine." Said the other: "I see myself (in a dream) carrying bread on my head, and birds are eating, thereof." "Tell us" (they said) "the truth and meaning thereof: for we see thou art one that doth good (to all)." He said: "Before any food comes (in due course) to feed either of you, I will surely reveal to you the truth and meaning of this ere it befall you: that is part of the (duty) which my Lord hath taught me. I have (I assure you) abandoned the ways of a people that believe not in Allah and that (even) deny the hereafter. And I follow the ways of my fathers, – Abraham, Isaac, and Jacob; and never could we attribute any partners whatever to Allah: that (comes) of the grace of Allah to us and to mankind: yet most men are not grateful. O my two companions of the prison! (I ask you): are many lords differing among themselves better, or the One Allah, Supreme and Irresistible? If not Him, ye worship nothing but names which ye have named, – ye and your fathers, – for which Allah hath sent down no authority: the command is for none but Allah: He hath commanded that ye worship none but Him: that is the right religion, but most men understand not . . . O my two companions of the prison! As to one of you, he will pour out the wine for his lord to drink: as for the other, he will hang from the cross, and the birds will eat from off his head. (so) hath been decreed that matter whereof ye twain do enquire" . . . And of the two, to that one whom he considers about to be saved, he said: "Mention me to thy lord." But Satan made him forget to mention him to his lord: and (Joseph) lingered in prison a few (more) years.

Act 5

Scene 1 (vv 43–45). Pharaoh's dream is overheard by the butler.

The king (of Egypt) said: "I do see (in a vision) seven fat kine, whom seven lean ones devour, and seven green ears of corn, and seven (others) withered. O ye chiefs! Expound to me my vision if it be that ye can interpret visions." They said: "A confused medley of dreams: and we are not skilled in the interpretation of dreams." But the man who had been released, one of the two (who had been in prison) and who now bethought him after (so long) a space of time, said: "I will tell you the truth of its interpretation: send ye me (therefore)."

Scene 2 (vv 46–49). The butler visits Joseph in prison to get the interpretation.

"O Joseph!" (he said) "O man of truth! Expound to us (the dream) of seven fat kine whom seven lean ones devour, and of seven green ears of corn and (seven) others withered: that I may return to the people, and that they may understand." (Joseph) said: "For seven years shall ye diligently sow as is your wont: and the harvests that ye reap, ye shall leave them in the ear, – except a little, of which ye shall eat. Then will come after that (period) seven dreadful (years), which will devour what ye shall have laid by in advance for them, – (all) except a little which ye shall have (specially) guarded. Then will come after that (period) a year in which the people will have abundant water, and in which they will press (wine and oil)."

Scene 3 (v 50). Joseph refuses to leave prison until declared innocent.

So the king said: "Bring ye him unto me." But when the messenger came to him, (Joseph) said: "Go thou back to thy lord, and ask him, 'What is the state of mind of the ladies who cut their hands?' For my Lord is certainly well aware of their snare."

Scene 4 (v 51). The butler, the king and the women.

(The king) said (to the ladies): "What was your affair when ye did seek to seduce Joseph from his (true) self?" The ladies said: "Allah preserve us! No evil know we against him!" Said the 'Aziz's wife: "Now is the truth manifest (to all): it was I who sought to seduce him from his (true) self: He is indeed of those who are (ever) true (and virtuous)."

Scene 5 (vv 52–53). Joseph speaking to the butler on his third visit to the prison.

"This (say I), in order that He may know that I have never been false to him in his absence, and that Allah will never guide the snare of the false ones. Nor do I absolve my own self (of blame): the (human) soul is certainly prone to evil, unless my Lord do bestow His Mercy: but surely my Lord is Oft-forgiving, Most Merciful."

Scene 6 (vv 54–55). Joseph before the king, and his promotion.

So the king said: "Bring him unto me; I will take him specially to serve about my own person." Therefore when he had spoken to him, he said: "Be assured this day, thou art, before our own presence, with rank firmly established, and fidelity fully proved!" (Joseph) said: "Set me over the store-houses of the land: I will indeed guard them, as one that knows (their importance)."

Act 6

Divine interjection (vv 56–57).

Thus did We give established power to Joseph in the land, to take possession therein as, when, or where he pleased. We bestow of our Mercy on whom We please, and We suffer not, to be lost, the reward of those who do good. But verily the reward of the hereafter is the best, for those who believe, and are constant in righteousness.

Scene 1 (vv 58–62). Joseph's brothers (minus Benjamin) in Egypt.

Then came Joseph's brethren: they entered his presence, and he knew them, but they knew him not. And when he had furnished them forth with provisions (suitable) for them, he said: "Bring unto me a brother ye have, of the same father as yourselves, (but a different mother): see ye not that I pay out full measure, and that I do provide the best hospitality? Now if ye bring him not to me, ye shall have no measure (of corn) from me, nor shall ye (even) come near me." They said: "We shall certainly seek to get our wish about him from his father: Indeed we shall do it." And (Joseph) told his servants to put their stock-in-trade (with which they had bartered) into their saddle-bags, so they should know it only when they returned to their people, in order that they might come back.

Act 7

Scene 1 (vv 63–67). The brothers back with Jacob in Canaan.

Now when they returned to their father, they said: "O our father! No more measure of grain shall we get (unless we take our brother): So send our brother with us, that we may get our measure; and we will indeed take every care of him." He said: "Shall I trust you with him with any result other than when I trusted you with his brother aforetime? But Allah is the best to take care (of him), and He is the Most Merciful of those who show mercy!" Then when they opened their baggage, they found their stock-in-trade had been returned to them. They said: "O our father! What (more) can we desire? This our stock-in-trade has been returned to us: so we shall get (more) food for our family; we shall take care of our brother; and add (at the same time) a full camel's load (of grain to our provisions). This is but a small quantity." (Jacob) said: "Never will I send him with you until ye swear a solemn oath to me, in Allah's name, that ye will be sure to bring him back to me unless ye are yourselves hemmed in (and made powerless)." And when they had sworn their solemn oath, he said: "Over all that we say, be Allah the witness and guardian!" Further he said: "O my sons! Enter not all by one gate: enter ye by different gates. Not that I can profit you aught against Allah (with my advice): None can command except Allah: On Him do I put my trust: and let all that trust put their trust on Him."

Divine interjection (v 68).

And when they entered in the manner their father had enjoined, it did not profit them in the least against (the plan of) Allah: It was but a necessity of Jacob's soul, which he discharged. For he was, by Our instruction, full of knowledge (and experience): but most men know not.

Act 8

Scene 1 (v 69). Brothers plus Benjamin in Egypt.

Now when they came into Joseph's presence, he received his (full) brother to stay with him. He said (to him): "Behold! I am thy (own) brother; so grieve not at aught of their doings."

Scene 2 (vv 70–76a). The crier and the brothers; Benjamin entrapped.

At length when he had furnished them forth with provisions (suitable) for them, he put the drinking cup into his brother's saddle-bag. Then shouted out a crier: "O ye (in) the caravan! Behold! Ye are thieves, without doubt!" They said, turning towards them: "What is it that ye miss?" They said: "We miss the great beaker of the king; for him who produces it, is (the reward of) a camel load; I will be bound by it." (The brothers) said: "By Allah! well ye know that we came not to make mischief in the land, and we are no thieves!" (The Egyptians) said: "What then shall be the penalty of this, if ye are (proved) to have lied?" They said: "The penalty should be that he in whose saddle-bag it is found, should be held (as bondman) to atone for the (crime). Thus it is we punish the wrong-doers!" So he began (the search) with their baggage, before (he came to) the baggage of his brother: at length he brought it out of his brother's baggage.

Divine interjection (v 76b).

Thus did We plan for Joseph. He could not take his brother by the law of the king except that Allah willed it (so). We raise to degrees (of wisdom) whom We please: but over all endued with knowledge is one, the All-Knowing.

Scene 3 (vv 77–79). The brothers back with Joseph.

They said: "If he steals, there was a brother of his who did steal before (him)." But these things did Joseph keep locked in his heart, revealing not the secrets to them. He (simply) said (to himself): "Ye are the worse situated; and Allah knoweth best the truth of what ye assert!" They said: "O exalted one! Behold! He has a father, aged and venerable, (who will grieve for him); so take one of us in his place; for we see that thou art (gracious) in doing good." He said: "Allah forbid that we take other than him with whom we found our property: indeed (if we did so), we should be acting wrongfully."

Act 9

Scene 1 (vv 80–87). Most of the brothers return to Jacob who grieves.

Now when they saw no hope of his (yielding), they held a conference in private. The leader among them said: "Know ye not that your father did take an oath from you in Allah's name, and how, before this, ye did fail in your duty with Joseph? Therefore will I not leave this land until my father permits me, or Allah commands me; and He is the best to command. Turn ye back to your father, and say, 'O our father! Behold! Thy son committed theft! We bear witness only to what we know, and we could not well guard against the unseen! Ask at the town where we have been and the caravan in which we returned, and (you will find) we are indeed telling the truth." Jacob said: "Nay, but ye have yourselves contrived a story (good enough) for you. So patience is most fitting (for me). Maybe Allah will bring them (back) all to me (in the end). For He is indeed full of knowledge and wisdom." And he turned away from them, and said: "How great is my grief for Joseph!" And his eyes became white with sorrow, and he fell into silent melancholy. They said: "By Allah! (Never) wilt thou cease to remember Joseph until thou reach the last extremity of illness, or until thou die!" He said: "I only complain of my distraction and anguish to Allah, and I know from Allah that which ye know not . . . O my sons! Go ye and enquire about Joseph and his brother, and never give up hope of Allah's Soothing Mercy: truly no one despairs of Allah's Soothing Mercy, except those who have no faith."

Act 10

Scene 1 (vv 88–93). The brothers in Egypt with Joseph.

Then, when they came (back) into (Joseph's) presence they said: "O exalted one! Distress has seized us and our family: we have (now) brought but scanty capital: so pay us full measure, (we pray thee), and treat it as charity to us: for Allah doth reward the charitable." He said: "Know ye how ye dealt with Joseph and his brother, not knowing (what ye were doing)?" They said: "Art thou indeed Joseph?" He said, "I am Joseph, and this is my brother: Allah has indeed been gracious to us (all): behold, he that is righteous and patient, – never will Allah suffer the reward to be lost, of those who do right." They said: "By Allah! Indeed has Allah preferred thee above us, and we certainly have been guilty of sin!" He said: "This day let no reproach be (cast) on you: Allah will forgive you, and He is the Most Merciful of those who show mercy! Go with this my shirt, and cast it over the face of my father: he will come to see (clearly). Then come ye (here) to me together with all your family."

Act 11

Scene 1 (vv 94–95). In Canaan, Jacob awaits his sons.

When the caravan left (Egypt), their father said: "I do indeed scent the presence of Joseph: Nay, think me not a dotard." They said: "By Allah! Truly thou art in thine old wandering mind."

Scene 2 (vv 96–98). Jacob gets news of Joseph.

Then when the bearer of the good news came, He cast (the shirt) over his face, and he forthwith regained clear sight. He said: "Did I not say to you, 'I know from Allah that which ye know not?' " They said: "O our father! Ask for us forgiveness for our sins, for we were truly at fault." He said: "Soon will I ask my Lord for forgiveness for you: for he is indeed Oft-Forgiving, Most Merciful."

Scene 3 (vv 99–101). Jacob and family travel to Egypt.

Then when they entered the presence of Joseph, he provided a home for his parents with himself, and said: "Enter ye Egypt (all) in safety if it please Allah." And he raised his parents high on the throne (of dignity), and they fell down in prostration, (all) before him. He said: "O my father! This is the fulfilment of my vision of old! Allah hath made it come true! He was indeed good to me when He took me out of prison and brought you (all here) out of the desert, (even) after Satan had sown enmity between me and my brothers. Verily my Lord understandeth best the mysteries of all that He planneth to do, for verily He is full of knowledge and wisdom. O my Lord! Thou hast indeed bestowed on me some power, and taught me something of the interpretation of dreams and events, – O Thou Creator of the heavens and the earth! Thou art my Protector in this world and in the Hereafter. Take Thou my soul (at death) as one submitting to Thy will (as a Muslim), and unite me with the righteous."

Concluding verses (vv 102–111).

Such is one of the stories of what happened unseen, which We reveal by inspiration unto thee; nor wast thou (present) with them then when they concerted their plans together in the process of weaving their plots. Yet no faith will the greater part of mankind have, however ardently thou dost desire it. And no reward dost thou ask of them for this: it is no less than a message for all creatures. And how many Signs in the heavens and the earth do they pass by? Yet they turn (their faces) away from them! And most of them believe not in Allah without associating (other as partners) with Him! Do they then feel secure from the coming against them of the covering veil of the wrath of Allah, – or of the coming against them of the (final) Hour all of a sudden while they perceive not? Say thou: "This is my way: I do invite unto Allah, – on evidence clear as the seeing with one's eyes, – I and whoever follows me. Glory to Allah! and never will I join gods with Allah!" Nor did We send before thee (as messengers) any but men, whom we did inspire, – (men) living in human habitations. Do they not travel through the earth, and see what was the end of those before them? But the home of the hereafter is best, for those who do right. Will ye not then understand? (Respite will be granted) until, when the messengers give up hope (of their people) and (come to) think that they were treated as liars, there reaches them Our help, and those whom We will are delivered into safety. But never will be warded off our punishment from those who are in sin. There is, in their stories, instruction for men endued with understanding. It is not a tale invented, but a confirmation of what went before it, – a detailed exposition of all things, and a guide and a mercy to any such as believe.

The story of Joseph is told with great imagination for detail of conversation. Some kind of appreciation of the dialogues going on is necessary in order to make sense of the concentrated verses. Inserted into the ensuing human story are "asides", as it were, spoken by God to make the point. I have called some of the larger of those asides "divine interjections" in the sura as set out here. The verses given later in Medina emphasise this point: they constitute a concluding aside, as it were.

Medinan verses (vv 1–3, 7).

Alif, Lam, Rar. These are the symbols (or Verses) of the perspicuous Book. We have sent it down as an Arabic Qur'an, in order that ye may learn wisdom. We do relate unto thee the most beautiful of stories, in that We reveal to thee this (portion of the) Qur'an: before this, thou too was among those who knew it not . . . Verily in Joseph and his brethren are signs (or symbols) for seekers (after Truth).

HEARING THE TEXT

My first purpose, as we step back from this lively story, is to illustrate how the text itself can carry a variety of possible interpretations.

In Act 1, scene 2, for example, as the brothers are overheard making their plot, it becomes evident that the murder of Joseph is intended (v 9): "Slay ye Joseph . . ."[2] urges a voice, or voices. Commentators differ as to whose voice lies behind the urging to kill. Al-Bayḍâwî suggests it is the plural voice of all the brothers except for the one who will say "Don't kill" (v 10), while al-Râzî maintains

[2] *uqtulû yûsufa.*

that "Slay" is uttered by only one of the brothers – supposedly Simeon or Dan – whilst the rest simply assent.[3] The text is heard slightly differently by these two *tafsîr* producers.

In Act 2, scene 1, the following phrase occurs in Arabic: "Yâ bushrâ" (v 19). It occurs at that point in the story where Joseph has been thrown down the well and the brothers have retired to consider what to do with him. While they are deliberating, a camel caravan arrives at the waterhole. The thirsty travellers let down a bucket to collect water. Instead of water, up comes young Joseph in the bucket! One of the travellers declares: "Yâ bushrâ!" What is he saying? Well he could be saying, as many commentators suggest, "Ah there! Good news!" Or he could be addressing his companion, who has the known name Bushrâ, getting his attention to what the bucket is bringing up from the well. Al-Bayḍâwî acknowledges both interpretations of the phrase and goes on to record alternative "readings"[4] of the text itself at this point.[5]

In Act 5, scenes 4 and 5, the majority of the commentators see verses 52 and 53 as following a break from verse 51 so that now Joseph himself starts to speak:

> (The king) said (to the ladies): "What was your affair when ye did seek to seduce Joseph from his (true) self?" The ladies said: "Allah preserve us! no evil know we against him!" Said the 'Aziz's wife: "Now is the truth manifest (to all): it was I who sought to seduce him from his (true) self: He is indeed of those who are (ever) true (and virtuous)" [v 51]. "This (say I [Joseph]), in order that He may know that I have never been false to him in his absence, and that Allah will never guide the snare of the false ones [52]. Nor do I absolve my own self (of blame): the (human) soul is certainly prone to evil, unless my Lord do bestow His Mercy: but surely my Lord is Oft-forgiving, Most Merciful" [53].

The sense of the verse in this case would be that Joseph is referring to his faithfulness towards the 'Azîz, namely that he has never taken advantage of his lord's absence to seduce the man's wife, even

[3] As noted by A.H. Johns, *op. cit.*, p 45. The view of al-Bayḍâwî is found in Bayḍâwî, 'Abd Allah ibn 'Umar, *Baiḍâwî's Commentary on Sûrah 12 of the Qur'ân* (text, accompanied by an interpretative rendering and notes by A.F.L. Beeston), Clarendon Press: Oxford (1963), p 6. The understanding of al-Râzî is expressed in his *Tafsîr*, 18:95.

[4] See chapter 8 for a discussion concerning various early "readings" of the Qur'ân.

[5] Al-Bayḍâwî writes: "Readers other than the Kufans read *bushrâya* 'my good luck' with genitive [pronoun] attached. Ḥamza and Kisâ'î pronounce *imâlah* of the *â*; Warsh reads a pronunciation intermediate [between *imâlah* and *tafkhîm*]. There is also a reading *bushrayya* with assimilation [of the *alif* of prologation into the following *y*], but this is dialectical. A further reading is *bushrây*, with the intention of producing a pausal form." In al-Bayḍâwî, *op. cit.*, p 11.

though he (Joseph) is human and liable to err.[6] A few commentators view verses 52 and 53 as constituting a continuation of Zulaykha's giving of her own defence. In effect, by this interpretation, Zulaykha admits her guilty conduct on this occasion but claims that overall, she has been faithful to her (eunuch) husband. This understanding of the text would seem harder to maintain in that it would seem likely that by this time the 'Azîz has died (see verse 54). Maybe Zulaykha is reflecting on the past. Certainly, by verse 78 Joseph himself is being addressed as 'Azîz.

In Act 7, scene 1, the brothers use the same deceitful words about their intended care of Benjamin as they had of their intended care of Joseph (v 63). The word used by them is *laḥâfiẓûna*: it is a loaded word in Arabic from which the idea of *ḥâfiẓ* ("guardian") would come to be applied to those Muslims who memorised the whole of the Qur'ân. The text here dramatically reinforces the sense of evil in the hearts of the ten brothers towards both Joseph and Benjamin.[7]

In his commentary on Act 10, scene 1, al-Râzî emphasises the point made by Joseph about his brothers' previous behaviour: they were *jâhilûn*, ignorant (v 89).[8] The brothers exhibit behaviour that clearly declares that they are a long way from being *muslim*, or submitted to God. Al-Bayḍâwî suggests that the ignorance of the brothers was that of "irresponsible youths".[9]

Verse 110 occurs in a short section at the end of the sura that looks back on the whole story and draws a conclusion from it:

> (Respite will be granted) until, when the messengers give up hope (of their people) and (come to) think that they were treated as liars, there reaches them Our help, and those whom We will are delivered into safety. But never will be warded off our punishment from those who are in sin.

Yusuf Ali comments on this verse: "*kuẓibû* is the usual reading, though *kuẓẓibû*, the alternative reading, also rests on good authority."[10] Ali prefers the more common reading, with its interpretation:

[6] Al-Bayḍâwî promotes this understanding in his commentary on verse 52: "This is what Joseph said when the messenger returned to him and told him of the women's statement; the meaning is 'that confirmation is in order that 'Azîz may recognize [the truth of Joseph's account]'." In al-Bayḍâwî *op. cit.*, p 29.

[7] Part of the text of this verse reads "No more measure of grain shall we get" unless Jacob sends Benjamin with us [ie the brothers]. Al-Bayḍâwî comments that "Ḥamza and al-Kisâ'î read it [*naktal*] in the third person sing., the subject in that case being the brother [Benjamin], ie he will receive his quota for himself, so that his entitlement will be added to ours."

[8] A.H. Johns, *op.cit.*, p 64, quoting al-Râzî's *Tafsîr*, 18:203–204.

[9] Al-Bayḍâwî, *op. cit.*, p 46.

[10] A. Yusuf Ali (trans.), *The Glorious Qur'an*, American Trust Publications (1977), p 590, note 1795. Al-Bayḍâwî makes the point that "Readers other than the Kufans read [*kudhdhibû*]

> . . . that God gives plenty of rope to the wicked (as in Joseph's story) until His own Messengers feel almost that it will be hopeless to preach to them and come to consider themselves branded as liars by an unbelieving world; that the breaking-point is then reached; that God's help then comes swiftly to His men, and they are delivered from persecution and danger, while the wrath of God overtakes sinners, and nothing can then ward it off.[11]

Ali concludes: "This interpretation has good authority behind it, though there are differences of opinion."[12]

My second purpose is to suggest that the Qur'ân is more concerned with the conclusions to be drawn from this story – especially for Prophet Muḥammad – than with the progression of the story itself. So, for example, the text focuses on the interpretation of the dreams of the butler and baker (v 36) rather than on the details of those dreams. Why? In order that the Qur'ân might present, via Joseph at this point, a strong call to monotheism:

> He said: "Before any food comes (in due course) to feed either of you, I will surely reveal to you the truth and meaning of this ere it befall you: that is part of the (duty) which my Lord hath taught me. I have (I assure you) abandoned the ways of a people that believe not in Allah and that (even) deny the Hereafter. And I follow the ways of my fathers, – Abraham, Isaac, and Jacob; and never could we attribute any partners whatever to Allah: that (comes) of the grace of Allah to us and to mankind: yet most men are not grateful. O my two companions of the prison! (I ask you): are many lords differing among themselves better, or the One Allah, Supreme and Irresistible? If not Him, ye worship nothing but names which ye have named, – ye and your fathers, – for which Allah hath sent down no authority: the command is for none but Allah: He hath commanded that ye worship none but Him: that is the right religion, but most men understand not . . ." (Sura 12:37–40)

Joseph is thus presented as a preacher of monotheism. The revelation at this point assists Muḥammad in his mission for it declares that another prophet has been before where Muḥammad finds himself now vis-à-vis the Quraysh (Sura 12:111). So many parallels are presented. Joseph, for example, has the discernment to interpret what is going on

in the second form, ie 'the prophets thought that the folk regarded them as liars in the monitions they addressed to the folk'." Al-Bayḍâwî, *op. cit.*, p 54.

[11] A. Yusuf Ali (trans.), *op. cit.*, p 590, note 1795.

[12] *Ibid.* Al-Bayḍâwî elaborates: "There is yet another reading in the active of the first form, *kadhabû*, ie 'Men thought that the prophets had lied in what they related to their people, when [the fulfilment of the prophetic message] was delayed in coming to them and they could not detect its having any effect'." Al-Bayḍâwî, *op. cit.*, p 54.

in his life, especially by reference to what God is saying. Is the same not true of Muḥammad? The brothers, living in a state of "ignorance" (verse 89), find themselves unable to accept Joseph's right to special affection from Jacob. The Quraysh currently reflect this living in a state of ignorance. Joseph undergoes a kind of *hijra* in which he shifts away from persecution to a fresh start in Egypt. There, he eventually comes to power where his rulership is moral and contrasts strongly with those (his brothers) who intend only evil. Muḥammad's experience in *hijra* and calling to potential leadership of the Muslim community is similar. Is it too strong to suggest that in this former prophet, Muḥammad finds an encouraging blueprint for his mission?

My third purpose is to suggest that text and context especially meet in this sura in the sense that the story itself affords the opportunity for God to underline that Muḥammad is indeed his spokesman on earth. Fakhr al-Dîn al-Râzî elaborates on the circumstances of the giving of sura 12.[13] On the prompting of the Jews, the Quraysh challenge Muḥammad, should he indeed be a prophet, to tell them how Joseph came to transfer his residence from Canaan to Egypt, and what might be the details of that story. The challenge constitutes a test. The Jews are aware that the story of Joseph is (supposedly) unknown to the Arabs and that Muḥammad has not before made reference to it. In the event, their challenge is more than adequately answered, for God himself reveals the details of the story to Muḥammad through this sura. That God is the source of this revelation is strongly emphasised in verse 3 by the occurrence of the separate pronoun *naḥnu* or "We." The Prophet is assured that what he receives will be the proper version of the story. Muḥammad's successful answer to the challenge of the Quraysh puts the latter (and their Jewish backers) on the spot, for it raises the issue of what might happen to them if they are now caught maltreating another of God's prophets. In the telling of the story, Joseph makes prophetic statements to wider audiences than just those of his own day. His call is for men to believe in and submit to the one true God. The point of the story of Joseph is that God's providence in the direction of events on earth is inexorable. Such becomes Muḥammad's reply to the challenge about being a prophet.

[13] Fakhr al-Dîn al-Râzî, *al-Tafsîr al-Kabîr*, Dâr al-Kutub al-'Ilmiyya: Tehran (n.d.), 18:83, quoted in A.H. Johns, *op. cit.*, p 43.

THE "SATANIC VERSES"

Sura 53 – known as *al-Najm* or "the Star" – is celebrated in the *ḥadîth* for two reasons. Firstly, this sura is the first one in which a *sajda* or "prostration" is recorded as being required. Secondly, this is the first sura of the Qur'ân that is recited – according to Ibn Mas'ûd – before an assembly of the Quraysh at which both believers and non-believers were present. It is suggested that, at the end of the recitation, when Muḥammad declared that a prostration was required – and he himself fell down to the ground to prostrate – the whole assembly also fell down in prostration with him: "But fall ye down in prostration to Allah, and adore (Him)!" (Sura 53:62) Included in this act of self-humbling worship were those tribal chiefs who had until now strongly opposed the Prophet. Ibn Mas'ûd is recorded as declaring that he saw only one man (Umayya bin Khalaf) from among the non-believers who did not fall to the ground to prostrate. This man chose instead to pick up a little dust from the ground and rub it on his forehead, declaring in the act that that was as far as he could go in participating in the worship.

This sura was evidently revealed some five years into Muḥammad's prophetic ministry in Mecca. Until now, he had been reciting the revelations given to him within private or restricted settings. This sura, however, was recited by Muḥammad within the precincts of the *ka'ba*, where a large number of the Quraysh had gathered. It was a public recitation and the recording of it immediately became a public affair. That recording led to different views of what Muḥammad is supposed to have recited.

According to al-Ṭabarî, the Prophet at this point was longing for some revelation that would soften his constantly declared call to the Meccans to turn away from their gross polytheism towards a rigid monotheism:

> When the Messenger of God saw his people draw away from him, it gave him great pain to see what a distance separated them from the word of Allah which he brought to them. Then he longed in his heart to receive a word from Allah which would bring him closer to his people. Because of his care for them and the love he had for them, he would gladly have seen those things that bore too harshly on them softened a little, so much so that he kept saying it to himself, and desiring it and wishing for it. It was then that Allah revealed to him the *sûrah* of the Star.[14]

[14] Al-Ṭabarî, *Annales* (ed. M.J. de Goeje et al). E.J. Brill: Leiden (1879), vol 1, chap 3,

Muḥammad's longing was allegedly mirrored by a tentative negotiation by some of the Quraysh about how Muḥammad might elicit a more favourable response to his preaching from them:

> Quraysh said to the Messenger of God (God bless and preserve him), "Those who sit beside you are merely the slave of so-and-so and the client of so-and-so. If you made some mention of our goddesses, we would sit beside you; for the nobles of the Arabs come to you, and when they see that those who sit beside you are the nobles of your tribe, they will have more liking for you." So Satan threw (something) into his formulation, and these verses were revealed, "Have ye considered al-Lât and al-'Uzzâ, And Manât, the third, the other?" and Satan caused to come upon his tongue, "These are the swans exalted, Whose intercession is to be hoped for, Such as they do not forget (or 'are not forgotten')." Then, when he had recited them, the Prophet (God bless and preserve him) prostrated himself, and the Muslims and the idolaters prostrated themselves along with him."[15]

The original version of this sura thus allowed worship of three of the prime idols of the Quraysh tribe. When Muḥammad announced such a (first) version of the Sura of the Star, the Meccans reportedly prostrated themselves with enthusiasm. Soon, however, Muḥammad was taken to task by God, who replaced the verses allowing worship of the three idols with an uncompromising statement of monotheism (vv 19–23):

> Have ye seen Lât, and 'Uzzâ, And another, the third (goddess), Manât? What! for you the male sex, and for Him, the female? Behold, such would be indeed a division most unfair! These are nothing but names which ye have devised, – ye and your fathers, – for which Allah has sent down no authority (whatever). They follow nothing but conjecture and what their own souls desire! – Even though there has already come to them Guidance from their Lord!

The Prophet then understood that Satan had whispered the alternative verses in his ear as he was receiving revelation from Gabriel: they were the "satanic verses":

> When he knew what Satan had caused to come upon his tongue, that weighed upon him; and God revealed, "And We have not sent before thee any messenger or prophet but that when he formed his desire Satan threw

pp 1192–1193. Quoted in Maxime Rodinson, *Muhammad* (trans. Anne Carter), Penguin: London (1971), pp 106–107.

[15] W. Montgomery Watt, *Muhammad at Mecca*, Oxford University Press: Karachi (1953), p 102.

Figure 11

"The Satanic verses"

Verses suggested by Satan	Correcting verses from God
Have ye considered al-Lât and al-ʿUzzâ, And Manât, the third, the other? and Satan caused to come upon his tongue, "These are the swans exalted, Whose intercession is to be hoped for, Such as they do not forget (or 'are not forgotten')."	Have ye seen Lât, and ʿUzzâ, And another, the third (goddess), Manât? What! for you the male sex, and for Him, the female? Behold, such would be indeed a division most unfair! These are nothing but names which ye have devised, – ye and your fathers, – for which Allah has sent down no authority (whatever). They follow nothing but conjecture and what their own souls desire! – Even though there has already come to them Guidance from their Lord!

> (something) into his formulation . . ." to the words ". . . and God is knowing, wise."[16]

Both versions of the sura were proclaimed publicly and the incident is well known by Muslims under the catchphrase "The Satanic Verses" (see figure 11).

Mawdûdî's interpretation of the story of this sura's recitation is that Prophet Muḥammad's presentation of it (that is, of the sura as it stands, now, in the Qur'ân) was so intense that his opponents were overwhelmed. At its conclusion, when he prostrated himself, they also fell down with him in prostration. Later they regretted their moment of weakness. Eventually they concocted a story to rescue their reputation as opponents of Muḥammad's self-declared prophethood. They announced, suggests Mawdûdî, the following:

> After he had recited *afaraʿ ait-ul Lata wal Uzza wa Manat ath-thalitha-al ukhra*, we heard from Muḥammad the words: *tilk al-gharoniqa-tal-ʿula, wa anna shafaʿat-u-hunna latarja*: "They are exalted goddesses: indeed their intercession may be expected." From this we understood that Muḥammad had returned to our faith.[17]

The real sting in Salman Rushdie's infamous book, *The Satanic Verses*, comes precisely over the issue of revelation or inspiration as it is highlighted in this sura. Rushdie embellishes the well-known

[16] *Ibid.*, p 64.

[17] Sayyid Abû'l-ʿAlâ Mawdûdî, "Commentary on *Sura an-Najm*." In Jamal al-Nasir, *Qur'an Viewer*, DivineIslam (2002), Sura 53, "The Star". See website at www.DivineIslam.com.

story, taken from the Traditions as cited here, concerning the giving of the Sura of the Star (Sura 53). We need to note that Rushdie speaks as a privileged "insider," knowing full well both the *ḥadîth* and the sensitivity of feeling about it within Islam. Rushdie's none too subtle "joke" is that actually the alternative "revelations" of sura 53 are neither of them due to God's activity or Satan's. Rushdie has Gibreel (Gabriel) pronounce to the reader his (Rushdie's) view on the Islamic concept of revelation:

> Gibreel, hovering-watching from his highest camera angle, knows one small detail, just one tiny thing that's a bit of a problem here, namely that *it was me both times, baba, me first and second also me*. From my mouth, both the statement and the repudiation, verses and converses, universes and reverses, the whole thing, and we all know how my mouth got worked.[18]

Gibreel gets his mouth worked by "Mahound" (Muḥammad) who forces Gibreel's face open and makes the voice pour out of him "like sick". It is Mahound's own voice, his own desires. The Qur'ân is simply a record of self-revelation. Not only Satan, but also God, are outside Rushdie's view of what "revelation" might entail. It is far from sending down or *tanzîl*; it is self-projection by a fairly sick or slick human being. Such a view is scandalous to Muslims. Little wonder it led to book-burnings and worse.

The point for my argument here is that the conveying of revelation in Islam is not so "automatic" or "non-engaging" of the human vehicle as might seem to be the case at first glance. In the incident of "the Satanic verses", God encourages the Prophet immediately after the fiasco by declaring that the risk of Satanic intervention goes with the job of being a prophet:

> Never did We send a messenger or a prophet before thee, but, when he framed a desire, Satan threw some (vanity) into his desire: but Allah will cancel anything (vain) that Satan throws in, and Allah will confirm (and establish) His Signs: for Allah is full of Knowledge and Wisdom . . . (Sura 22:52)

Satan evidently can intervene in the sending down of the Qur'ân or any other holy book. That might be by his whispering into Muḥammad's ear an alternative to the words that God was seeking to convey. Or it might be by his making it seem to Muḥammad's hearers that the Prophet was declaring "extra" material that they very much wanted to hear.

[18] Salman Rushdie, *The Satanic Verses*, Viking: London (1988), p 123.

"NIGHT JOURNEY" OR "CHILDREN OF ISRAEL"?

The seventeenth sura of the Qur'ân is famous for its description of Prophet Muḥammad's "night journey":

> Glory to (Allah) Who did take His servant for a Journey by night from the Sacred Mosque to the farthest Mosque, whose precincts We did bless, – in order that We might show him some of Our Signs: for He is the One Who heareth and seeth (all things). (Sura 17:1)

The sura, however, is sometimes referred to by a title taken from its fourth verse:

> And We gave (Clear) Warning to the Children of Israel in the Book, that twice would they do mischief on the earth and be elated with mighty arrogance (and twice would they be punished)! (Sura 17:4)

"Children of Israel" forms the alternative title to this sura that reflects on a clear warning previously given by God to the children of Israel. Both "night journey" and "children of Israel" epitomise alternative focuses in this late Meccan sura.

Out of an emphasis on the focal centre of the sura being the "night journey" (*isrâ'*), a rich legend of what precisely happened during this night excursion has developed. *Isrâ'* is interpreted as a miraculous ride to Jerusalem followed by an ascent to heaven via *mi'râj* or "ladder". Ibn Kathîr includes in his commentary a report from Anas bin Malik concerning this miraculous ride, as conveyed by Imam Aḥmad:

> Al-Buraq was brought to me, and it was a white animal bigger than a donkey and smaller than a mule. One stride of this creature covered a distance as far as it could see. I rode on it and it took me to Bayt al-Maqdis (Jerusalem), where I tethered it at the hitching post of the Prophets. Then I entered and prayed two Rak'ahs there, and came out. Jibril brought me a vessel of wine and a vessel of milk, and I chose the milk. Jibril said: "You have chosen the Fiṭrah (natural instinct)." Then I was taken up to the first heaven and Jibril asked for it to be opened. It was said, "Who are you?" He said, "Jibril." It was said, "Who is with you?" He said, "Muḥammad." It was asked, "Has his Mission started?" He said, "His Mission has started." So it was opened for us, and there I saw Adam, who welcomed me and prayed for good for me. Then I was taken up to the second heaven and Jibril asked for it to be opened. It was said, "Who are you?" He said, "Jibril." It was said, "Who is with you?" He said, "Muḥammad." It was asked, "Has his Mission started?" He said, "His Mission has started." So

it was opened for us, and there I saw the two maternal cousins, Yahya and ʿIsa, who welcomed me and prayed good for me. Then I was taken up to the third heaven and Jibril asked for it to be opened. It was said, "Who are you?" He said, "Jibril." It was said, "Who is with you?" He said, "Muḥammad." It was asked, "Has his Mission started?" He said, "His Mission has started." So it was opened for us, and there I saw Yusuf, who had been given the beautiful half. He welcomed me and prayed good for me. Then I was taken up to the fourth heaven and Jibril asked for it to be opened. It was said, "Who are you?" He said, "Jibril." It was said, "Who is with you?" He said, "Muḥammad." It was asked, "Has his Mission started?" He said, "His Mission has started." So it was opened for us, and there I saw Idris, who welcomed me and prayed for good for me. Then (the Prophet) said: "Allah says: ('And We raised him to a high station') (19:57). [Then he resumed his narrative]: Then I was taken up to the fifth heaven ad Jibril asked for it to be opened. It was said, "Who are you?" He said, "Jibril." It was said, "Who is with you?" He said, "Muḥammad." It was asked, "Has his Mission started?" He said, "His Mission has started." So it was opened for us, and there I saw Harun, who welcomed me and prayed good for me. Then I was taken up to the sixth heaven and Jibril asked for it to be opened. It was said, "Who are you?" He said, "Jibril." It was said, "Who is with you?" He said, "Muḥammad." It was asked, "Has his Mission started?" He said, "His Mission has started." So it was opened for us, and there I saw Musa, who welcomed me and prayed for good for me. Then I was taken up to the seventh heaven and Jibril asked for it to be opened. It was said, "Who are you?" He said, "Jibril." It was said, "Who is with you?" He said, "Muḥammad." It was asked, "Has his Mission started?" He said, "His Mission has started." So it was opened for us, and there I saw Ibrahim, who was leaning back against the Much-Frequented House (*al-bayt al-maʿmur*). Every day seventy thousand angels enter it, then they never come back to it again. Then I was taken to the Sidrat al-Muntaha (the Lote tree beyond which none may pass), and its leaves were like the leaves [ears] of elephants and its fruits were like jugs, and when it was veiled with whatever it was veiled with by the command of Allah, it changed, and none of the creatures of Allah can describe it because it is so beautiful. Then Allah revealed that which He revealed to me. He enjoined on me fifty prayers every day and night. I came down until I reached Musa, and he said, "What did our Lord enjoin on your Ummah?" I said, "Fifty prayers every day and night." He said, "Go back to your Lord and ask Him to reduce (the burden) for your Ummah, for your Ummah will not be able to do that. I tested the Children of Israel and found out how they were." So I went back to my Lord and said, "O Lord, reduce (the burden) for my Ummah for they will never be able to do that." So He reduced it by five. I came back down until I met Musa and he asked me, "What did you do?" I said, "(My Lord) reduced (my burden) by five." He said, "Go back to your Lord and ask Him to reduce (the burden) for your Ummah." I kept

> going back between my Lord and Musa, and (my Lord) reduced it by five each time, until He said, "O Muḥammad, these are five prayers every day and night, and for every prayer there is (the reward of) ten, so they are (like) fifty prayers. Whoever wants to do something good then does not do it, one good deed will be recorded for him, and if he does it, ten good deeds will be recorded for him. Whoever wants to do something evil and does not do it, no evil deed will be recorded for him, and if he does it, one evil deed will be recorded for him." I came down until I reached Musa, and told him about this. He said, "Go back to your Lord and ask him to reduce (the burden) for your Ummah, for they will never be able to do that. I had kept going back to my Lord until I felt too shy.[19]

Associated with this story is the myth of the washing of Muḥammad's heart. Ibn Kathîr quotes the report of Anas bin Malik from Malik bin Saʿsaʿah in which the Prophet speaks about the night during which he was taken on the special journey:

> While I was lying down in al-Hatim (or maybe, Qatadah said, in al-Hijr), someone came to me and said to his companion, "The one who is in the middle of these three." He came to me and opened me. I [one of the narrators] heard Qatadah say, "Split me – from here to here." Qatadah said: "I said to al-Jarud, who was beside me, 'What does that mean?' He said, 'From the top of his chest to below his navel,' and I heard him say, 'from his throat to below his navel.' The Prophet said: 'He took out my heart and brought a golden vessel filled with faith and wisdom. He washed my heart then filled it up and put it back, then a white animal was brought to me that was smaller than a mule and larger than a donkey . . .'."[20]

From here, the account proceeds to tell the story of Muḥammad's journey through the heavens.

We need to note that Muḥammad's ascent to heaven is recalled as referring to an actual event in Muḥammad's experience. The *ḥadîth* specifically rehearse Muḥammad's defence of the reality of his journey. According to Ibn Kathîr, Imam Aḥmad recorded that Jabir bin ʿAbdullah said that he heard the Messenger of Allah say:

> When Quraysh did not believe that I had been taken on the Night Journey to Bayt al-Maqdis, I stood up in al-Hijr and Allah displayed Bayt al-Maqdis before me, so I told them about its features while I was looking at it.[21]

In other words, Muḥammad possessed knowledge of such details concerning the mosque in Jerusalem because he had actually been there. "Night journey" was a real night journey!

[19] Ibn Kathîr, *op. cit.*, Sura 17: "The Report of Anas bin Malik."
[20] *Ibid.*, "The Report of Anas bin Malik from Malik bin Saʿsaʿah."
[21] *Ibid.*, "The Report of Jabir bin ʿAbdallah."

What about the alternative title to this sura? Out of an emphasis on the "children of Israel," a different message is promoted. The point in such an alternative reading of the verses is that the location of the journey is only indirectly mentioned – it is *al-masjid al-aqṣâ* ("the remote temple") as opposed to "the sacred temple" near at hand. Al-Ṭabarî therefore treats the story as a sleep-story. Muḥammad is translated to Jerusalem in a dream. What is the purpose of the dream? It is given so that God can show the prophet some of his (God's) signs. The corpus of the sura (verses 2 to 111) becomes, by this reading, a commentary on verse 1. Prophets are people who see signs. Moses was a prophet of God who saw signs. Muḥammad, another of the prophets, also sees God's signs: "For truly did he see, of the Signs of his Lord, the Greatest!" (Sura 53:18). Sura 17 presents Muḥammad and Moses in parallel, showing how each of them became recipients of God's signs. The sura (after verse 1) divides into three sections.

Section 1 (vv 2–21). A given Book is a Sign that comes via Moses and Muḥammad.

a) vv 2–8: a warning to the Jews.

We gave Moses the Book, and made it a Guide to the Children of Israel, (commanding): "Take not other than Me as Disposer of (your) affairs." O ye that are sprung from those whom We carried (in the Ark) with Noah! Verily he was a devotee most grateful. And We gave (Clear) Warning to the Children of Israel in the Book, that twice would they do mischief on the earth and be elated with mighty arrogance (and twice would they be punished)! When the first of the warnings came to pass, We sent against you Our servants given to terrible warfare: They entered the very inmost parts of your homes; and it was a warning (completely) fulfilled. Then did We grant you the Return as against them: We gave you increase in resources and sons, and made you the more numerous in man-power. If ye did well, ye did well for yourselves; if ye did evil, (ye did it) against yourselves. So when the second of the warnings came to pass, (We permitted your enemies) to disfigure your faces, and to enter your Temple as they had entered it before, and to visit with destruction all that fell into their power. It may be that your Lord may (yet) show Mercy unto you; but if ye revert (to your sins), We shall revert (to Our punishments): And we have made Hell a prison for those who reject (all Faith).

b) vv 9–21: the choice before humankind.

Verily this Qur'an doth guide to that which is most right (or stable), and giveth the Glad Tidings to the Believers who work deeds of righteousness, that they shall have a magnificent reward; And to those who believe not in the Hereafter, (it announceth) that We have prepared for them a Penalty Grievous (indeed). The prayer that man should make for good, he maketh for evil; for man is given to hasty (deeds). We have made the Night and the Day as two (of Our) Signs: the Sign of the Night have We obscured, while the Sign of the Day We have made to enlighten you; that ye may seek bounty from your Lord, and that ye may know the number and count of the years: all things have We explained in detail. Every man's fate We have fastened on his own neck: On the Day of Judgment We shall bring out for him a scroll, which he will see spread open. (It will be said to him:) "Read thine (own) record: Sufficient is thy soul this day to make out an account against thee." Who receiveth guidance, receiveth it for his own benefit: who goeth astray doth so to his own loss: No bearer of burdens can bear the burden of another: nor would We visit with Our Wrath until We had sent an messenger (to give warning). When We decide to destroy a population, We (first) send a definite order to those among them who are given the good things of this life and yet transgress; so that the word is proved true against them: then (it is) We destroy them utterly. How many generations have We destroyed after Noah? and enough is thy Lord to note and see the sins of His servants. If any do wish for the transitory things (of this life), We readily grant them – such things as We will, to such person as We will: in the end have We provided Hell for them: they will burn therein, disgraced and rejected. Those who do wish for the (things of) the Hereafter, and strive therefore with all due striving, and have Faith, – they are the ones whose striving is acceptable (to Allah). Of the bounties of thy Lord We bestow freely on all – These as well as those: The bounties of thy Lord are not closed (to anyone). See how We have bestowed more on some than on others; but verily the Hereafter is more in rank and gradation and more in excellence.

Section 2 (vv 22–81). Signs from God (like the "ten commandments" referred to here) are mostly received with disbelief.

a) vv 22–39: the duties of believers.

Take not with Allah another object of worship; or thou (O man!) wilt sit in disgrace and destitution. Thy Lord hath decreed that ye worship none but Him, and that ye be kind to parents. Whether one or both of them attain old age in thy life, say not to them a word of contempt, nor repel them, but address them in terms of honour. And, out of kindness, lower to them the wing of humility, and say: "My Lord! bestow on them thy Mercy even as they cherished me in childhood." Your Lord knoweth best what is in your hearts: If ye do deeds of righteousness, verily He is Most Forgiving to those who turn to Him again and again (in true penitence). And render to the kindred their due rights, as (also) to those in want, and to the wayfarer: But squander not (your wealth) in the manner of a spendthrift. Verily spendthrifts are brothers of the Evil Ones; and the Evil One is to his Lord (himself) ungrateful. And even if thou hast to turn away from them in pursuit of the Mercy from thy Lord which thou dost expect, yet speak to them a word of easy kindness. Make not thy hand tied (like a niggard's) to thy neck, nor stretch it forth to its utmost reach, so that thou become blameworthy and destitute. Verily thy Lord doth provide sustenance in abundance for whom He pleaseth, and He provideth in a just measure. For He doth know and regard all His servants. Kill not your children for fear of want: We shall provide sustenance for them as well as for you. Verily the killing of them is a great sin. Nor come nigh to adultery: for it is a shameful (deed) and an evil, opening the road (to other evils). Nor take life – which Allah has made sacred – except for just cause. And if anyone is slain wrongfully, we have given his heir authority (to demand *qisas* or to forgive): but let him not exceed bounds in the matter of taking life; for he is helped (by the Law). Come not nigh to the orphan's property except to improve it, until he attains the age of full strength; and fulfil (every) engagement, for (every) engagement will be enquired into (on the Day of Reckoning). Give full measure when ye measure, and weigh with a balance that is straight: that is the most fitting and the most advantageous in the final determination. And pursue not that of which thou hast no knowledge; for every act of hearing, or of seeing or of (feeling in) the heart will be enquired into (on the Day of Reckoning). Nor walk on the earth with insolence: for thou canst not rend the earth asunder, nor reach the mountains in height. Of all such things the evil is hateful in the sight of thy Lord. These are among the (precepts of) wisdom, which thy Lord has revealed to thee. Take not, with Allah, another object of worship, lest thou shouldst be thrown into Hell, blameworthy and rejected.

b) vv 40–60: arguments with unbelievers.

Has then your Lord (O Pagans!) preferred for you sons, and taken for Himself daughters among the angels? Truly ye utter a most dreadful saying! We have explained (things) in various (ways) in this Qur'an, in order that they may receive admonition, but it only increases their flight (from the Truth)! Say: If there had been (other) gods with Him, as they say, – behold, they would certainly have sought out a way to the Lord of the Throne! Glory to Him! He is high above all that they say! – Exalted and Great (beyond measure)! The seven heavens and the earth, and all beings therein, declare His glory: there is not a thing but celebrates His praise; And yet ye understand not how they declare His glory! Verily He is Oft-Forbear, Most Forgiving! When thou dost recite the Qur'an, We put, between thee and those who believe not in the Hereafter, a veil invisible: And We put coverings over their hearts (and minds) lest they should understand the Qur'an, and deafness into their ears: when thou dost commemorate thy Lord and Him alone in the Qur'an, they turn on their backs, fleeing (from the Truth). We know best why it is they listen, when they listen to thee; and when they meet in private conference, behold, the wicked say, "Ye follow none other than a man bewitched!" See what similes they strike for thee: but they have gone astray, and never can they find a way. They say: "What! when we are reduced to bones and dust, should we really be raised up (to be) a new creation?" Say: "(Nay!) be ye stones or iron, "Or created matter which, in your minds, is hardest (to be raised up), – (Yet shall ye be raised up)!" then will they say: "Who will cause us to return?" Say: "He who created you first!" Then will they wag their heads towards thee, and say, "When will that be?" Say, "May be it will be quite soon! It will be on a Day when He will call you, and ye will answer (His call) with (words of) His praise, and ye will think that ye tarried but a little while!" Say to My servants that they should (only) say those things that are best: for Satan doth sow dissensions among them: For Satan is to man an avowed enemy. It is your Lord that knoweth you best: If He please, He granteth you mercy, or if He please, punishment: We have not sent thee to be a disposer of their affairs for them. And it is your Lord that knoweth best all beings that are in the heavens and on earth: We did bestow on some prophets more (and other) gifts than on others: and We gave to David (the gift of) the Psalms. Say: "Call on those – besides Him – whom ye fancy: they have neither the power to remove your troubles from you nor to change them." Those whom they call upon do desire (for themselves) means of access to their Lord, – even those who are nearest: they hope for His Mercy and fear His Wrath: for the Wrath of thy Lord is something to take heed of. There is not a population but We shall destroy it before the Day of Judgment or punish it with a dreadful Penalty: that is written in the (eternal) Record. And We refrain from sending the signs, only because the men of former generations treated them as false: We sent the she-camel to the Thamud to open their eyes, but they treated her wrongfully: We only send the Signs by way of terror (and warning from evil). Behold! We told thee that thy Lord doth encompass mankind round about: We granted the vision which We showed thee, but as a trial for men, – as also the Cursed Tree (mentioned) in the Qur'an: We put terror (and warning) into them, but it only increases their inordinate transgression!

c) vv 61–72: Iblis (Satan), opponent of God's goodness.

Behold! We said to the angels: "Bow down unto Adam": They bowed down except Iblis: He said, "Shall I bow down to one whom Thou didst create from clay?" He said: "Seest Thou? this is the one whom Thou hast honoured above me! If Thou wilt but respite me to the Day of Judgment, I will surely bring his descendants under my sway – all but a few!" (Allah) said: "Go thy way; if any of them follow thee, verily Hell will be the recompense of you (all) – an ample recompense. "Lead to destruction those whom thou canst among them, with thy (seductive) voice; make assaults on them with thy cavalry and thy infantry; mutually share with them wealth and children; and make promises to them." But Satan promises them nothing but deceit. "As for My servants, no authority shalt thou have over them:" Enough is thy Lord for a Disposer of affairs. Your Lord is He That maketh the Ship go smoothly for you through the sea, in order that ye may seek of his Bounty. For he is unto you most Merciful. When distress seizes you at sea, those that ye call upon – besides Himself – leave you in the lurch! but when He brings you back safe to land, ye turn away (from Him). Most ungrateful is man! Do ye then feel secure that He will not cause you to be swallowed up beneath the earth when ye are on land, or that He will not send against you a violent tornado (with showers of stones) so that ye shall find no one to carry out your affairs for you? Or do ye feel secure that He will not send you back a second time to sea and send against you a heavy gale to drown you because of your ingratitude, so that ye find no helper. Therein against Us? We have honoured the sons of Adam; provided them with transport on land and sea; given them for sustenance things good and pure; and conferred on them special favours, above a great part of our creation. One day We shall call together all human beings with their (respective) Imams: those who are given their record in their right hand will read it (with pleasure), and they will not be dealt with unjustly in the least. But those who were blind in this world, will be blind in the hereafter, and most astray from the Path.

d) vv 73–81: Muḥammad tempted to compromise.

And their purpose was to tempt thee away from that which We had revealed unto thee, to substitute in our name something quite different; (in that case), behold! they would certainly have made thee (their) friend! And had We not given thee strength, thou wouldst nearly have inclined to them a little. In that case We should have made thee taste an equal portion (of punishment) in this life, and an equal portion in death: and moreover thou wouldst have found none to help thee against Us! Their purpose was to scare thee off the land, in order to expel thee; but in that case they would not have stayed (therein) after thee, except for a little while. (This was Our) way with the messengers We sent before thee: thou wilt find no change in Our ways. Establish regular prayers – at the sun's decline till the darkness of the night, and the morning prayer and reading: for the prayer and reading in the morning carry their testimony. And pray in the small watches of the morning: (it would be) an additional prayer (or spiritual profit) for thee: soon will thy Lord raise thee to a Station of Praise and Glory! Say: "O my Lord! Let my entry be by the Gate of Truth and Honour, and likewise my exit by the Gate of Truth and Honour; and grant me from Thy Presence an authority to aid (me)." And say: "Truth has (now) arrived, and Falsehood perished: for Falsehood is (by its nature) bound to perish."

Section 3 (vv 82–111). "Book" as sign leads to controversy in the case of both Moses and Muḥammad.

a) vv 82–100: the uniqueness of the Qur'ân; objections to God's messengers.

We send down (stage by stage) in the Qur'an that which is a healing and a mercy to those who believe: to the unjust it causes nothing but loss after loss. Yet when We bestow Our favours on man, he turns away and becomes remote on his side (instead of coming to Us), and when evil seizes him he gives himself up to despair! Say: "Everyone acts according to his own disposition: But your Lord knows best who it is that is best guided on the Way." They ask thee concerning the Spirit (of inspiration). Say: "The Spirit (cometh) by command of my Lord: of knowledge it is only a little that is communicated to you, (O men!)." If it were Our Will, We could take away that which We have sent thee by inspiration: then wouldst thou find none to plead thy affair in that matter as against Us, – Except for Mercy from thy Lord: for his bounty is to thee (indeed) great. Say: "If the whole of mankind and Jinns were to gather together to produce the like of this Qur'an, they could not produce the like thereof, even if they backed up each other with help and support. And We have explained to man, in this Qur'an, every kind of similitude: yet the greater part of men refuse (to receive it) except with ingratitude! They say: "We shall not believe in thee, until thou cause a spring to gush forth for us from the earth, "Or (until) thou have a garden of date trees and vines, and cause rivers to gush forth in their midst, carrying abundant water; Or thou cause the sky to fall in pieces, as thou sayest (will happen), against us; or thou bring Allah and the angels before (us) face to face: Or thou have a house adorned with gold, or thou mount a ladder right into the skies. No, we shall not even believe in thy mounting until thou send down to us a book that we could read." Say: "Glory to my Lord! Am I aught but a man, – a messenger?" What kept men back from belief when Guidance came to them, was nothing but this: they said, "Has Allah sent a man (like us) to be (His) Messenger?" Say, "If there were settled, on earth, angels walking about in peace and quiet, We should certainly have sent them down from the heavens an angel for a messenger." Say: "Enough is Allah for a witness between me and you: for He is well acquainted with His servants, and He sees (all things). It is he whom Allah guides, that is on true Guidance; but he whom He leaves astray – for such wilt thou find no protector besides Him. On the Day of Judgment We shall gather, them together, prone on their faces, blind, dumb, and deaf: their abode will be Hell: every time it shows abatement, We shall increase from them the fierceness of the Fire. That is their recompense, because they rejected Our signs, and said, "When we are reduced to bones and broken dust, should we really be raised up (to be) a new Creation?" See they not that Allah, Who created the heavens and the earth, has power to create the like of them (anew)? Only He has decreed a term appointed, of which there is no doubt. But the unjust refuse (to receive it) except with ingratitude. Say: "If ye had control of the Treasures of the Mercy of my Lord, behold, ye would keep them back, for fear of spending them: for man is (every) niggardly!"

b) vv 101–111: Moses' experience; Muḥammad's experience of passing on the Qur'ân.

To Moses We did give Nine Clear Signs: As the Children of Israel: when he came to them, Pharaoh said to him: "O Moses! I consider thee, indeed, to have been worked upon by sorcery! Moses said, "Thou knowest well that these things have been sent down by none but the Lord of the heavens and the earth as eye-opening evidence: and I consider thee indeed, O Pharaoh, to be one doomed to destruction!" So he resolved to remove them from the face of the earth: but We did drown him and all who were with him. And We said thereafter to the Children of Israel, "Dwell securely in the land (of promise)": but when the second of the warnings came to pass, We gathered you together in a mingled crowd. We sent down the (Qur'an) in Truth, and in Truth has it descended: and We sent thee but to give Glad Tidings and to warn (sinners). (It is) a Qur'an which We have divided (into parts from time to time), in order that thou mightest recite it to men at intervals: We have revealed it by stages. Say: "Whether ye believe in it or not, it is true that those who were given knowledge beforehand, when it is recited to them, fall down on their faces in humble prostration, And they say: 'Glory to our Lord! Truly has the promise of our Lord been fulfilled!'" They fall down on their faces in tears, and it increases their (earnest) humility. Say: "Call upon Allah, or call upon Rahman: by whatever name ye call upon Him, (it is well): for to Him belong the Most Beautiful Names. Neither speak thy Prayer aloud, nor speak it in a low tone, but seek a middle course between." Say: "Praise be to Allah, who begets no son, and has no partner in (His) dominion: Nor (needs) He any to protect Him from humiliation: yea, magnify Him for His greatness and glory!"

This sura was revealed in the last stage of Muḥammad's prophethood in Mecca, where opposition was constantly increasing.[22] One year before the *hijra* came Prophet Muḥammad's dream-ascension. Arising from that experience, the direction for five times of daily prayer in *ṣalât* became the norm for the Muslim community. The Prophet was also given the closing verse of Sura 2 and God's promise of forgiveness for those committing "major sins", as Ibn Kathîr records:

Al-Ḥâfiẓ Abû Bakr al-Bayhaqi reported that 'Abdullah bin Mas'ûd said: "When the Messenger of Allah was taken on the Night Journey, he went

[22] Different commentators assign various verses (including 12, 23–41, 76–82, 87) to the Medinan period.

> as far as Sidrat al-Muntaha, which is in the sixth heaven. Everything that ascends stops there, until it is taken from that point, and everything that comes down stops there, until it is taken from there." (When that covered as-Sidrat al-Muntaha which did cover it!) [53:16] Ibn Mas'ûd said: "It is covered with gold butterflies. The Messenger of Allah was given the five prayers and the final Ayat of surat al-Baqarah, and forgiveness was granted for major sins to those who do not associate anything in worship with Allah."[23]

The seventeenth sura of the Qur'ân can be read differently according to what is felt to be the main point of the revelation. What the words describe (real journey or dream journey) depends upon how the commentator hears the text or what he brings to his reading of it. The overall conclusion may be the same – as it was in Moses' experience, so it is in Muḥammad's – but "what the text means" in each interpretation is quite different. Are we being given a travel guide to the night ascension of the prophet or a history lesson from the annals of the children of Israel?

Text and context bear a symbiotic and open-to-interpretation relationship in the giving/receiving of the Qur'ân. What might that dynamic relationship say about the nature of the word being "sent down"? Is it so rigidly "fixed" or weighted as is traditionally claimed? Or is it capable of carrying various nuances of meaning with their subtly different intentions?

[23] Ibn Kathîr, *op. cit.*, Sura 17; "The Report of 'Abdullah bin Mas'ûd."

Chapter 6

Relying on a text

THERE are parallels to such kinds of consideration of formation and understanding of text in terms of our appreciation of the Bible. The Old Testament is preserved for us in Greek – the Septuagint – and in Hebrew – the Masoretic Text. The New Testament is provided via some major codices in the Greek language dating from the fourth century AD, with input from a myriad of smaller manuscripts or fragments of manuscripts in Greek and other languages. We will look at how the canons of the Old and New Testaments came to be formalised in chapter 7. Here, we are concerned with some of the variety of textual detail in those early, contributive sources.

OLD TESTAMENT: HEBREW OR GREEK?

The Septuagint translation (from Hebrew into Koiné Greek) of the Old Testament dates from the third century BC. It is the oldest and most important, complete translation of the Hebrew Bible made by Jews. It is the version of the Old Testament from which Jesus and the apostles quoted. It became the basis for translations made into Arabic, Ethiopic, Armenian, Old Latin, Coptic, Georgian and Old Church Slavonic.[1] The Samaritan text of the Pentateuch (in Hebrew) dates from the same period as the Septuagint. The Masoretic Text is the Hebrew text of the *Tanakh* (our Old Testament) that is approved for general use in Judaism. It is also widely used in translations of the Old Testament into other languages. It was primarily compiled, edited and distributed by a group of Jews known as the Masoretes between the first and tenth centuries AD.[2]

[1] The Septuagint did *not* provide the base for the Syriac version (known as the Peshitta), which is a pre-Christian translation based directly upon the Hebrew, or for Jerome's Latin translation, which is also based on the Hebrew.

[2] The oldest, extant, complete Hebrew manuscript of the Jewish Bible is *Codex B19A*, which is now in the public library in St Petersburg. The scribe's colophon states that it was written in AD 1008 in Cairo. It constitutes the best preserved manuscript of the whole Hebrew biblical text, and is the basis of most scholarly editions. It is exceeded in quality only by the *Aleppo Codex*, which is a few decades older but of which a quarter has been lost since 1948.

Figure 12

Masoretic Text versus Samaritan Pentateuch, Septuagint and New Testament

Text	Exodus 12:40	Hosea 13:14
Masoretic Text	Now the length of time the Israelite people lived in Egypt was 430 years. (Exodus 12:40)	I will ransom them from the power of the grave; I will redeem them from death: O death, I will be thy plagues; O grave, I will be thy destruction: repentance shall be hid from mine eyes. (Hosea 13:14)
Samaritan Pentateuch	Now the length of time the Israelite people lived in Egypt and Canaan was 430 years. (Exodus 12:40)	
Septuagint	Now the length of time the Israelite people lived in Egypt and Canaan was 430 years. (Exodus 12:40)	I will deliver them out of the power of Hades, and will redeem them from death: where is thy penalty, O death? O Hades, where is thy sting? Comfort is hidden from mine eyes. (Hosea 13:14)
New Testament	What I mean is this: The law, introduced 430 years later, does not set aside the covenant previously established by God and thus do away with the promise. (Galatians 3:17)	O death, where is thy sting? O grave, where is thy victory? (1 Corinthians 15:55)

There are numerous differences between the Septuagint *Vorlage* – that is, the presumed underlying Hebrew text from which the Septuagint derived – and the Masoretic Text. Most of those differences are quite minor but some are major. It would seem, in many cases, that the Septuagint is based on a version of the Hebrew different from the later, standard, Masoretic Text. The Samaritan text of the Pentateuch has nearly two thousand differences from the Masoretic Text in common with the Septuagint, yet in many places it differs from the Septuagint and agrees with the Masoretic Text! When the New Testament quotes from the first five books of the Bible, it usually agrees with the Samaritan Pentateuch where that differs from the Masoretic Text. Indeed, when there is a difference between the Septuagint and the Masoretic Text generally, the New

Testament is found to be closer to the Septuagint in over 90% of the cases (see figure 12). Probably the most well-known example of such "bias towards the Septuagint" is found in Matthew 1:23 where Isaiah 7:14 is quoted in the Septuagint version: "Therefore the Lord himself shall give you a sign; behold, a virgin shall conceive in the womb, and shall bring forth a son, and thou shalt call his name Emmanuel." The Septuagint uses the Greek word for "virgin", while the Masoretic Text uses a Hebrew word meaning "woman".

The Septuagint differs from the Masoretic Text not only in details of language, but in the form in which various books are presented. The books of Daniel and Esther are much longer in the Septuagint version, in contrast to the prophecy of Jeremiah which is about one-eighth shorter than its equivalent in the Masoretic Text. The ordering of the chapters in the two versions of Jeremiah is different. The Septuagint version of Job is about one-sixth smaller than the Masoretic Text version, but it includes an ending not extant in the Hebrew (see figure 13).

Figure 13

Ending of Job 42 in Masoretic Text and Septuagint

Masoretic Text	Septuagint
So Job died, old and full of days.	And Job died, an old man and full of days: and it is written that he will rise again with those whom the Lord raises up. This man is described in the Syriac book as living in the land of Ausis, on the borders of Idumea and Arabia: and his name before was Jobab; and having taken an Arabian wife, he begot a son whose name was Ennon. And he himself was the son of his father Zare, one of the sons of Esau, and of his mother Bosorrha, so that he was the fifth from Abraam. And these were the kings who reigned in Edom, which country he also ruled over: first, Balac, the son of Beor, and the name of his city was Dennaba: but after Balac, Jobab, who is called Job: and after him Asom, who was governor out of the country of Thaeman: and after him Adad, the son of Barad, who destroyed Madiam in the plain of Moab; and the name of his city was Gethaim. And his friends who came to him were Eliphaz, of the children of Esau, king of the Thaemanites, Baldad sovereign of the Sauchaeans, Sophar king of the Minaeans.

Almost half of the verses in "Septuagint" Esther are not found in "Masoretic Text" Esther. Exodus differs between the Masoretic Text and the Septuagint in many places according to the order of verses and the inclusion or exclusion of words and other material. It is often suggested, in an attempt to explain such differences, that the Septuagint reflects a very early Hebrew text no longer available to us.

The difficult question that these different texts raise is, of course, which is the more original? Or, perhaps, how – through them all – might an original text be deduced? Should precedence be given to the Hebrew text? If so, then to which text is it to be given – the Masoretic Text or the *Vorlage* (the assumed Hebrew text from which the Septuagint was translated)? The New Testament writers and the emerging Gentile Christian church opted for the accessibility and reliability of the Septuagint. Within the Jewish community – especially after the destruction of the Second Temple in Jerusalem during AD 70 – alternative translations of the proto-Masoretic Text were made in place of the Septuagint for Greek-speaking Jews. Gradually such Greek texts came to be sidelined in favour of the Hebrew, Masoretic Text.

The contemporary path to original text would seem to lead by way of a comparison between the Masoretic Text and the Samaritan Pentateuch, the Qumran fragments[3] and supremely the Septuagint. Along that way, choices have to be made by researchers, translators and editors of text. Some of those choices have significant bearing upon the meaning of the text. We have already noted the alternative possibilities of Isaiah 7:14 as rendered in Septuagint and Masoretic Text. Often, in our English translations of the Old Testament, a footnote will offer an alternative version of a verse as given in the Masoretic Text, or the Septuagint, or the Samaritan Pentateuch, or the Syriac, or the Vulgate, or the Dead Sea Scrolls, or the Peshitta. Someone, then, is choosing what they deem to be the closest meaning to the original. That choosing is made with great care, but it

[3] With the exception of the book of Esther, all the books of the Bible were represented in the Qumran finds (AD 1947–1956), even if only in tiny fragments. A complete scroll of the prophecy of Isaiah was found. The majority of the fragments date from the first and second centuries BC, but some go back to the third century BC. The proto-Masoretic text is represented in the finds, showing that this text which came to be exclusively used in the Jewish community from the end of the first century AD, is not an edited revision but a form of the text with its own history. Some of the Qumran fragments are close to the Samaritan form of the text (the Samaritan Pentateuch). Among the earliest manuscripts are some that correspond to the Hebrew *Vorlage* origin of the Septuagint translation. These manuscripts show how closely the Greek Septuagint translation followed the Hebrew on which it was based.

illustrates a certain fluidity of conviction about the formation of holy text.

EXEGETES TO THE RESCUE

Sometimes the text in itself is not very clear and may carry a variety of meanings. We are given an exegete's strong help, for example, in the book of Nahum. This vivid prophecy is delivered in three waves. In the first wave, the prophet describes the avenging wrath of *Yahweh* (1:2–10). In the second wave, he alternates between words of reproach addressed to an unnamed foe and promises of comfort directed towards Judah (1:11–2:3). In the third wave, he paints a picture of the soon-coming destruction of Nineveh (2:4–3:19).

The first chapter of Nahum's prophecy is more or less served up in Hebrew as an alphabetic acrostic, with verse two of the chapter beginning with the first letter of the Hebrew alphabet, verse three with the second letter of the Hebrew alphabet, and so on. Altogether, fifteen lines begin with successive letters of the Hebrew alphabet in their natural order. The result is a tightly-structured poem in which a vivid impression is given of *Yahweh's* wrath and a strong incentive is proffered to his people to persevere in trusting in the Lord. Beyond the acrostic poem, the whole first wave of Nahum's prophecy consists in warning (Nineveh) and encouraging (Judah). The two addressees (the city of Nineveh and the people of Judah) are for the most part unnamed in the text, so the prophecy as it appears in English Bibles includes the exegetical addition of "Nineveh" and "Judah" to help the reader understand whom is being addressed in different verses:

> The LORD is a jealous and avenging God;
> the LORD takes vengeance and is filled with wrath.
> The LORD takes vengeance on his foes
> and maintains his wrath against his enemies.
> The LORD is slow to anger and great in power;
> the LORD will not leave the guilty unpunished.
> His way is in the whirlwind and the storm,
> and clouds are the dust of his feet.
> He rebukes the sea and dries it up;
> he makes all the rivers run dry.
> Bashan and Carmel wither
> and the blossoms of Lebanon fade.

The mountains quake before him
and the hills melt away.
The earth trembles at his presence,
the world and all who live in it.
Who can withstand his indignation?
Who can endure his fierce anger?
His wrath is poured out like fire;
the rocks are shattered before him.
The LORD is good,
a refuge in times of trouble.
He cares for those who trust in him,
but with an overwhelming flood
he will make an end of →Nineveh←;
he will pursue his foes into darkness.
Whatever they plot against the LORD
he will bring to an end;
trouble will not come a second time.
They will be entangled among thorns
and drunk from their wine;
they will be consumed like dry stubble.

From you, →O Nineveh←, has one come forth
who plots evil against the LORD
and counsels wickedness.
This is what the LORD says:
"Although they have allies and are numerous,
they will be cut off and pass away.
Although I have afflicted you, →O Judah←,
I will afflict you no more.
Now I will break their yoke from your neck
and tear your shackles away."

The LORD has given a command concerning you, →Nineveh←:
"You will have no descendants to bear your name.
I will destroy the carved images and cast idols
that are in the temple of your gods.
I will prepare your grave,
for you are vile."

Look, there on the mountains,
the feet of one who brings good news,
who proclaims peace!
Celebrate your festivals, O Judah,
and fulfill your vows.
No more will the wicked invade you;
they will be completely destroyed.

An attacker advances against you, →Nineveh←.
Guard the fortress,
watch the road,
brace yourselves,
marshal all your strength! (Nahum 1:2–2:1)

The Hebrew phrases in the acrostic part of the first chapter of Nahum are quite dense and difficult, consequently, to comprehend. Images are supplied in phrases that are compressed into a specific meter, leaving quite a bit of leeway for variations of interpretation as to what precisely is in the prophet's mind. Verse 10 comprises a good example. Literally, the verse reads:

> For unto thorns entangled and like their drink soaked, they will be devoured like fully dried straw.

As one commentator suggests, "As it stands in the Masoretic text, this verse is wholly unintelligible".[4] It is usually interpreted as meaning that even though the enemies of *Yahweh* are, like tangled thorns, difficult and dangerous to approach and hard to destroy and like drenched thorns difficult to burn, yet before *Yahweh's* might they will be made to disappear as easily as fire consumes straw. The verse, however, might validly be interpreted as meaning that like drunkards who fall into the flames as though desiring in their drunkenness to do so, the enemies of *Yahweh* will be consumed as easily as fully dried straw. "No translation affording any connected sense is possible within the limits of ordinary grammatical interpretation", declares John Smith.[5] The New International Version simply offers a note to its rendering of the verse that reads: "The meaning of the Hebrew for this verse is uncertain." The specific meaning of the text in such a case has therefore to be conjectured, even though the general purport of the passage is clear. Is the point being made by the prophet/poet that the enemies of *Yahweh* are like a patch of thorns laid low by the sickle and ready for the fire – an image expressed elsewhere in the prophetic books of the Old Testament (such as Isaiah 33:11–12)?

Verses 11 and 12 are not much easier to comprehend. The Hebrew does not include the words "O Nineveh" in verse 11 or "O Judah" in verse 12. So whom does the prophet have in mind in each verse? If

[4] John M. P. Smith, *A Critical and Exegetical Commentary on Nahum*, T & T Clark: Edinburgh (1974), p 294.
[5] *Ibid.*, p 294.

verse 11 is referring to Nineveh and the one who has come out of her – most likely Sennacherib – then verse 12 could validly be read as referring also to Nineveh. This is the sense, perhaps, of the Masoretic Text:

> I will afflict you [Nineveh] so that I will not afflict you again.

In other words, *Yahweh* is about to utterly destroy the Assyrians, to afflict them beyond needing to afflict them ever again. Alternatively, verse 11 could refer to Nineveh and verse 12 to Judah, with the first half of verse 12 reading:

> Indeed, the days of my contention are completed; yes, they are over and gone.

The sense here would be that *Yahweh* no longer needs to punish Judah for her sins. If verse 12 refers to Judah, however, who does "their" in verse 13 refer to? Nineveh will fall in 612 BC. Nahum is prophesying about 630 BC. By that time, the Assyrian empire has already diminished in prestige and power. The Scythian invasion (about 626 BC) will sound the death knell of Assyria. The city itself will be overrun by the Babylonians in 612 BC. The Assyrians will move their capital to Harran until that too is captured by the Babylonians. The capital will then move to Carchemish. Egypt, allied to Assyria, will march to Assyria's aid in 609 BC. On the way, the army of Pharaoh Necho II will be delayed at Megiddo by the forces of King Josiah of Judah. Josiah will be killed and his army defeated. Egypt and Assyria will be crushed at Carchemish by the Babylonians. By the time of Nahum's prophesying, the Babylonians and Medes are already emerging as the new superpower of the day. The "their" of verse 13 could arguably refer to Assyria or Babylon or Egypt.

My point is that the prophecy of Nahum illustrates the difficulties, sometimes, of discerning what constitutes the text of the Bible and what that constituted text might mean. Exegesis is often part and parcel of the process of determining both what makes up the text and how that text is to be explained. In the case of an English translation of Nahum, without the exegetical help (indicated by the words within facing arrows in the long passage quoted earlier), a sense of what the prophecy is about would be hard to grasp. Such exegetical "help" is predicated upon an interpretation of what the (sometimes non-explicit) Hebrew or Greek text seems to be trying to convey. That interpretation forms part of a dialogue with alternative sources as to what constitutes the original text.

WHICH TEXT IS "HOLY TEXT"?

Back to our consideration of how the text of the Bible came to be established in the form in which we inherit it today. In the case of the New Testament, there are thousands of surviving manuscripts, though none of them constitutes a complete autograph in itself. The Gospel of Mark is usually seen as comprising an early, abridged account of the life of Jesus, composed by Mark from the recollections of Peter. Mark's Gospel is evidently one of the sources used by both Matthew and Luke. The conviction that Mark's Gospel is the earliest of the four Gospels to come to fruition is based, amongst other considerations, on the fact that Mark does not mention the pre-existence of Christ (unlike the reference to the eternal *Logos* or "Word" of John's Gospel), nor the (virgin) birth of Jesus (unlike the accounts of Jesus' origins in Matthew and Luke), nor indeed any accounts featuring the bodily appearance of the resurrected Jesus.

Our discussion, in these central paragraphs of this chapter, concerns variant readings of Mark's Gospel as they have survived in early manuscripts. We will consider, firstly, variant readings from the end of the Gospel.[6] In Mark 16:1–8, the Gospel-writer offers his account of the resurrection. It focuses upon an announcement by an angel of Jesus having risen:

> When the Sabbath was over, Mary Magdalene, Mary the mother of James, and Salome bought spices so that they might go to anoint Jesus' body. Very early on the first day of the week, just after sunrise, they were on their way to the tomb and they asked each other, "Who will roll the stone away from the entrance of the tomb?" But when they looked up, they saw that the stone, which was very large, had been rolled away. As they entered the tomb, they saw a young man dressed in a white robe sitting on the right side, and they were alarmed. "Don't be alarmed," he said. "You are looking for Jesus the Nazarene, who was crucified. He has risen! He is not here. See the place where they laid him. But go, tell his disciples and Peter, 'He is going ahead of you into Galilee. There you will see him, just as he told you.' " Trembling and bewildered, the women went out and fled from the tomb. They said nothing to anyone, because they were afraid.

[6] See Ezra Gould, *Critical and Exegetical Commentary on the Gospel According to St. Mark*, T & T Clark: Edinburgh (1983), pp 301–308.

The account – and the Gospel – ends at verse 8 on a rather negative note. The women are restrained by their fear from telling anyone the stupendous news that Christ has risen! All that Mark tells us of the resurrection of Jesus, therefore, is the announcement of it by an angel and the promise that Jesus would appear to his disciples in Galilee.

At some early stage, two different, revised endings to Mark's Gospel emerged. They are known as the "Short Ending" (v 9) and the "Long Ending" (vv 9–20). The Short Ending reads:

> And they reported briefly to Peter and those in his company all the things commanded. And after these things Jesus himself also sent forth through them from the east even to the west the holy and incorruptible message of eternal salvation.

The Long Ending reads:

> When Jesus rose early on the first day of the week, he appeared first to Mary Magdalene, out of whom he had driven seven demons. She went and told those who had been with him and who were mourning and weeping. When they heard that Jesus was alive and that she had seen him, they did not believe it. Afterward Jesus appeared in a different form to two of them while they were walking in the country. These returned and reported it to the rest; but they did not believe them either. Later Jesus appeared to the Eleven as they were eating; he rebuked them for their lack of faith and their stubborn refusal to believe those who had seen him after he had risen. He said to them, "Go into all the world and preach the good news to all creation. Whoever believes and is baptized will be saved, but whoever does not believe will be condemned. And these signs will accompany those who believe: In my name they will drive out demons; they will speak in new tongues; they will pick up snakes with their hands; and when they drink deadly poison, it will not hurt them at all; they will place their hands on sick people, and they will get well." After the Lord Jesus had spoken to them, he was taken up into heaven and he sat at the right hand of God. Then the disciples went out and preached everywhere, and the Lord worked with them and confirmed his word by the signs that accompanied it.

Interestingly, the longer ending gives no account of an appearance by Jesus in Galilee, contrary to what one might expect after the angel's words at the tomb. It offers, instead, appearances of Jesus within Jerusalem and in its vicinity. Other, "internal" evidence strongly suggests that the "extra" verses were not written by the same person who produced the rest of the Gospel. I'm thinking here of Greek words that are used in this tiny section that appear nowhere else in Mark's Gospel, and so on. What is more, the Long and Short endings do not fit Mark's style in the manner that the abrupt ending at verse 8 does. By and large, Mark focuses on the active part of Jesus' life, from the beginning of the Galilean ministry to the crucifixion. The introduction to that career, including the ministry of John the Baptist, the baptism of Jesus and the temptation of Jesus, is very briefly told. Mark excludes long discourses by Jesus. Instead, he offers a fast-moving and full narrative of the active ministry of Jesus. After the crucifixion, Mark again reverts to brevity. He gives merely the announcement of the resurrection to the women by the angels and then closes his account. He acts consistently in so doing. The most important "external" evidence to the text – or in this case the lack of it beyond verse 8 – comes from the authoritative Codex Sinaiticus and Codex Vaticanus, along with several other witnesses.

At the end of Mark's Gospel, then, no one is absolutely sure how the account ends. My New International Version separates the Long Ending from the body of the text and prefaces it with the words: "The two most reliable early manuscripts do not have Mark 16:9–20."[7]

At the other extremity of the Gospel, a (well-attested) variant reading occurs at its very opening: "The beginning of the gospel about Jesus Christ, the Son of God" (Mark 1:1). The phrase ". . . the Son of God" is missing in several important witnesses including Codex Sinaiticus, Codex Koridethi, MSS 28[c] and 1555, the Palestinian Syriac and so on. The title of Jesus in these manuscripts is simply "Jesus Christ." How can the difference be explained? Often it is suggested that the original had the full phrase and that the shorter reading was created by accident (see figure 14).

[7] A few analysts see a significant textual history for Mark 15:34, concerning the words describing Jesus' cry of desolation from the cross: "My God, my God, why have you forsaken me?" There are surviving manuscript fragments that have a variant reading for the person addressed in Jesus' words. Analysts who hold those variant possibilities to be more original posit the possibility that the early text of Mark's Gospel perhaps allowed the Gnostic conviction that Jesus died alone after the divine Christ had left him in order to return into the Pleroma. The (later) apocryphal *Gospel of Peter* certainly maintained such an interpretation: "My power, Oh power, you have left me!" (*Gospel of Peter*: 19). In his comprehensive treatise against heretics, Irenaeus claims that certain Gnostics used Mark 15:34 to portray Sophia's irretrievable separation from the Pleroma (*Irenaeus Against Heresies*, Kessenger Publishing [e-book], vol 1, chap 8, part 2, p 24). Does Mark, therefore, in his own day – or those compiling his Gospel in the years after his death – provide a paraphrased reading of the Hebrew of Psalm 22 deliberately to counter an incipient Gnostic reading of Jesus' supposed words?

Figure 14

Mark 1:1

Longer phrase	Shorter phrase
Ιησου χριστου υιου θεου	*Ιησου χριστου*

The technical term for the kind of error posited is "parablepsis" (an "eye-slip") brought about by "homoeoteleuton" (words "ending in the same way"). So the copying scribe's eye, by this hypothesis, slipped from the "*ou*" of "*christou*" to the "*ou*" of "*theou*". Undermining this explanation is the fact that the alternative reading of Mark 1:1 was made independently by scribes early on, over a widespread area and in an unrelated manner. Moreover, why should this kind of "eye-slip" occur within the first six words of a Gospel when, presumably, a scribe would be at his most wakeful?

Another way of explaining the early variant readings of Mark 1:1 is to suggest that the difference did not occur by accident. As Bart D. Ehrman proposes:

> . . . whether the phrase 'Son of God' was added to a text that originally lacked it or deleted from a text that originally had it, the change was apparently made intentionally.[8]

It is unlikely that the phrase "Son of God" would be deleted from a text. It is quite understandable that at some early stage of the producing of the Gospel it might be added. All rather depends on what the shorter term "the gospel about Jesus Christ" managed to convey despite its brevity. Both Mark and (especially) Luke evidently use "messiah" terminology in their Gospels as quite adequate in itself to convey the idea of Jesus' divinity, indeed of his Sonship. In so doing they differ considerably from Matthew, more so Luke than Mark (see figure 15). Their "messiah" terminology focuses on Jesus' role as Lord and Saviour. It carries their conviction that Jesus is divine, while Matthew has to spell out that equation – "Christ" equals "divine Son" – more deliberately. In Matthew's recounting to a Jewish audience, he records, for example, Peter's famous confession

[8] Bart D. Ehrman, "The Text of Mark in the Hands of the Orthodox". In Mark S. Burrows & Paul Rorem (eds.), *Biblical Hermeneutics in Historical Perspective*, Eerdmans: Grand Rapids (1991), p 28.

Figure 15

Terms used by the Synoptics to convey Jesus' divinity

Matthew	Mark	Luke
		"He will be great and will be called the Son of the Most High. The Lord God will give him the throne of his father David, and he will reign over the house of Jacob for ever; his kingdom will never end." (Luke 1:32–33) *The "messianic" sense of "Son" is brought out.* Moreover, demons came out of many people, shouting, "You are the Son of God!" But he rebuked them and would not allow them to speak, because they knew he was the Christ. (Luke 4:41)
Simon Peter answered, "You are the Christ, the Son of the living God." (Matthew 16:16)	Peter answered, "You are the Christ." (Mark 8:29)	Peter answered, "The Christ of God." (Luke 9:20)
"Come down from the cross, if you are the Son of God!" (Matthew 27:40)		"He saved others; let him save himself if he is the Christ of God, the Chosen One." (Luke 23:35)

in full: " 'You are the Christ, the Son of the living God' " (Matthew 16:16). Jesus agrees with Peter's statement, but then warns his disciples "not to tell anyone that he was the Christ" (Matthew 16:20). Mark and Luke respectively conflate Peter's fulsome words to "You are the Christ" (Mark 8:29) and "The Christ of God" (Luke 9:20). In Mark and Luke's understanding of their audiences, the "messiah" terminology was apparently enough to convey the semantic content of the term "Son of the living God."[9]

Back to my argument about the change of text at the beginning of Mark's Gospel. Did the "messiah" terminology, after initially carrying sufficient overtones of divinity, gradually lose the ability to

[9] See Rick Brown's helpful articles that inform some of my thoughts here: "Explaining the Biblical Term 'Son(s) of God' in Muslim Contexts" in *International Journal of Frontier Missions*, vol. 22, no. 3 (2005), pp 91–96; and "Translating the Biblical Term 'Son(s) of God' in Muslim Contexts" in *International Journal of Frontier Missions*, vol. 22, no. 4 (2005), pp 135–145.

do so? Without the insertion of "the Son of God", it was possible (and evidently the historical case) that an adoptionist[10] reading of Mark's Gospel – beginning with the account of Jesus' baptism – could reasonably be derived from the text introduced as simply "the gospel of Jesus Christ". With the addition of the phrase ". . . the Son of God", Jesus' status as divine is once again firmly established prior to his baptism – prior, even, to the mention of John the Baptist, the forerunner of Jesus.

Perhaps, also, the striking use by Mark of the word *euaggeliou* or "gospel" lost some of its implicit pointedness over time. The word originally belonged to the announcement of news of victory, especially in Roman military battles. It came to be utilised in Roman propaganda about its emperors. Each Caesar was eulogised as a "divine man" and news of his birth was proclaimed as "gospel". For Mark, the word *euaggeliou* is sufficient in itself to serve notice on the Roman system that now a new "divine man" is on the scene. Mark does not need the extra words "Son of God" to make that subtle but massive claim, though maybe, fairly soon, many of his readers would. Hence the later expansion of the phrase.

The textual history is not clear and literary critics are not agreed as to what processes might have occurred that adequately explain the existence, at an early date, of variant readings of this hinge verse in the Gospel of Mark. It is reasonable to allow the possibility that exegetical explanation, in some respects, went alongside the formation of the text – in a way parallel to what might be discerned to be the case in the unfolding of the Qur'ân. In the case of Mark's Gospel, it is ironic that a rendering of the text without the whole phrase "Jesus Christ, the Son of God" at its outset, would make it a far more attractive Gospel to offer to Muslims! There would be no baulking by them at its initial introduction of Jesus Christ if the delicate words "Son of God" did not appear so blatantly.

A RANSOM FOR WHOM?

We have previously had a look at one of Jesus' famous "Son of Man" statements, concerning Lordship over the Sabbath. Here we will briefly consider another – concerning self-sacrifice – as it illustrates some of the delicate connections between language, context,

[10] Such a reading sees Jesus as a human being finding himself being adopted as Son of God.

Gospel authorship and other matters of interpretation and exegesis. Along with the eucharistic words of institution (at the Last Supper), the "ransom saying" in Mark 10:45 comprises one of very few comments made by Jesus concerning his impending self-sacrifice:

> For even the Son of Man did not come to be served, but to serve, and to give his life as a ransom for many.

Mark uses the Greek word *lutron* for "ransom". How do we know what he (or before him, Jesus) might mean by that word? The word only appears here (and at the equivalent point in Matthew's Gospel) in the New Testament. Some Bible commentators pick up a related word as it appears in Paul's writings and suggest that "Mark" reflects here the later-than-Jesus, systematised, theologising of Paul the apostle:

> For there is one God and one mediator between God and men, the man Christ Jesus, who gave himself as a ransom [*antilutron*] for all men – the testimony given in its proper time. (1 Timothy 2:5–6)

Other commentators say, "No! You can easily translate the Greek sentence (Mark 10:45) back into Aramaic." Their conclusion from that fact is that the influence went in the opposite direction – from the Semitic thought-form of Jesus/Mark to the Greek thought-form of Paul in 1 Timothy. The significance of such a suggestion is that it concentrates attention strongly on what Jesus/Mark might then be meaning by choosing to use this rare word.

Exegetes make suggestions here concerning the radical undermining by Jesus' choice of vocabulary of the popular presuppositions about the character of their expected Messiah. Jesus dares to link the title "Son of Man" with *lutron*! It is an unthinkable connection! The apocalyptic figure of Daniel 7, described as one "like the Son of Man" who comes on the clouds of heaven to be presented before the throne of God, and who receives everlasting dominion and authority (Daniel 7:13–14) is well-known and well-liked. Such a "Son of Man" is the kind of Messiah the Jews are expecting to come and rescue them from Roman overlordship. Instead of such a popular, triumphant, political Messiah restoring David's rule, Jesus instead promotes a picture of Messiah as servant, indeed as servant-unto-death. He is, in effect, here predicting his own passion and dying. The "ransom" language suggests the matter of substitution. The Son of Man will offer himself as a substitute for humankind, for "many". The "Son of Man" language invokes the person who is to be the recipient of such a ransoming act – namely God. In a process of self-offering in the place of others, even as far as innocent death, Jesus renders his obedience to his heavenly Father.

This Son of Man saying in Mark's Gospel (paralleled in Matthew 20:28) occurs in the context of a battle for prestige that takes place among Jesus' disciples. James and John, the sons of Zebedee, are asking Jesus for special privilege at the time of his rulership, and their colleagues are very angry with them. Mark (with Matthew) places this incident on the journey to Jerusalem. Luke places it – or places an equivalent incident – differently. The context of the Lucan incident, as far as the disciples' behaviour is concerned however, is the same as in Mark and Matthew. In Luke's account (Luke 22:24–30), they are again arguing about which of them might be considered the greatest. Jesus responds:

> "The greatest among you should be like the youngest, and the one who rules like the one who serves. For who is greater, the one who is at the table or the one who serves? Is it not the one who is at the table? But I am among you as one who serves." (Luke 22:26–27)

Luke does not quote Jesus as using the word *lutron* here. It would seem that Luke's concern is likely to have been to avoid completely any possible association, via the idea of "ransom" or "sacrifice", with the sacrificial system of the Old Testament. Jesus/Luke is not referring in these words to any kind of cultic sacrifice or ransom. He is not speaking about an exaction of a penalty in blood. Rather, he is referring to the absolute serving aspect of a person who is totally obedient. Why is that so significant? It is significant because Luke places his account of these words of Jesus at the heart of the institution of the eucharist. In the establishing of the Lord's Supper, Jesus/Luke is at pains to say: "This fellowship meal is not about cultic sacrifice but about obedient service." The transformation of Passover that Jesus intends is not, primarily, about him becoming a passive victim to be slaughtered to appease an upset God – a cultic perspective – but rather about him being a vigorous agent of God's active redemption through his (Jesus') willed obedience unto death.

Why am I introducing these differing, yet connected, accounts of Jesus' words about serving? My intention is to show how a look at the texts-in-context perhaps explains why different views of "redemption" or "atonement" might arise. This is a "hot" subject in Christian thinking today!

Abbot Anselm of Canterbury wrote up his interpretation of the crucifixion of Christ at the end of the eleventh century in a thesis entitled *Cur Deus Homo* or *Why God Became Man.*[11] Central to Anselm's view of atonement, as we shall see in a moment, was the idea of satisfaction. Someone or something needed satisfaction for the sinfulness of humankind. This idea has informed Western traditions of Christianity ever since in their understanding of Christ's death as sacrifice. That view has been increasingly questioned over the years, not least by Islamic theologians. From an Islamic perspective, moral questions are asked: "What is just or right in demanding price-paying by a non-guilty party?" Or: "Why should God not simply choose to forgive sin without demanding the death of an alleged divine Son?" From a Christian perspective a slightly different, theological matter is focused upon:

> Generally the phrase *atonement doctrine* implies a chain of related themes and ideas with subtle shading between them: namely, sacrifice, expiation, propitiation, penal substitution, vicarious suffering, satisfaction. However, all these usages in respect of the Crucified imply an exchange value in Christ's death, whereby something is gained in return for the life lost, and by means of an eternal order or economy that demands it.[12]

By such readings of atonement, the Cross has come to be primarily seen through the lens of sacred violence: the devil is paid off, or the Father's wrath is satisfied. The creditor in this transaction could be either the devil or God the Father.

Augustine, and other theologians trained in Roman law, tended to see the Son of Man giving up his life as a ransom to the devil:

> In this redemption the blood of Christ was as it were the price given for us (but the devil on receiving it was not enriched but bound), in order that we might be loosed from his chains . . . and that he might not . . . draw with himself to the ruin of the second and eternal death, anyone of those whom Christ, free from all debt, had redeemed by pouring out his own blood without being obliged to do so.[13]

[11] See Brian Davies and G.R. Evans (eds.), *Anselm of Canterbury: The Major Works*, Oxford University Press: Oxford (1998), pp 260–356.

[12] Anthony W. Bartlett, *Cross Purposes: The Violent Grammar of Christian Atonement*, Trinity Press International: Harrisburg (2001), p 3.

[13] Augustine, *De Trinitate*, vol 13, chap 15 in *St Augustine, The Trinity* (trans. Stephen McKenna), *The Fathers of the Church*, vol 45, Catholic University of America Press: Washington D.C. (1963), pp 397–398. Tertullian, Cyprian and Ambrose also held this view of transaction, in ransoming humankind, with the devil.

Origen, Gregory of Nazianzus, Athanasius, and Anselm himself, tended to see "ransom" as constituting a satisfying of God's justified wrath or anger with sinful humanity. Anselm summarises his thesis as to why God became man:

> You have . . . shown that it was not right that the restoration of human nature should be left undone, and that it could not have been brought about unless man repaid what he owed to God. This debt was so large that, although no one but man owed it, only God was capable of repaying it, assuming that there should be a man identical with God.[14]

Christ, by Anselm's reading, behaves as a perfect feudal knight, delivering himself up to death for the sake of God's honour.[15] The Father thus finds himself under obligation to repay the Son. The Son, however, has everything already (as divine), so the merits of his dying are passed on to humanity. Christ's death becomes, by this "feudal" reading, a displacement or substitution for the revenge of God rightly owing to humanity:

> From Anselm onward penal substitution simply leaps the formal steps of satisfaction, moving at once to the point of wrath that lies behind the whole, and making Christ bear this passively rather than offer compensation actively.[16]

The question is whether that, or any other view highlighted in the last few paragraphs, is the perspective on atonement that the New Testament proposes. Does it add up to what Jesus thought his death entailed?

My suggestion here is that one might possibly deduce some such "substitutionary" view of atonement from Mark's rendering of this incident in the ministry of Jesus. Jesus conceived of the glorious Son of Man living out his authoritative rule by choosing a path of obedience unto voluntary death on behalf of others. Even in Mark's rendering, however, the deliberate use of the term "ransom" links more to Isaiah 43:3 ("I give Egypt for your ransom") than to, say, Isaiah 53:5 ("the punishment that brought us peace was upon him"). Luke, however, will deliberately not allow us to go down the cultic sacrifice road. He is clearly allowing no interpretation of the transformed Passover – now eucharistic meal – as celebrating a satisfying

14 Davies and Evans, *op. cit.*, p 348.

15 "The way in which this giving has to be understood, therefore, is this: that in some way he will be laying aside himself, or something from himself, to the honour of God, since he will not be a debtor." In *ibid.*, p 330.

16 Bartlett, *op. cit.*, p 85.

of divine wrath or a paying off of the devil. Rather, Jesus would seem to be presented here as someone who saw himself as an agent of God's gracious redemption. The price of seeing that redemption into reality would be a surrendering of his own will in obedience to his heavenly Father to whatever degree the Father chose.

At the heart of the Christian gospel lie a message and an understanding about Christ dying on behalf of sinful humanity. How that message and understanding comes to be expressed depends on a dynamic relationship between Jesus himself, his biographers, the interpreters of such biography and ourselves. Jesus-in-context, Mark or Luke-in-context, Augustine or Anselm-in-context, ourselves-in-context – all contribute to the dynamic of discerning what the word of the Lord may be about.

Choices about sources – especially Greek and Hebrew sources for the Old Testament – have a large impact on the formation of holy text. Exegesis (as with Nahum) constitutes part of the process of making explicable the (sometimes inadequate and alternative) raw data of texts. Theological intention and the meaning that words (such as "Christ") might carry appear to contribute to what finally ends up as holy text (as with the beginning and ending of Mark's Gospel). Interpretation of meaning sits behind the discerning of Jesus' self-understanding, or Mark and Luke's different approaches to describing Jesus' self-understanding – especially with regard to his "obedience unto death". Texts referring to the same, or similar, incident(s) are subtly altered to convey different nuances of meaning. Upon such nuances are built theological interpretations that sometimes contradict rather than complement one another.

Chapter 7

Securing a holy Bible?

HOW do human beings come to possess "holy books" – books of revelation? Some religions, of course, have no sacred writings. Others have sacred writings, but those writings are not canonised. Others still – as in Judaism, Christianity and Islam – possess canonical scriptures. Within this last group of monotheistic faiths, the formulating of an authorised text proceeds in quite different ways. The Jewish and Christian histories differ radically from the Islamic experience.

JEWISH INHERITANCE . . .

It is not possible to know precisely how the Old Testament came together to make up the collection of books that comprise the Jewish Scriptures. The Jews have a strong tradition that the scribe Ezra (about 425 BC) arranged and collected the books of the Old Testament, though collections of the first five books (the "books of Moses" or Pentateuch) and records of the declarations of the prophets plus wisdom writings (Psalms, Proverbs and so on) were in existence much earlier. Josephus considered the Jewish canon of Scripture as fixed from the days of Ezra. A rabbinical discussion on the canonical status of Ecclesiastes and the Song of Songs occurred at Yabneh (or Jamnia) in AD 90. A canon of scripture and a view of what "canonisation" meant was evidently well formulated by then.

The Jewish Scriptures were arranged in three groups, as figure 16 illustrates. Five books comprised the Law or *Torah*. Eight books comprised the Prophets (*Nebi'îm*), former and latter, with 1 and 2 Samuel and 1 and 2 Kings each making up one book; and with the twelve "minor prophets" making up one book between them. Eleven books made up the Writings (*Kethubîm*), with Ezra-Nehemiah and 1 and 2 Chronicles each as one book. All twenty-four books of the Jewish Scriptures amount to the same as the thirty-nine books of the Christian's "Old Testament", as a comparison between the columns labelled "Jewish" and "Protestant" in figure 16 will show.

The New Testament contains some three hundred quotations from these Jewish Scriptures. The only other Hebrew material outside these Jewish Scriptures quoted in the New Testament is provided in the brief extracts from *The Assumption of Moses* and the *Book of Enoch* in the letter of Jude.[1]

Early Christian apostles and teachers relied on the Old Testament as a revelation of God, from God. References in the New Testament which incorporated the phrase ". . . according to the Scriptures . . ." meant, of course, the Old Testament Scriptures. Paul, for example, sought to underline for Corinthian Christians that the gospel which he had personally received and which he had subsequently shared with them had as one of its central elements a statement about the resurrection of Jesus of Nazareth (1 Corinthians 15:3). That historical reality was perfectly reconciled with what the Hebrew Scriptures led one to expect: the contemporary facts fulfilled the earlier predictions precisely. The common strategy of Peter and Paul in their evangelistic arguments with Jewish audiences was to depict from the Old Testament the expected circumstances that would identify Messiah when he came. They then went on to show how Jesus of Nazareth fulfilled those expectations in the details of his living, dying and rising again. All was ". . . according to the Scriptures . . ."

. . . IN GREEK CLOTHING

Almost exclusively, however, the early Christians read and quoted the Old Testament, not in its original Hebrew version, but in its Greek translation – a translation known as the Septuagint.

A thriving Jewish community in Alexandria began translating the Hebrew Scriptures into Greek in the early third century BC. The Greek king in Egypt, Ptolemy II (285–247 BC), is reputed to have personally sponsored the initial translation of the Torah and to have summoned seventy elders from Jerusalem to travel to Egypt to do the work. The Greek translation of the Hebrew Scriptures came to be known as the Septuagint (meaning "Seventy") after the seventy

[1] Jude 9 reads: But even the archangel Michael, when he was disputing with the devil about the body of Moses, did not dare to bring a slanderous accusation against him, but said, "The Lord rebuke you!" Jude 14–15 reads: Enoch, the seventh from Adam, prophesied about these men: "See, the Lord is coming with thousands upon thousands of his holy ones to judge everyone, and to convict all the ungodly of all the ungodly acts they have done in the ungodly way, and of all the harsh words ungodly sinners have spoken against him."

original translators. The Septuagint translators re-classified the books of the Hebrew Scriptures according to subject matter (historical, poetical, prophetic). They also added various, extra, "apocryphal" books originating from the third to the first century BC, which by that time had become well-known in the Jewish, Greek-speaking world. These new, apocryphal books were given the same respect as the other books in the Septuagint (Greek) version of the Old Testament.

Interestingly, Jesus and the early Christians who relied so heavily on the Greek translation of the Hebrew Scriptures (apocryphal material included) did not once leave us a quotation from that apocryphal material, though there are plenty of allusions to it contained within the New Testament.

Figure 16

The Old Testament

Jewish	Protestant	Roman Catholic
Law (*Torah*)	**Law (*Pentateuch*)**	***Pentateuch***
Genesis	Genesis	Genesis
Exodus	Exodus	Exodus
Leviticus	Leviticus	Leviticus
Numbers	Numbers	Numbers
Deuteronomy	Deuteronomy	Deuteronomy
Prophets (*Nebi'îm*)		
FORMER PROPHETS:	**The Historical Books**	**The Historical Books**
Joshua	Joshua	Joshua
Judges	Judges	Judges
	Ruth	Ruth
1 & 2 Samuel	1 & 2 Samuel	1 & 2 Samuel
1 & 2 Kings	1 & 2 Kings	1 & 2 Kings
	1 & 2 Chronicles	1 & 2 Chronicles
LATTER PROPHETS:	Ezra	Ezra
	Nehemiah	Nehemiah
Isaiah		Tobit
Jeremiah		Judith
Ezekiel	Esther	Esther + additions[2]
Hosea, Joel, Amos, Obadiah, Jonah, Micah, Nahum, Habakkuk, Zephaniah, Haggai, Zechariah, Malachi		1 & 2 Maccabees

[2] Additions to Esther come in six sections and include prayers of Esther and Mordecai.

Jewish	Protestant	Roman Catholic
Writings (*Kethubîm*)	**The Poetical Books**	**The Wisdom Books**
Poetical Writings:	Job	Job
Psalms	Psalms	Psalms
Proverbs	Proverbs	Proverbs
Job	Ecclesiastes	Ecclesiastes
	Song of Solomon	Song of Songs
Five Scrolls:		Book of Wisdom
		Ecclesiasticus
Song of Songs		
Ruth		
Lamentations	**The Major Prophets**	**The Prophets**
Ecclesiastes		
Esther	Isaiah	Isaiah
	Jeremiah	Jeremiah
Historical Books:	Lamentations	Lamentations
		Baruch[3]
Daniel	Ezekiel	Ezekiel
Ezra-Nehemiah	Daniel	Daniel + additions[4]
1 & 2 Chronicles		
	The Minor Prophets	
	Hosea, Joel, Amos, Obadiah, Jonah, Micah, Nahum, Habakkuk, Zephaniah, Haggai, Zechariah, Malachi	Hosea, Joel, Amos, Obadiah, Jonah, Micah, Nahum, Habakkuk, Zephaniah, Haggai, Zechariah, Malachi

OLD TESTAMENT CANON, ACCORDING TO CHRISTIANS

During the centuries after Christ, the church gradually fixed the "canon" of Scripture – the material that became our Bible. Christians inherited a choice of perspective from the Jews of the texts that might be held to comprise the Old Testament. A list of twenty-four inspired books – twenty-two if custom followed Josephus' technique of combining Ruth with Judges and Lamentations with Jeremiah in order to make the list of books correspond to the number of letters in the Hebrew alphabet – seems to have been current among Palestinian

[3] Baruch includes the Letter of Jeremiah.

[4] Additions to Daniel include The Song of the Three Young Men, Susanna, and Bel & the Dragon. We need to note also that the Greek canon of Scripture includes 1 & 2 Esdras and The Prayer of Manasseh as well.

Jews by the end of the first Christian century. This shorter, or Eastern, canon was the preference of many prominent Christian writers.

However, another and longer list also persisted because in the Greek version of the Old Testament, as we have seen, the Jews included material which did not exist in the Hebrew corpus. This extra material is referred to as the "Apocrypha" or the "Deutero-canonical books". In figure 16, the extra books that appear in the "Roman Catholic" list comprising Old Testament Scripture make up the balance of this longer list. When the Bible was translated into Latin by Jerome in the second century AD, although he translated the Old Testament from the Hebrew, he had available to him the Greek Septuagint version of the Old Testament also. As a result, he included the extra, apocryphal books in his Latin "Vulgate" version.

A double tradition of shorter and longer canon of the Old Testament consequently persisted through the time of the early church Fathers down to the sixteenth century Renaissance period. In AD 1546, the Ecumenical Council summoned by Pope Sixtus and sitting at Trent in Italy, issued one of its decrees on April 8th. The longer canon of the Old Testament was made a rule of faith – the extra books from the Greek version were divinely inspired. A distinction was made, however. The Pope differentiated between those Old Testament books which were "canonical now and in the past" and those which were "canonical now but previously not universally accepted." The shorter canon was nicknamed "protocanonical" – first order Scripture! The extra texts in the longer canon were nicknamed "deuterocanonical" – second order Scripture!

Roman Catholics reserve the term "apocrypha" for Jewish religious literature which neither Jews nor Christians consider canonical in any sense. Protestants tend to label this kind of literature as "pseudepigrapha". Figure 17 illustrates the different terminology used by Protestants and Roman Catholics to refer to the various texts.

The oldest manuscripts of the Christian Scriptures contain the apocryphal or deuterocanonical books (or most of them). Jerome, who, as we have seen, translated the extra material from Greek into Latin and included it with his translation of the Hebrew Scriptures, thought that the additional material was valuable for reading in church. Again as we have noted, the apocryphal books came to be distributed in the Old Testament among the historical, prophetic and wisdom sections as illustrated in the "Roman Catholic" column

Figure 17

Protestant and Roman Catholic terminology

Material referred to:	Protestant terminology	Roman Catholic terminology
Books comprising the Hebrew Scriptures	Canonical	Protocanonical
Extra books found in the Greek translation of the Hebrew Scriptures (the Septuagint)	Apocryphal	Deuterocanonical
Works of similar character and date to the apocryphal or deuterocanonical literature, but which have never been considered by Jew or Christian to be part of Scripture.	Pseudepigraphal	Apocryphal

of figure 16. Luther, in his Bible of AD 1534, extracted them and had them printed at the end of the Old Testament under the heading: "Apocrypha: these are books which are not held equal to the Sacred Scriptures and yet are useful and good for reading."

The apocryphal or deuterocanonical books survived this drawn-out canonisation process as significant and they remain as part of the authentic Bible for many Christians today. They contain primary resources in terms of history (1 and 2 Maccabees) and a wealth of material illustrating the best in Israel's "Wisdom" tradition. They constitute about one-sixth of the length of the Old Testament and consist of seven complete books plus other portions. The "books" are those of Tobit, Judith, The First Book of Maccabees, The Second Book of Maccabees, The Book of Wisdom, Ecclesiasticus and Baruch. The portions comprise some additions to Esther included in Esther, the Letter of Jeremiah included in Baruch and the Song of the Three Young Men, Susanna, plus Bel and the Dragon all added to Daniel. The seven books, plus the additions to other books, just named, comprise all of the deuterocanonical material as accepted by the Roman Catholic Church. Protestants include all of the above books and portions in their definition of the Apocrypha plus First and Second Esdras and the Prayer of Manasseh – books and a portion inherited from the Greek

Orthodox canon of Scripture, but not included in the Roman Catholic canon.

The books of the apocrypha form a varied collection of Jewish literature dating from the period between 300 BC and AD 100. The majority of such books were originally written in Hebrew but have only survived through their translation (originally as part of the Septuagint) and use in Greek and other translations by the early Church.

I hope that my summary of the intricacies involved in the formation of Old Testament Scripture is clear!

NEW TESTAMENT CANON

The coming together of the New Testament illustrates even more vividly the miraculous mix of Holy Spirit, human personality, cultural context and communal patience in the formation of an authoritative corpus of texts.

As far as the canon of (New Testament) Scripture is concerned, the limit of what comprised authenticated "Scripture" was not officially finalised until late in the fourth century. The documents that eventually made up the New Testament, however, seem to have been in general circulation by AD 200. By that date the Christian church was using the four Gospels – and no others, despite the fact that many fictitious tales about Jesus and writings by other, post-apostolic Christian leaders were in circulation. There are hints in the New Testament itself that, while the apostles themselves were still alive, and under their supervision, collections of their letters were being made for public reading in the churches:

> After this letter has been read to you, see that it is also read in the church of the Laodiceans and that you in turn read the letter from Laodicea. (Colossians 4:16)

> I charge you before the Lord to have this letter read to all the brothers. (1 Thessalonians 5:27)

The possibility of what came to be the Gospels being considered as "Scripture" was mooted early in apostolic times. In the first letter to Timothy, the sentence: "The worker deserves his wages" is quoted as "Scripture" (1 Timothy 5:18). The only places where this sentence occurs in the Bible are Matthew 10:10 and Luke 10:7, evidence that

Figure 18

Geographical foci of New Testament texts

Geographical focus of text	**Palestine**	**Asia Minor**	**Greece**	**Crete**	**Rome**
New Testament Books	Matthew James Hebrews (?)	John Galatians Ephesians Colossians 1 Timothy 2 Timothy Philemon 1 Peter 2 Peter 1 John 2 John 3 John Jude Revelation	1 Corinthians 2 Corinthians Philippians 1 Thessalonians 2 Thessalonians Luke (?)	Titus	Mark Acts Romans

Matthew and/or Luke was then in existence, and regarded as Scripture. Clement of Rome, in his *Letter to the Corinthians* (AD 96) quotes from, or refers to, Matthew, Luke, Romans, Corinthians, Hebrews, 1 Timothy and 1 Peter.

Different New Testament books surfaced in different geographical areas, according to where the authors or recipients resided, and each tended to be accepted more quickly by Christians residing "on site" as it were. Figure 18 illustrates the likely geographical foci of various New Testament texts. The evolution to a common core of texts was slow and gradual, a process made more difficult in a climate of non-acceptance of Christianity, even open persecution, by both Jewish leaders and Roman officials. Nevertheless, a general appreciation of the variety of New Testament material available spread inexorably throughout the Mediterranean basin.

Tertullian of Carthage (AD 160–220), living while the original manuscripts of the various Epistles were likely still in existence, speaks of the Christian Scriptures as the "New Testament", almost the first known author to do so. In Tertullian's extant writings there are nearly two thousand quotations from New Testament books. He cites all the books of (our) New Testament with the exception of 2 Peter, James, 2 John and 3 John. In his work *The Prescription Against Heretics*, he challenges his opponents:

> If you are willing to exercise your curiosity profitably in the business of your salvation, visit the Apostolic churches in which the very chairs of the apostles still preside in their places; in which their very authentic Epistles are read, sounding forth the voice and representing the countenance of each of them. Is Achaia near you? You have Corinth. If you are not far from Macedonia, you have Philippi and Thessalonica. If you can go to Asia, you have Ephesus. If you are near Italy, you have Rome.[5]

Eusebius (AD 264–340) was for many years bishop of Caesarea. He was also a careful historian of the development of the Christian church up until his day. He was imprisoned during Diocletian's persecution of Christians – that last attempt by Rome to blot out Christianity. Part of Diocletian's strategy involved the finding and burning of Bibles over a ten year period. Eusebius survived into the reign of Constantine and became the emperor's chief religious adviser. One of Constantine's first acts on ascending the throne was to order fifty Bibles for the churches of Constantinople. The Bibles were to be prepared under the direction of his adviser, Eusebius. Eusebius carefully researched the matter, seeking to determine which books had been generally accepted by the churches. His primary yardstick in effect was: "What do Christians-in-community believe to be the word of God?" In his *Ecclesiastical History*,[6] he categorised four types of book amongst those competing for recognition as "Scripture": those universally accepted, those disputed, spurious books and forgeries (see figure 19).

It is clear that the evolution of the canon of the New Testament proceeded gradually and in the context of a plethora of fictitious tales concerning Jesus (some fifty spurious "Gospels" are now known about) or relating supposed acts and instructions of the early apostles. A sample of some of the best-known of such spurious or apocryphal "Gospels", "Acts" and "Letters" is given in figure 20.

However strongly these aprocryphal texts spoke out on behalf of Christianity, the early church's concern for authenticity and compatibility with apostolic teaching – the "Tradition" – predominated.

Not only were plenty of spurious materials in circulation, but there were also available to the churches many mature writings composed by Christian leaders who lived after the apostles (people

[5] Tertullian, *The Prescription Against Heretics*, Kessenger Publishing [e-books], chap 36, p 40.

[6] Eusebius Pamphili (trans. Roy J. Deferrari), *Ecclesiastical History: Books 1–5*, Catholic University of America Press: Washington D.C. (1953), book 3, chap 25, pp 178–180.

Figure 19

Eusebius' categorisation of books available for inclusion in the New Testament

Category of book	Detail
Universally accepted books	All the canonical books except those in the "disputed" category.
Disputed books	James, 2 Peter, Jude, 2 John, 3 John – though included in Eusebius' own Bible, and though affirmed by churches where they first appeared, these were doubted by some.
Spurious books	Eusebius mentions the Acts of Paul, the Shepherd of Hermas, the Apocalypse of Peter, the Epistle of Barnabas and the Didache.
Heretical books	Eusebius mentions the Gospel of Peter, the Gospel of Thomas, the Gospel of Matthias, the Acts of Andrew and the Acts of John.

known as the "Apostolic Fathers") and whose lives overlapped with those of the apostles. Not many of these writings remain in existence but they are known to us through quotation by others. They provided valuable links between the apostles and later generations of Christians.

Some of the Apostolic Fathers were so highly regarded that, in different local contexts, their compositions were temporarily regarded as Scripture. Clement's *Letter to the Corinthians*, for example, was read publicly in many churches down to the fourth century and was included at the end of the New Testament in the Alexandrian manuscript of the Bible. Clement was a companion of Paul and Peter and was most probably acquainted with John. He wrote his letter from Rome to address a situation in Corinth in which division was (once again!) damaging the church there. Figure 21 lists some of the significant writings of the Apostolic Fathers and identifies those that were at different times and in different places included as part of the New Testament.

No early church council arbitrarily decided that certain books comprised the New Testament. Rather, over a lengthy period of time the church discovered that certain writings had a clear and general authority. Christians actually needed to heed one another – from

Figure 20

Apocryphal New Testament books

Gospel of Nicodemus	includes "Acts of Pilate" *2nd century*
Protevangelium of James	birth of Mary to slaughter of innocents *2nd century*
Gospel of Hebrews	alleged sayings of Jesus *100 AD*
Gospel of Ebionites	compiled from Synoptics *2nd–4th century*
Gospel of Egyptians	conversations between Jesus and Salome *140 AD*
Gospel of Peter	based on canonical Gospels *150 AD*
Gospel of Pseudo-Matthew	childhood miracles of Jesus *5th century*
Gospel of Thomas	Jesus from 5 to 12 years old; teaching; early versions of some parables *2nd century*
Nativity of Mary	visits of angels to Mary *6th century*
Arabic Gospel of Infancy	miracles during sojourn in Egypt *7th century*
Gospel of Joseph the Carpenter	Glorification of Joseph *4th century*
Assumption of Mary	story of assumption to paradise *4th century*
Apocalypse of Peter	visions of heaven and hell
Acts of Paul	contains the supposed lost letter to the Corinthians *2nd century*
Acts of Peter	love affair of Peter's daughter; contains the "quo vadis" story *end of 2nd century*
Acts of John	visit to Rome *end of 2nd century*
Acts of Andrew	story of Andrew persuading Maximilla to refrain from intercourse with her husband, resulting in his martyrdom
Acts of Thomas	travel-romance *end of 2nd century*
Letter of Peter to James	violent attack on Paul from Ebionite position *end of 2nd century*
Epistle to Laodicea	professes to be one referred to in Colossians 4:16 *end of 2nd century*
Letters of Paul to Seneca	commending Christianity to followers of Seneca *4th century*
Abgarus Letters	Jesus' message to the king of Edessa

Figure 21

Significant writings of the Apostolic Fathers

Apostolic Father	Writing	Significance
Clement: Bishop of Rome AD 91–100; companion of Paul and Peter	*Letter to the Corinthians*	Read publicly in churches; found at end of New Testament in Alexandrine manuscript of Bible
Polycarp: Bishop of Smyrna; pupil of John	*Letter to the Philippians*	Reply to letter from the church; only extant writing of Polycarp, c AD 110
Ignatius: Bishop of Antioch; pupil of John	*Letters to the: Ephesians, Magnesians, Trallians, Philadelphians, Smyrnans, Romans, Polycarp*	Written in Asia Minor on his way to martyrdom in Rome AD 110
Barnabas: written AD 90–120; probably not the Barnabas of Scripture	*Letter of Barnabas*	Contains an outline interpretation of Septuagint; found in the Sinaitic manuscript of the Bible
Papias: Bishop of Hierapolis; pupil of John	*Explanation of the Sayings of the Lord*	Extant until thirteenth century; now only fragments quoted by later theologians
	The Didache (Teaching of the Twelve)	Written AD 80–120; statement by unknown author of the teaching of the apostles
	Shepherd of Hermas	Written AD 100–140 in Rome; allegory; read in many churches to time of Jerome; contained in Sinaitic manuscript of the Bible at end of New Testament
Justin Martyr: Philosopher, AD 100–167	*Apologies* *Dialogue with Trypho*	Apologist
Unknown author; self-styled a "disciple of the Apostles"	*Letter to Diognetus*	Vindication of Christianity

many different Mediterranean backgrounds – in order for a general consensus to emerge of what might constitute, collectively, their scripture.

Even with agreed-upon texts, such as the four Gospels, there were different convictions about their order. In the western Mediterranean, the early Latin manuscripts set out the books as Matthew–John–Luke–Mark. The Greek writers at the eastern end of the Mediterranean set them out as Matthew–Mark–Luke–John. Eventually, at the Council of Laodicea (AD 363) and the Council of Carthage (AD 397) the bishops agreed on a list of books identical to our New Testament, except that at Laodicea the book of Revelation was left out. Jerome (about AD 400) tidied up the order of the Gospels, opting for the eastern version in his Latin translation of the Bible – called the Vulgate. Today, all Bibles contain the same twenty-seven New Testament books. We are greatly indebted to those earlier generations of Christians for allowing the Holy Spirit to dictate the pace at which agreement of view was reached – several hundred years!

PRODUCING HOLY TEXT

The strong Christian claim that its scripture derives directly from God is based upon Paul's words to Timothy:

> All Scripture is God-breathed and is useful for teaching, rebuking, correcting and training in righteousness . . . (2 Timothy 3:16)

The Greek word translated "God-breathed" (*theopneustos*) literally means "breathed out by God". Such divine breathing out encompasses a whole range of human skills and processes in receiving and processing such "breath". For the most part, it is evident that human authors of scripture simply performed their task through the exercise of abilities with which they were naturally endowed. They did not necessarily know that they were producing canonical scripture, even though they were convinced of God's involvement in what they were speaking or writing. Indeed, some contributors to scripture may not have been at all aware that they were responding to, or being caught up in, a divine initiative towards scripture. One thinks here of the Song of Solomon, or Agur's oracle (Proverbs 30), or the *maskil* of Heman the Ezrahite (Psalm 88). Luke's Gospel, moreover, might be deemed to fall into this kind of category – the author himself tells us that his motive for writing it was because "it seemed good . . . to me" (Luke 1:3).

Inspired documents of different kinds can constitute scripture in the biblical sense. Luke's Gospel is really the writing-up of a piece of first-hand, historical research. Chronicles seems to be a re-write of Kings, composed to bring to the surface powerful underlying motifs in the history of the relationship between *Yahweh* and the people of Israel. Proverbs appears to have undergone various editions and recensions on the way to reaching the form in which we inherit it (see the editorial notes within the text at Proverbs 10:1; 24:23; 25:1). There is evidence of wholesale borrowing between the authors of 2 Peter and Jude, yet both books – along with others mentioned in this paragraph – are acknowledged as scripture.

J.I. Packer summarises the idea of inspiration as God accommodating himself to different people who deliver different genres of material. The whole process, under God's providence, unerringly produces holy scripture:

> We are to think of the Spirit's inspiring activity . . . as (to use an old but valuable technical term) *concursive*; that is, as exercised in, through and by means of the writers' own activity, in such a way that their thinking and writing was *both* free and spontaneous on their part *and* divinely elicited and controlled, and what they wrote was not only their own work, but also God's work.[7]

The inspiration is, consequently, "verbal". It has to do with the words that are deduced and handed on. The texts that record those words may contain some problems within them – corruptions, or missing words, or evidence of editorial process en route to the "final" product. But the original and orthodox Christian conviction about inerrancy coheres in a confidence that the text is sufficiently trustworthy not to lead the reader or hearer into error.

[7] J. I. Packer, *"Fundamentalism" and the Word of God*, Eerdmans: Grand Rapids (1958), p 80.

Chapter 8

Ascertaining a holy Qur'ân?

HOW different from the cases of Jewish and Christian canonisation of holy text is the experience of Islam! Or so it would seem! The Muslim account of the authorisation of the Qur'ân focuses in a revelatory act via one individual and proceeds quickly to a consolidation of the resulting text within a generation. We shall review here the Muslim story of the producing of the Qur'ân and, in passing, allow some questions to be asked of it.

ANGELIC REVISION CLASSES

During Prophet Muḥammad's life, no complete, written copy of the Qur'ân existed. According to a well-known tradition or *ḥadîth*, the angel Gabriel used to check the recitation with the Prophet – the latter speaking from memory – every Ramaḍân, and in the final year of Muḥammad's life he rehearsed it with him twice:

> Fâṭima said, 'The Prophet told me secretly, "Gabriel used to recite the Qur'ân to me and I to him once a year, but this year he recited the whole Qur'ân with me twice. I don't think but that my death is approaching".'[1]

The recitations gradually came to be jotted down on tablets, parchment, bones, leaves and skins though mostly they continued to be retained within the memories of men and women. Some of Muḥammad's closest companions devoted themselves to learning the text of the Qur'ân by heart. I intend no questioning of the reliability of "remembered" scripture. In oral cultures, learning by rote is as accurate a form of recording as any writing or printing might be in contemporary Western cultures. The "text" remembered, however, could evidently be recited in different ways by different companions:

> Narrated 'Umar bin al-Khaṭṭâb: I heard Hishâm bin Ḥakîm bin Ḥizâm reciting Sûrat-al-Furqân in a way different to that of mine. Allâh's Apostle had taught it to me (in a different way). So, I was about to quarrel with him

[1] Recorded in al-Bukhârî, *al-Ṣaḥîḥ*, vol 6, book 61, chap 7, trad 518, p 485.

(during the prayer) but I waited till he finished, then I tied his garment round his neck and seized him by it and brought him to Allâh's Apostle and said, "I have heard him reciting Sûrat-al-Furqân in a way different to the way you taught it to me." The Prophet ordered me to release him and asked Hishâm to recite it. When he recited it, Allâh's Apostle said, "It was revealed in this way." He then asked me to recite it. When I recited it, he said, "It was revealed in this way. The Qur'ân has been revealed in seven different ways, so recite it in the way that is easier for you."[2]

We shall return to consider such different ways of reciting the Qur'ân in a moment. A major difficulty arose for the early Muslim community after Prophet Muḥammad's demise because people who had committed the Qur'ân to memory were dying or being martyred. According to the *ḥadîth*, the earliest written compilation of the whole Qur'ân was made by Zaid ibn Thâbit at the instruction of Abû Bakr, first caliph or leader of the Muslim community after Prophet Muḥammad's death in AD 632. Abû Bakr was urged to instigate this action by 'Umar, the man who would succeed him as caliph:

Narrated Zaid bin Thâbit: Abû Bakr Aṣ-Ṣiddîq sent for me when the people of Yamâma had been killed (i.e., a number of the Prophet's companions who fought against Musailama). (I went to him) and found 'Umar bin Al-Khaṭṭâb sitting with him. Abû Bakr then said (to me), "'Umar has come to me and said: 'Casualties were heavy among the Qurrâ' of the Qur'ân (i.e. those who knew the Qur'ân by heart) on the day of the Battle of Yamâma, and I am afraid that more heavy casualties may take place among the Qurrâ' on other battlefields, whereby a large part of the Qur'ân may be lost. Therefore I suggest, you (Abû Bakr) order that the Qur'ân be collected.' I said to 'Umar, 'How can you do something which Allâh's Apostle did not do?' 'Umar said, 'By Allâh, that is a good project.' 'Umar kept on urging me to accept his proposal till Allâh opened my chest for it and I began to realise the good in the idea which 'Umar had realised." Then Abû Bakr said (to me). "You are a wise young man and we do not have any suspicion about you, and you used to write the Divine Inspiration for Allâh's Apostle. So you should search for (the fragmentary scripts of) the Qur'ân and collect it (in one book)." By Allâh! If they had ordered me to shift one of the mountains, it would not have been heavier for me than this ordering me to collect the Qur'ân. Then I said to Abû Bakr, "How will you do something which Allâh's Apostle did not do?" Abû Bakr replied, "By Allâh, it is a good project." Abû Bakr kept on urging me to accept his idea until Allâh opened my chest for what He had opened the chests of Abû Bakr and 'Umar. So I started looking for the

[2] Recorded in al-Bukhârî, *al-Ṣaḥîḥ*, vol 3, book 41, chap 23, trad 601, p 355.

> Qur'ân and collecting it from (what was written on) palm-leaf stalks, thin white stones and also from the men who knew it by heart, till I found the last Verse of Sûrat At-Tauba (Repentance) with Abî Khuzaima Al-Anṣârî, and I did not find it with anybody other than him. The Verse is: Verily there has come unto you an Apostle (Muḥammad) from amongst yourselves. It grieves him that you should receive any injury or difficulty . . . (till the end of Sûrat-Barâ'a (At-Tauba) 9:128–129). Then the complete manuscripts (copy) of the Qur'ân remained with Abû Bakr till he died, then with 'Umar till the end of his life, and then with Ḥafṣa, the daughter of 'Umar.[3]

Zaid's written compilation was kept with Abû Bakr and then with Ḥafṣa, daughter of the next caliph, 'Umar. This text came to be referred to as "Ḥafṣa's copy". Leone Caetani questions the reliability of the claim (from tradition) that during Abû Bakr's caliphate such a first compilation of the Qur'ân was thus made. He asks why, if the death of so many Muslims at al-Yamâma endangered the preservation of the text, would Abû Bakr practically conceal the copy commissioned by him from Zaid ibn Thâbit, entrusting it to the guardianship of a woman? It seems odd, moreover, that the compilation would be entrusted to Zaid ibn Thâbit rather than one of the four men whom Prophet Muḥammad himself had recommended as reliable teachers of the Qur'ân:

> Narrated Masrûq: 'Abdullâh bin 'Amr mentioned 'Abdullâh bin Mas'ûd and said, "I shall ever love that man, for I heard the Prophet saying, 'Take (learn) the Qur'ân from four: 'Abdullâh bin Mas'ûd, Sâlim, Mu'adh and Ubaî bin Ka'b'."[4]

Caetani suggests that "Ḥafṣa's copy" is an invention made to justify the corrections of the compilation subsequently made under 'Uthmân. Nonetheless, Caetani allows the possibility of a copy of the Qur'ân being prepared at Medina during the time of Abû Bakr and 'Umar – a copy in which no verse of the text was accepted which was not authenticated by at least two witnesses who could declare that they themselves had heard it from the Prophet.

Caetani's investigation is prompted by his assumption that the official canonical redaction undertaken at 'Uthmân's command was due to uncertainty at the time with regard to the text of the Qur'ân – an uncertainty posed by the different "readings" referred to earlier. Caetani is interested in the tensions that existed between champions

[3] Recorded in al-Bukhârî, *al-Ṣaḥîḥ*, vol 6, book 61, chap 3, trad 509, pp 477–478.
[4] Recorded in al-Bukhârî, *al-Ṣaḥîḥ*, vol 6, book 61, chap 8, trad 521, pp 486–487.

of the provincial copies of the text (copies that would evidently be deliberately destroyed by fire after 'Uthmân's redaction was completed) and the caliph in al-Kufa with his promotion of a Medinan text. Caetani also investigates the roles of the *qurrâ'* (Qur'ân-readers) themselves vis à vis the emerging central authority of the caliphate. He reads 'Uthmân's commissioning of an "authentic" text as an open challenge to the *qurrâ'* and, indeed, as a successful attempt to end the monopoly that they claimed over the sacred text.[5]

The manuscript of the Qur'ân, as compiled by Zaid ibn Thâbit remained, it is claimed, with Ḥafṣa. In the provinces, different reciters (*qurrâ'*) of the Qur'ân continued to offer different renderings of the revelation according to what they had heard from the Prophet or learned from those who had. Soon, the differences began to cause friction within the emerging Muslim community:

> Narrated Anas bin Mâlik: Ḥudhaifa bin al-Yamân came to 'Uthmân at the time when the people of Shâm and the people of 'Irâq were waging war to conquer Armînya and Âdharbîjân. Ḥudhaifa was afraid of their (the people of Shâm and 'Irâq) differences in the recitation of the Qur'ân, so he said to 'Uthmân, "O chief of the Believers! Save this nation before they differ about the Book (Qur'ân) as Jews and Christians did before." So 'Uthmân sent a message to Ḥafṣa saying, "Send us the manuscripts of the Qur'ân so that we may compile the Qur'ânic materials in perfect copies and return the manuscripts to you." Ḥafṣa sent it to 'Uthmân. 'Uthmân then ordered Zaid bin Thâbit, 'Abdullah bin Az-Zubair, Saîd bin Al-'Âṣ and 'Abdur-Raḥmân bin Ḥârith bin Hishâm to rewrite the manuscripts in perfect copies. 'Uthmân said to the three Quraishî men, "In case you disagree with Zaid bin Thâbit on any point in the Qur'ân, then write it in the dialect of the Quraish as the Qur'ân was revealed in their tongue." They did so, and when they had written many copies, 'Uthmân returned the original manuscripts to Ḥafṣa. 'Uthmân sent to every Muslim province one copy of what they had copied, and ordered that all the other Qur'ânic materials, whether written in fragmentary manuscripts or whole copies, be burnt. Zaid bin Thâbit added, "A Verse from Sûrat Aḥzâb was missed by me when we copied the Qur'ân and I used to hear Allâh's Apostle reciting it. So we searched for it and found it with Khuzaima bin Thâbit Al-Anṣârî. (That Verse was): 'Among the Believers are men who have been true in their covenant with Allâh.' (33:23).[6]

According to Anas bin Mâlik, al-Yamân appeals to 'Uthmân to "save the nation" because the Muslims differed about the wording of

[5] See Leone Caetani, "Uthman and the Recension of the Koran," in *The Moslem World*, vol 5 (1915), pp 380–390.

[6] Recorded in al-Bukhârî, *al-Ṣaḥîḥ*, vol 6, book 61, chap 3, trad 510, pp 478–479.

the Qur'ân. A variety of readings was causing misunderstanding and dispute within the *umma*. The situation was seen as serious. It was not just out in the provinces that different readings of the Qur'ân were causing trouble:

> During the reign of 'Uthmân, teachers were teaching this or that reading to their students. When the students met and disagreed about the reading, they reported the differences to their teachers. They would defend their readings, condemning the others as heretical. News of this came to 'Uthmân's ears and he addressed the people, 'You who are here around me are disputing as to the Qur'ân, and pronouncing it differently. It follows that those who are distant in the various regional centres of Islam are even more widely divided. Companions of Muḥammad! Act in unison; come together and write out an *imam* for the Muslims.'[7]

According to this account, there appear to have been disputes concerning the true content of the revelation not only between Muslims in Medina and those in the provinces, but even between Muslims in Medina themselves. Those "here around me" – that is within Medina – were also caught up in the disputes over how the Qur'ân should be recited.

ALLOWING ONE TEXT

'Uthmân's solution to the growing problem was to aim at uniting all Muslims on the basis of a single text of the Qur'ân. He decided to make Ḥafṣa's copy the official text. If there should be any disagreement among the scribes who copied that text concerning how to recite it, the bias should be in favour of the Qurayshi[8] dialect. Other copies or fragments of the Qur'ân were then to be destroyed, presumably in order to minimise the risk of different readings surviving. Seven readings, even though authenticated by Prophet Muḥammad himself, early appear difficult to cope with. The solution, decided upon by Caliph 'Uthmân, is to determine one single, official Qur'ân.

The alleged comparison with "Ḥafṣa's copy" in the process of revision is sometimes disputed because no mention is made of that

[7] In Abû Bakr 'Abdullâh ibn Abî Da'ûd, *Kitâb al-Masâhif* (ed. Arthur Jeffery), Cairo (1936), p 21 and quoted in John Burton, *The Collection of the Qur'ân*, Cambridge University Press: Cambridge (1977), p 143.

[8] The Quraysh constituted the Arabian tribe of which Muḥammad was a member and to which the majority of Meccans belonged.

copy in the recorded descriptions given of the collection and consultation process. Difficulties also remain in reconciling seemingly incompatible contentions concerning the formulating of a single text of the Qur'ân. The contentions include the following: the Qur'ân was first collected by Abû Bakr; the Qur'ân was first collected by 'Umar; the Qur'ân's collection was begun by Abû Bakr and completed by 'Umar; the Qur'ân's collection was begun by 'Umar and completed by 'Uthmân; the Qur'ân was solely collected by 'Uthmân.[9]

The independent sources consulted by Zaid ibn Thâbit comprised various codices emanating from different places such as Basra, Kufa and Syria. Figure 22 lists the major source texts involved in this process. Three of these versions derived from the men whom Prophet Muḥammad had indicated as reliable teachers of the Qur'ân.

From the researches made by Zaid and his companions, a definitive text was produced. Within that production, the suras were finally ordered and the text was restricted to a single (Quraysh) dialect. In effect, by such a process, a Medinan text was established as standard – and Medina was, of course, the seat of 'Uthmân's

Figure 22

Significant codices of the Qur'ân consulted by Zaid ibn Thâbit

Source	Place of Origin
Zaid ibn Thâbit, a native of Medina; one of the *Anṣâr* and Muḥammad's amanuensis.	Medina
'Abd Allâh ibn Mas'ûd, a Companion; one of the "illustrious ten" to whom Muḥammad gave an assurance of paradise.	Kufa
Mu'adh ibn Jabal (sometimes referred to as Miqdad ibn al-Aswad), one of the most famous of the Companions. Ubay ibn Ka'b, a secretary of Muḥammad about whom the *Ṣaḥîḥ* of al-Bukhârî states that of all the Muslims he was acknowledged to be one of the best Qur'ân reciters.[10]	Damascus and Homs elsewhere in Syria
Abû Mûsâ Ash'ari, one of the early authorities on the Qur'ân.	Basra

[9] See Burton, *op. cit.*, p 225.
[10] Recorded in al-Bukhârî, *al-Ṣaḥîḥ*, vol 6, book 61, chap 8, trad 527, p 489.

government! A single copy of the subsequent, definitive text was sent to each Muslim province with instructions that all other qur'ânic materials – fragments or whole copies – were to be burnt.

HINTS OF OTHER TEXTS?

Details about the major codices consulted in this process, plus many others extant at the time but not consulted by Zaid ibn Thâbit, may easily be garnered from various later Islamic theological writings in which alternative renderings of words or verses of the Qur'ân were drawn from those different codices. Arthur Jeffery, for example, records the known differences of readings in qur'ânic codices that were destroyed under 'Uthmân in his *Materials for the History of the Text of the Quran.*[11] Jeffery presents in this comprehensive list of codices the *Kitâb al-Masâhif* of Ibn Abî Da'ûd, plus a collection of variant readings from the codices of Ibn Mas'ûd, Ubai, 'Ali ibn 'Abbas, Anas, Abû Mûsâ and other early qur'ânic authorities. The codices provide evidence of texts that were different and earlier than 'Uthmân's canonical text. John Burton comments on the significance of later proponents of the "legal sciences" within Islam in their appeal to such codices:

> . . . it soon becomes apparent that, far from being identical with the so-called 'Uthmânic text, the *suhuf* of Ḥafṣa, like the *suhuf* of 'Â'isha or the *suhuf* of a third widow of the Prophet, Umm Salama, played a role analogous to that conferred upon the *mushaf* of 'Abdullâh, of Abû Mûsâ, of Ubayy, of Miqdâd (or Mu'âd). Like all of these, Ḥafṣa's codex had occasional exegetical value in the scholars' attempts to decide issues left 'unclear' in the 'Uthmân text.[12]

Even within Abdullah Yusuf Ali's translation of the Qur'ân into English there appears evidence of the survival of "readings" of the Qur'ân different from 'Uthmân's standardised text. Sura 33:6 reads:

[11] See Arthur Jeffrey (ed), *Materials for the History of the Text of the Quran*, Leiden: Brill (1937).

[12] Burton, *op. cit.*, p 227. See also Arthur Jeffery, "The Textual History of the Qur'an," a lecture delivered in October 1946 at a meeting of the Middle East Society of Jerusalem and published in *The Qur'an and Scripture*, R.F. Moore Co: New York (1952). John Gilchrist offers a summary of the process of codification of the qur'ânic text in his *Jam' al-Qur'an: The Codification of the Qur'an Text*, TMFMT: Warley (1989).

> The Prophet is closer to the Believers than their own selves, and his wives are their mothers. Blood-relations among each other have closer personal ties, in the Decree of God, than (the Brotherhood of) Believers and Muhajirs: nevertheless do ye what is just to your closest friends: such is the writing in the Decree (of God).

Ali includes a footnote referring to a recitation ("reading") from Ubaî ibn Ka'b, one of the four men whom Prophet Muḥammad had recommended as the best teachers of the Qur'ân. That reading adds a phrase after the word "selves":

> In some Qirâats, like that of Ubai ibn Ka'b, occur also the words "and he is a father to them" which imply his spiritual relationship and connect on with the words "and his wives are their mothers."[13]

Sura 23:112 reads as follows in Yusuf Ali's translation: He will say: "What number of years did ye stay on earth?" Here, Ali includes a footnote concerning the phrase "He will say" which in Arabic is rendered by a single word:

> The usual Indian reading is "Qala", "He will say". This follows the Kûfa Qirâat. The Basra Qirâat reads "Qul", "Say" (in the imperative). The point is only one of grammatical construction.[14]

Similar footnotes are given by Yusuf Ali at other stages of his translation.[15] The point for the meaning of the text is that such differences are very minor. The point for the claim that there has only ever been one version of the qur'ânic text is that that claim looks to be somewhat exaggerated.

The text of the Qur'ân in its earliest days was written in a script that did not have dots or vowel marks – just bare, sometimes undifferentiated, consonants. During the period that 'Uthmân sought to standardise the Qur'ân, such diacritical markings were still not yet employed. They were, in fact, added later, with the result that many variations became available and used by Muslims over the years. Different written transmissions of various readings of the Qur'ân eventuated in different parts of the Muslim world. That is why Yusuf Ali is able to refer to a "usual Indian reading" in which a Kûfan textual tradition is reflected.

Today, there are two qur'ânic Arabic texts that are popular: that of Warsh (deriving from the recitation by Nafi) and that of Hafs

[13] A. Yusuf Ali (trans), *The Glorious Qur'an*, American Trust Publications (1977), Sura 33:6, note 3674, p 1104.

[14] *Ibid.*, Sura 23:112, note 2948, p 893.

[15] *Ibid.*, e.g. Suras 21:4, 112.

(deriving from the recitation by Asim). The variations between the texts are minor and do not vitally change the meaning of the Qur'ân. Their existence and history, however, suggest that authority for today's text of the Qur'ân cannot simply lie in a claim that the current Arabic Qur'ân contains the exact words of God as dictated or confirmed by the angel Gabriel to Prophet Muḥammad. That would appear to be a claim too far.

Relatively quickly, then, the Muslim community came to possess a single authoritative version of the Qur'ân. The standard story of that version's definition and promulgation is accepted as part of the Muslim case for strong confidence about the authenticity of the text that it inherits. Beneath the surface, however, one may discern that the redacting and editing process involved human choices as to what the unified text should finally look like.

THE QUR'ÂN: A SPECIAL CASE?

Within Judaism and Christianity, the process of canonising their religious texts lasted for several centuries. The religious texts themselves came from the lips and pens of many men whose lives spanned vast areas of land and periods of time. By contrast, the Qur'ân was mediated via one individual during 23 years of his lifetime. Relatively quickly, after his demise, a "single" authoritative text came to be given canonical status. The claim is frequently made by Muslims today, as we have seen, that the text in front of them now is the same as that which was sent down via Prophet Muḥammad.

Against the background of this rapid process of revelation-leading-to-canonisation, and arising from an analysis of the unique qualities of qur'ânic versification, has grown the doctrine of *i'jâz al-Qur'ân*. It is clearly predicted within the Qur'ân that it comprises a phenomenon that neither jinn nor men could ever emulate:

> Say: "If the whole of mankind and Jinns were to gather together to produce the like of this Qur'an, they could not produce the like thereof, even if they backed up each other with help and support." (Sura 17:88)

The qur'ânic revelation is conceived as having a miraculous quality. The text has a unique resonance that renders people incapable of imitating it either in form or content:

> The superb style of the Qur'ân has a tremendous effect on its readers. It totally changes the pattern of life of those who believe and practise its teachings. It leaves a soothing effect on the mind of the reader, even if he does not fully understand its meaning.[16]

A fascinating example of this acclaimed quality of the Qur'ân is found in M.Y. Alam's novel, *Kilo*. The fictional story is set in Alam's home town of Bradford and it explores the painful experience of dual cultural identity. Khalil, the main character, is British born from Pakistani parents. His family suffers from racial abuse and violent racketeering from without. It suffers from an unbridgeable generation gap from within. Khalil reinvents himself as Kilo, clever player in the big money world of the Bradford drug scene. As Kilo climbs higher in the underworld of local street crime, he has an awakening of conscience that derives from his roots as a Muslim. The Qur'ân is the catalyst for his subsequent transformation:

> And so, after bathing, I came back downstairs, sat on the floor, cross-legged, opened the book at random and I read. One line in Arabic followed by a line of interpretation. I never understood any of it as a kid. I'd go to mosque, read a few pages and then I'd go home like all the other kids. Like them, I knew how to read, how to pronounce, where to pause and where not to, but I never understood like I should have understood . . . But that day, as I sat there, reading in one tongue then another, I did get a certain sense of relevance. Sounds weird, sounds like a lie coming from someone like me, but I did get a sense of meaning, a sense of place in the universe, and yes, I even felt a sense of purpose that day. First time for everything.[17]

We might comprehend, simply from an evaluation of the acclaimed process of Qur'ân-formulation, why the hermeneutical issue within Islam has largely been a settled one. Added to that is the weight given to the resultant text through the theological conviction concerning *tanzîl* or "sending down". God's word has been consistently delivered to and through the Prophets such as Abraham, Moses, David and Jesus. The messages that they passed on were the same, though their listeners came to doctor or forget them. A final "sending down" (*tanzîl*) by God of his unchanging word has been given via Prophet Muḥammad. That word or "recitation" (*qur'ân*) constitutes the original and correcting word from God to humankind. In the process of its being "sent down", Prophet

[16] Sarwar, *op. cit.*, p 34.
[17] M Y Alam, *Kilo*, Route: Glasshoughton (2002), p 204.

Muḥammad provides the mouthpiece for the revelation but he in no way cognitively participates in the process. The resulting word on earth is to be received and obeyed as miraculously and clearly "God's word." There is no question of it being interrogated, evaluated or criticised. John Wansbrough neatly summarises the consequence of such a conviction about the delivery and quality of the Qur'ân:

> As a record of Muslim revelation the book requires no introduction. As a document susceptible of (*sic*) analysis by the instruments and techniques of Biblical criticism it is virtually unknown.[18]

The idea that a contemporary Muslim theologian might investigate the text of the Qur'ân for whispers of "the historical Muḥammad" in a way parallel to the quest within the New Testament for "the historical Jesus" is laughable and risky. Mind you, that sort of quest has not always been quite so off-limits as might be thought. The revered encyclopaedist Jalâl al-Dîn al-Suyûtî (died AD 1505) stated that Prophet Muḥammad received revelation (that is the Qur'ân) only in content, while the actual phrasing of the Qur'ân came from the man himself. The human contribution to the wording of the Qur'ân, by this understanding, was considerable and opens up all sorts of lines of linguistic and historical enquiry. However, as one contemporary professor of Arabic studies asserts:

> Today, such an idea cannot be discussed, nor even mentioned, publicly. People have lost their lives for speaking out in this manner.[19]

Those few Muslim authors who have published thoughtful speculation about the (human) sources of the Qur'ân have found themselves condemned in decrees declaring them to be apostates and beyond the pale of Islam. The traditional view – the traditional hermeneutic – predominates. God's word in the Qur'ân is simply a rendering on earth of the eternal text inscribed "in a tablet preserved" (Sura 85:22). It is in essence a "recitation" – the Arabic word *qur'ân* comes from *qara'*, meaning "to recite". That, after all, is how it began for Prophet Muḥammad, as recorded in the first (chronological) sura: "Proclaim! (or Read!) in the name of thy Lord and Cherisher . . ." (Sura 96:1)[20]

[18] John Wansbrough, *Quranic Studies. Sources and Methods of Scriptural Interpretation*, Oxford University Press: Oxford (1977), p ix.

[19] Abu Zaid (2004), *op. cit.*, p 201.

[20] The Arabic word for "Proclaim" is *iqra'*. It derives from *qara'* and could equally well be translated "Recite!" The whole sura is named *Iqra'*.

For the Muslim, then, recitation simply *is* revelation. Wansbrough insightfully proposes that "the elaboration of Islam may be seen as a co-ordination of three generically distinct factors: canon, prophet, and sacred language."[21] Through the medium of a recitation, unimpeded in the process by any conscious human participation, the divine (Arabic) word is mediated to human listeners. A canonical scripture is delivered to earth. Listeners to the recitation, down the ages, may be certain of the origin of the revelation for the process of revelation stands guarantee to its reliability. The hermeneutic is one of certainty.

On the surface, the history of the development of the Qur'ân appears neat and tidy and quickly settled. Under the surface, however, one might infer instances of human hesitation, or provocation, or at the very least involvement in the revelatory process, that are similar to those pertaining to the producing of Old and New Testaments.

[21] Wansbrough, *op. cit.*, p 19.

Chapter 9

The clear and the not so clear

NOT only does the concept of *tanzîl* engender in Muslims a "recipient-only" attitude in their appreciation of the Qur'ân, but the text itself clearly and frequently defines how this holy book is to be appreciated. In the words of Stefan Wild, "the Qur'an is the most metatextual, most self-referential holy text known in the history of world religions."[1] Where it comes from, how it comes, what it leads to – all are carefully defined within its pages. Such definition, mind you, leads to some tricky questions about how all the different hints might be seen to come together. We shall look at a few of those questions later in this chapter.

THE QUR'ÂN ON "THE QUR'ÂN"

The Qur'ân is revealed "in clear Arabic" (Sura 26:195) but such "clarity" does not evidently extend to a transparency of meaning in all its parts. We have already discovered that some understanding of immediate human context (as with Sura 53 concerning the "Satanic verses") or an appreciation of the different "voices" of the text (as in Sura 12 concerning Joseph), assists in making clear what might otherwise seem opaque. The Qur'ân also announces quite forthrightly that it contains both unambiguous and ambiguous material:

> He it is Who has sent down to thee the Book: In it are verses basic or fundamental (of established meaning); they are the foundation of the Book: others are allegorical. But those in whose hearts is perversity follow the part thereof that is allegorical, seeking discord, and searching for its hidden meanings, but no one knows its hidden meanings except Allah. And those who are firmly grounded in knowledge say: "We believe in the Book; the whole of it is from our Lord:" and none will grasp the Message except men of understanding. (Sura 3:7)

[1] Stefan Wild, "The Self-Referentiality of the Qur'ân: Sura 3:7 as an Exegetical Challenge". In Jane Dammen McAuliffe, Barry D. Walfish & Joseph W. Goering (eds.), *With Reverence for the Word. Medieval Scriptural Exegesis in Judaism, Christianity, and Islam*, Oxford University Press: Oxford (2003), pp 422–436.

This important verse of the Qur'ân typifies in itself the delicate problem of how the text might be received. There are two ways in which the words of this verse can be read in Arabic, each giving a different meaning. If the verse is recited with a pause (*waqf*), its sense becomes ". . . and none knows its interpretation, save only God. And those firmly rooted in knowledge say . . ." This interpretation suggests that part of the qur'ânic revelation is interpretable only by God – only God knows its meaning. If the same words in Arabic are recited without a pause, the sense of the sentence is continued forward (*wasl*), giving the different idea ". . . and none knows its interpretation, save only God and those firmly rooted in knowledge. They say . . ." This interpretation of the reading of the text proposes that some human beings, along with God, might be able to interpret parts of the Qur'ân not interpretable by other humans.

With regard to the details of what is being suggested within Sura 3:7, a lot of discussion arises as to the meaning of the different words. What, for example, is meant by "clear verses" (*âyât muḥkamât*) and "ambiguous verses" (*âyât mutashâbiḥât*)? Concerning the import of "clear verses", we learn elsewhere that God exercises a divine care for the revealed word:

> Alif, Lam, Rar. (This is) a Book, with verses basic or fundamental (of established meaning), further explained in detail, – from One Who is Wise and Well-acquainted (with all things). (Sura 11:1)

God evidently abrogates and corrects any unfortunate Satanic intervention that might sully or compromise that word:

> Never did We send a messenger or a prophet before thee, but, when he framed a desire, Satan threw some (vanity) into his desire: but Allah will cancel anything (vain) that Satan throws in, and Allah will confirm (and establish) His Signs: for Allah is full of Knowledge and Wisdom: That He may make the suggestions thrown in by Satan, but a trial for those in whose hearts is a disease and who are hardened of heart: verily the wrong-doers are in a schism far (from the Truth). (Sura 22:52–53)

Through the revealed word, God sends a clear, unambiguous message, allowing hearers no excuse for prevaricating over its demands:

> Those who believe say, "Why is not a sura sent down (for us)?" But when a sura of basic or categorical meaning is revealed, and fighting is mentioned therein, thou wilt see those in whose hearts is a disease looking at thee with a look of one in swoon at the approach of death. But more fitting for them – Were it to obey and say what is just, and when a matter is resolved on, it were best for them if they were true to Allah. (Sura 47:20–21)

Ibn Kathîr presents one interpretation of what *muḥkamât* (clear) and *mutashâbiḥât* (ambiguous) might mean, and gives an illustration of how the two might relate to Christian claims that the divinity of Jesus is potentially acknowledged in the Qur'ân:

> The Muḥkamât are the Ayât that explain the abrogating rulings, the allowed, prohibited, laws, limits, obligations and rulings that should be believed in and implemented. As for the Mutashâbiḥât Ayât, they include the abrogated Ayât, parables, oaths, and what should be believed in, but not implemented . . . Therefore Allah said, (So as for those in whose hearts there is a deviation) meaning, those who are misguided and deviate from truth to falsehood, (they follow that which is not entirely clear thereof) meaning, they refer to the Mutashabiḥ, because they are able to alter its meanings to conform with their false interpretation since the wordings of the Mutashâbiḥât encompass such a wide area of meanings. As for the Muḥkam Ayât, they cannot be altered because they are clear and, thus, constitute unequivocal proof against the misguided people. This is why Allah said, (seeking Al-Fiṭnâh) meaning, they seek to misguide their following by pretending to prove their innovation by relying on the Qur'ân – the Mutashâbiḥ of it – but, this proof is against and not for them. For instance, Christians might claim that ['Isa is divine because] the Qur'ân states that he is Ruhullah and His Word, which He gave to Mary, all the while ignoring Allah's statements, (He ['Isa] was not more than a servant. We granted Our favour to him.) [43:59] . . .[2]

In other words, the clear verses describing Jesus as certainly not divine take precedence over ambiguous verses that refer to Jesus as "Spirit of God" or "His Word". In such a manner the references to Jesus in the Qur'ân that would seem to provide bridges to a Christian understanding of Christ are subsumed under other statements, more adamantly qur'ânic in their orientation.

Similarly with *umm al-kitâb*, ("essence", literally "mother", of the Book) – what does this phrase mean? Usually "the mother of the Book" is identified with a heavenly pre-scripture. Other suras appear to confirm such a suggestion:

> Allah doth blot out or confirm what He pleaseth: with Him is the Mother of the Book. (Sura 13:39).

> And verily, it is in the Mother of the Book, in Our Presence, high (in dignity), full of wisdom. (Sura 43:4)

Is this verse (3:7) saying, then, that only the *muḥkamât* verses constitute the eternally-existing word? Or does "ambiguous verses"

[2] Ibn Kathîr, *op. cit.*, Sura 3: "The Mutashâbiḥât and Muḥkamât Ayât."

in this context refer to qur'ânic revelations that resembled but were not identical with passages in the Jewish and Christian scriptures?

Again, with the phrase *al-râsikhûna fî'l-'ilm* ("those firmly rooted in knowledge") – to whom does this refer? In the context of the delivery of this sura, it might be suggested that it refers to Medinan Jews who acknowledged the prophethood of Muḥammad. Ibn Kathîr suggests that the ones firmly rooted in knowledge are those who receive both the *muḥkamât* and the *mutashâbiḥât* as true and authentic, and "each one of them testifies to the truth of the other. This is because they both are from Allah and nothing that comes from Allah is ever met by contradiction or discrepancy."[3] Such receivers of the divine word – clear or not so clear – tend to be humble, says Ibn Kathîr. He goes on to quote Ibn al-Mundhir who records in his work of interpretation that Nafi' bin Yazid said:

> "Those firmly grounded in knowledge are those who are modest for Allah's sake, humbly seek his pleasure, and do not exaggerate regarding those above them, or belittle those below them."[4]

The purpose of the last paragraphs is not to deduce a definition of what the terms "clear" (*muḥkam*) and "ambiguous" (*mutashâbiḥ*) might amount to, but to demonstrate that interpretation is an essential facet of receiving, and responding to, the revelation given from heaven. In the history of *tafsîr*, there developed various opinions as to whether each qur'ânic verse might be either clear or ambiguous or whether the terms were mutually exclusive. Sometimes the "clear" verses are defined as those pertaining to legal matters covering human behaviour, while the "ambiguous" verses are said to deal with matters of belief. The Islamic exegetical tradition evinces many attempts either to establish one correct interpretation, or in many cases to accept a multitude of equally acceptable correct interpretations. Muhammad Asad (died AD 1992), born Leopold Weiss, famous recent Jewish convert to Islam, designated this verse a key to any understanding of the Qur'ân. It is evidently a strongly self-referential verse, and it raises as many questions as it answers.

[3] Ibn Kathîr, *op. cit.*, Sura 3: "Only Allah Knows the True Ta'wîl (Interpretation) of the Mutashâbiḥât."

[4] *Ibid.*

NOT ALL CLEAR

Not everything is simple, then, in the witness that the Qur'ân bears towards itself. Simplicity is definitely lacking in another internal Muslim debate concerning the nature of the Qur'ân. As we have discovered, before the divine word was sent down by God's decree, it had something like a resting-place in heaven: "Nay, this is a Glorious Qur'an, (Inscribed) in a Tablet Preserved!" (Sura 85:21–22) Questions about the quality of the Qur'ân have arisen from this hint of what Wild refers to as a "divine pre-history of the Qur'anic text."[5]

We begin with a simple question: "Is the Qur'ân itself eternal or created?" We are told that God sent down the verses of the "clear Book" as "an Arabic Qur'ân" (Sura 12:1–2). Those verses comprise a recitation on earth of what is Word or Book in heaven. So, the Qur'ân exists in heaven – eternally! Islamic orthodoxy insists that the Qur'ân constitutes the uncreated speech or word of God. The orthodox point is that, because it always existed, it was never created. The doctrine of an unchanging, uncreated revelation obviously has implications for a Muslim view of previous "revelations". Contradictions between the surviving former scriptures and the Qur'ân have to be seen as the result of human corruption of the earlier divine revelations. The question of the createdness or not of the Qur'ân occupied the Mu'tazila, or "separatists" in the early years of the Islamic faith. The Mu'tazila comprised a sect founded by Wâsil ibn 'Atâ (died AD 748), who "separated" from the school of Ḥasan al-Basrî about 100 years after Prophet Muḥammad's death. Later, the Mu'tazila referred to themselves as *Ahl al-'Adl wa'l-Tawḥîd* (People of Justice and Monotheism), based on the theology that they advocated.[6] The Mu'tazila expanded on the logic and rationalism of Greek philosophy, seeking to combine them with Islamic

[5] Stefan Wild, " 'We have sent down to Thee the Book with the Truth . . .' Spatial and temporal implications of the Qur'anic concepts of *nuzûl*, *tanzîl*, and *'inzâl*." In Stefan Wild (ed.), *The Qur'an as Text*, E.J. Brill: Leiden (1996), p 145.

[6] Mu'tazila theologians disagreed on some points, but they were all in agreement on five fundamental principles. Those principles were God's justice, God's unity, the "intermediate position" (committing a grave sin does not automatically make one an infidel), God's irreversible threats and promises, and God's commanding the right and prohibiting the wrong. The principles were mostly worked out in response to rival theologians, especially those who held to a literal interpretation of the Qur'ân and those who believed in unqualified predestination.

doctrines. Their theology developed in the eighth century and by the early ninth century had become the official court belief of the 'Abbasid caliphate under al-Ma'mûn.[7] These rationalist theologians argued from the perspective of *tawḥîd*, or the unity of God, that nothing can be set alongside God's essence as eternal being. Not even the attributes of God may be equated with him. To assert that an attribute of God is eternal, declared Wâsil, amounts to declaring that there are two gods. It obviously follows that the Word of God must be only created, not eternal. It had come into existence at a specific time and in a specific place. God's essence – something eternal and beyond human comprehension – and God's word – created and accessible to human reason – are different. Wâsil's motive in declaring the createdness of the Qur'ân was a desire to defend the unity of God against the possibility that God could be perceived as accommodating any other eternally existing attributes or – as per Christians – persons. By the thirteenth century the theology of the Mu'tazila had virtually disappeared from Sunnî Islam. Their arguments, however, do raise the awkward question for orthodox theologians: how can there be an eternally existing phenomenon (the Word of God) besides God?

Questions also arise over the mechanics of *tanzîl*. How does God's word "come down"? We have heard the qur'ânic view that at various times and to various people via various prophets, the eternally-abiding text has been sent down by God. Supremely it has been revealed via Muḥammad in its original form – in Arabic, not translated. It is sent down an Arabic Qur'ân:

> We have made it a Qur'an in Arabic, that ye may be able to understand (and learn wisdom). (Sura 43:3)

But how does it come down? Well – through Prophet Muḥammad, over a period of 23 years:

> But those who believe and work deeds of righteousness, and believe in the (Revelation) sent down to Muḥammad – for it is the Truth from their Lord, – He will remove from them their ills and improve their condition. (Sura 47:2)

[7] Mu'tazilism tended to be fairly elitist, initially focusing on attacks on Islam from non-Muslims. Later it became focused on debating other theologies and sects within Islam. As a response to Mu'tazilism, Abû Ḥasan al-Ash'arî, initially a Mu'tazilî himself, developed his *kalâm* methodology that eventually issued in the Ash'arî school of theology. Several Shî'a sects, especially the "Twelver" sect, have adopted certain tenets of Mu'tazila beliefs and have incorporated them into their theology. Al-Zamakhsharî, a major exegete of the Qur'ân, was a Mu'tazilî.

Sending down through Prophet Muḥammad, however, is not the only description given of the process of *tanzîl*. Two other texts within the Qur'ân appear to offer a somewhat different account of that process:

> Ramadhân is the (month) in which was sent down the Qur'an, as a guide to mankind, also clear (Signs) for guidance and judgment (Between right and wrong). So every one of you who is present (at his home) during that month should spend it in fasting, but if any one is ill, or on a journey, the prescribed period (Should be made up) by days later. Allah intends every facility for you; He does not want to put you to difficulties. (He wants you) to complete the prescribed period, and to glorify Him in that He has guided you; and perchance ye shall be grateful. (Sura 2:185)

> We have indeed revealed this (Message) in the Night of Power: (Sura 97:1)

As Muḥammad 'Alî summarises, the Qur'ân by this self-describing "was revealed in the month of Ramadzân on a certain night which thenceforward received the name of *Lailat-al-Qadr* or the Grand Night".[8]

Different attempts have been made to reconcile these alternate views of how revelation proceeded. Al-Zamakhsharî proposes that the act of "sending down" takes place in two stages. Initially, the whole text is sent down from the highest heaven to the lowest heaven during the Night of Power. Then, over a period of some 23 years, the text is transmitted by the archangel Gabriel to and through Prophet Muḥammad:

> In the first stage, the holy word was sent down in one piece from the seventh heaven to the lowest heaven, which was closest to the earth and mankind. Then scribes were ordered to copy it in the *Laylat al-Qadr*, and then Gabriel took the written text piece by piece to the Prophet Muḥammad to recite it to him.[9]

This twofold process of "delivery", however, raises questions about each part of the process – the heavenly/eternal part and the earthly/temporal part. We have thought a little about some of the philosophical questions within Islam to do with asserting an eternally existing "Word" besides an only-existing God. There are also questions of the human/temporal side of the story. If the Qur'ân is God's uncreated speech existing from eternity, then it would seem to

[8] Muḥammad 'Alî, *op. cit.*, p 18. *Laylat al-Qadr* or "Night of Power" is one of three possible nights during the month of Ramaḍân: the night preceding the 25th, the 27th or the 29th of the month.

[9] Stefan Wild, (1996), *op. cit.*, p 150. "Scribes" refers to heavenly amanuenses.

be the case that all the events and conversations found within it were pre-ordained. Such a consideration is illustrated in a *ḥadîth* that purports to record Muḥammad's account of a dispute between Adam and Moses:

> Abû Hurayra reported Allah's Messenger (may peace be upon him) as saying: There was an argument between Adam and Moses (peace be upon both of them) in the presence of their Lord. Adam came the better of Moses. Moses said: Are you that Adam whom God created with His Hand and breathed into him His spirit, and commanded angels to fall in prostration before him and He made you live in Paradise with comfort and ease. Then you caused people to get down to the earth because of your lapse. Adam said: Are you that Moses whom Allah selected for His Messengership and for His conversation with him and conferred upon you the tablets, in which everything was clearly explained, and granted you the audience in order to have confidential talk with you. What is your opinion, how long Torah would have been written before I was created? Moses said: Forty years before. Adam said: Did you not see these words: Adam committed an error and he was enticed to (do so). He (Moses) said: Yes. Thereupon, he (Adam) said, Do you then blame me for an act which Allah had ordained for me forty years before He created me? Allah's Messenger (may peace be upon him) said: This is how Adam came the better of Moses.[10]

Adam concludes from Moses' recollection of the Book given to him that God (forty years prior to Adam's creation) had already ordained the Fall into which he was enticed. Yet, instead of quoting the Torah, the source quotes Sura 20:121 ("thus did Adam disobey his Lord, and allow himself to be seduced") of the Qur'ân! Maybe the assumption here is that in its pristine form, the *Torah* would have read the same as the Qur'ân. The question, however, is begged: what is the relationship between the Qur'ân and the revelations "sent down" before it? How are any differences between them to be explained in a convincing way?

A further paradox arises in the manner in which the eternally existing Qur'ân is proffered through Muḥammad. Why did Gabriel not just deliver the whole text to Muḥammad in one batch? Why take 23 years?

Such questions provoke Tariq Ramadan to distance himself from an overly literalist view of the Qur'ân. Despite his impeccable Islamist credentials (his maternal grandfather was Ḥasan al-Banna), Ramadan is concerned to explore the human facet of qur'ânic revelation:

[10] Recorded in Muslim, *al-Jâmi'al-Sahih*, vol 4, book 31, chap 603, trad 6411, p 1396.

Figure 23

Chronological revelations concerning interest/usury

Reference	Text
Sura 30:39	That which ye lay out for increase through the property of (other) people, will have no increase with Allah: but that which ye lay out for charity, seeking the Countenance of Allah, (will increase): it is these who will get a recompense multiplied.
Sura 4:160–162	For the iniquity of the Jews We made unlawful for them certain (foods) good and wholesome which had been lawful for them; – in that they hindered many from Allah's Way; – that they took usury, though they were forbidden; and that they devoured men's substance wrongfully; – we have prepared for those among them who reject faith a grievous punishment. But those among them who are well-grounded in knowledge, and the believers, believe in what hath been revealed to thee and what was revealed before thee: And (especially) those who establish regular prayer and practise regular charity and believe in Allah and in the Last Day: To them shall We soon give a great reward.
Sura 3: 130–132	O ye who believe! Devour not usury, doubled and multiplied; but fear Allah; that ye may (really) prosper. Fear the Fire, which is prepared for those who reject Faith: And obey Allah and the Messenger; that ye may obtain mercy.
Sura 2:275–281	Those who devour usury will not stand except as stand one whom the Evil one by his touch Hath driven to madness. That is because they say: "Trade is like usury," but Allah hath permitted trade and forbidden usury. Those who after receiving direction from their Lord, desist, shall be pardoned for the past; their case is for Allah (to judge); but those who repeat (The offence) are companions of the Fire: They will abide therein (for ever). Allah will deprive usury of all blessing, but will give increase for deeds of charity: For He loveth not creatures ungrateful and wicked. Those who believe, and do deeds of righteousness, and establish regular prayers and regular charity, will have their reward with their Lord: on them shall be no fear, nor shall they grieve. O ye who believe! Fear Allah, and give up what remains of your demand for usury, if ye are indeed believers. If ye do it not, Take notice of war from Allah and His Messenger: But if ye turn back, ye shall have your capital sums: Deal not unjustly, and ye shall not be dealt with unjustly. If the debtor is in a difficulty, grant him time Till it is easy for him to repay. But if ye remit it by way of charity, that is best for you if ye only knew. And fear the Day when ye shall be brought back to Allah. Then shall every soul be paid what it earned, and none shall be dealt with unjustly.

> It is, therefore, a question of reminding oneself that the Qur'ân was revealed over a span of 23 years; that there was the Makkan period and the Madinan period; that some verses precede others; that some prohibitions were revealed gradually (wine and *ribâ* for example); that, finally, the absoluteness of the Revealed Message is subject to an interpretation that takes into consideration the historical moment – and therefore relative – that gives it meaning.[11]

Ramadan points, for example, to the gradualist approach of the Qur'ân regarding the issues of interest and usury. That approach bespeaks an engagement at a human level with Muslims who, over a period, are given appropriate instructions about this aspect of their financial interaction (see figure 23). The revelation is progressive and interactive. It is relative and wrapped up with the historical moment.

The earthly side of the story of *tanzîl* at least raises the possibility that the Qur'ân is (if not the result) at least in part the record of the religious experience of Muḥammad. In that experience, personal relationships and contextual landscapes seem to play their part in promoting the sending down of relevant portions of the Qur'ân.

[11] Tariq Ramadan (trans. Saïd Amghar), *Islam, the West and the Challenges of Modernity*, The Islamic Foundation: Leicester (2001), p 336.

Chapter 10
The genius of genealogies

RECONCILING "CONTRADICTORY" PASSAGES

THE kind of questioning in chapter 9 of what it means for the Qur'ân to present a suggestion of *tanzîl* that appears in some respects to be composed of mutually incompatible elements is reflected in an equivalent interrogation of the text of the Bible. One of the major, early questions that arise when Muslims first read the New Testament concerns the genealogies of Jesus as presented by Matthew and Luke. It is a questioning that has long since preoccupied Christian exegetes. The two genealogies – of Matthew 1 and Luke 3 – are different (see figure 24).

King David constitutes a significant fulcrum-figure in both lists. Luke's genealogy begins with Adam and proceeds to David while Matthew's starts with Abraham and arrives at David. Then with David's successors, the two genealogies split. Matthew proceeds via David's son Solomon while Luke proceeds via David's son Nathan, each ending with Jesus. How can these different "lines" of heritage be explained?

One "explanation" has been constructed around the idea that in Luke's genealogy, "there are two sons improperly such".[1] The "sons" should really be called "sons-in-law" and then the two genealogies would fit together. The two culprits in Luke's listing are identified as Shealtiel, who is really son-in-law of Neri but son of Jeconiah (thus fitting with Matthew 1:12), and Joseph, who is really son-in-law of Heli but son of Jacob (thus fitting with Matthew 1:16). The making of these two amendments alone, we are informed:

> is sufficient to remove every difficulty. Thus it appears that Joseph, son of Jacob, according to Matthew, was son-in-law of Heli, according to Luke. And Salathiel [Shealtiel], son of Jechonias [Jeconiah], according to the former, was son-in-law of Neri, according to the latter. Mary therefore

[1] Gerhard Nehls and Walter Eric, *The Islamic Christian Controversy*, SIM: Nairobi (1996), p 27.

Figure 24

The genealogies of Jesus according to Matthew and Luke

Matthew (via Joseph)	Luke (via Mary)
	Adam, Seth, Enosh, Cainan, Mahalaleel, Jared, Enoch, Methuselah, Lamech, Noah, Shem, Arphaxad, Cainan, Shelah, Heber, Peleg, Reu, Serug, Nahor, Terah
Abraham, Isaac, Jacob, Judah, Perez, Hezron, Ram, Amminadab, Nahshon, Salmon, Boaz, Obed, Jesse, David	*Abraham, Isaac, Jacob, Judah, Perez, Hezron, Ram, Amminadab, Nahshon, Salmon, Boaz, Obed, Jesse, David*
Solomon	Nathan
Rehoboam, Abijah, Asa, Jehoshaphat, Joram, Uzziah, Jotham, Ahaz, Hezekiah, Manasseh, Amon, Josiah, Jeconiah	Mattatha, Menna, Melea, Eliakim, Jonam, Joseph, Judah, Simeon, Levi, Matthat, Jorim, Eliezer, Joshua, Er, Elmadam, Cosam, Addi, Melchi, Neri
Shealtiel, Zerubbabel	*Shealtiel, Zerubbabel*
Abihud	Rhesa
Eliakim, Azor, Zadok, Achim, Eliud, Eleazar, Matthan, Jacob	Joanan, Joda, Josech, Semein, Mattathias, Maath, Naggai, Hesli, Nahum, Amos, Mattathias, Joseph, Jannai, Melchi, Levi, Matthat, Heli
Joseph	*Joseph* ("as it was thought")
Jesus	*Jesus*

> appears to have been the daughter of Heli, so called by abbreviation for Heliachim, which is the same in Hebrew with Joachim. Joseph, son of Jacob, and Mary, daughter of Heli, were of the same family. Both came from Zerubbabel; Joseph from Abiud [Abihud], his eldest son, Mt 1.13; and Mary by Rhesa, the youngest.[2]

Another of the most common explanations is made by drawing a distinction between what is termed "the legal line" (described by Matthew as running from Abraham through David and Solomon to Jesus) and "the biological line" (described by Luke as running from

[2] *Ibid.*, p 28 where the authors quote Adam Clark, *Holy Bible: containing the old and new Testaments with a commentary and critical notes designed as a help to a better understanding of the sacred writings*, Abingdon (n.d.), vol 3, pp 861–862.

Adam through David and Nathan to Jesus). This idea of two different genres of genealogy is reinforced by an appeal to the phrase "so it was thought" in Luke 3:23:

> Now Jesus himself was about thirty years old when he began his ministry. He was the son, so it was thought, of Joseph . . .

The "so it was thought" phrase is taken to signify that, in fact, the genealogy that is about to follow is not that of Joseph but that of Mary. Why? Because Jesus cannot be considered the *biological* son of Joseph, but only of Mary. Moreover, the descendancy via Joseph (the genealogy from Matthew) is held to be compromised in another sense. Partway through the list from David to Joseph comes the name Jeconiah (Matthew 1:11–12). A famous prophesy by Jeremiah records a curse upon this man (there called Coniah), such that none of his descendants would ever "sit on the throne of David or rule anymore in Judah" (Jeremiah 22:30). The "curse" at least raises the possibility that true Messiah could not conceivably come via this man's line of descent. Matthew's genealogy concedes this possibility, making the neat point that Jesus is not in fact a biological descendant of Jeconiah. He is descended biologically from David via the other lineage, that of Mary (as offered by Luke). However, the legal adoption of Jesus by Joseph accrued the legal rights of Joseph (as a descendant of David) to Jesus as his "son". So Jesus is legally but not biologically a descendant of David through his adoptive human father, Joseph.

The "solutions" arrived at above proceed by seeking to harmonise the two Gospel accounts of Jesus' heritage. There may be merit in such harmonisation, especially if one feels that one single, overarching explanation is what is required. That kind of requirement does, however, beg the question of why the Holy Spirit thought that four independent (though to varying degrees related) accounts of Jesus' life and ministry were appropriate. Why does the Holy Spirit, in this instance, inspire two different approaches to defining Jesus' "heritage"? As Goldingay intimates:

> Matthew and Luke offer markedly different accounts of Jesus' birth, the beginning of his ministry, and his resurrection appearances. If the interpretive task concentrates on looking behind these differences or harmonizing them, it ceases to follow the story Matthew or Luke told and to open itself to the world they portrayed.[3]

[3] Goldingay, *op. cit.*, p 17.

It seems to me that the key clue to the two genealogies (of Matthew and Luke) lies precisely in their clear, individual constructions of that heritage: Matthew begins his list with Abraham and moves forward in contrived groups of names to Jesus, while Luke begins with Jesus and works backwards through many (biblically) unknown characters to Adam. Perhaps one might also ask why, if Matthew and Luke both had access to Mark's Gospel when they composed their own, did they each insist on adding a genealogical record? After all, Mark was content with Jesus' baptism as the starting-point for his life of Christ. Matthew, however, backs up and begins his Gospel with a genealogy, prior to describing the birth of Jesus. Luke, different again, gets as far as describing the baptism of Jesus, having begun with birth stories for not only Jesus but John the Baptist also, and then he suddenly inserts his genealogy of Jesus.

What is the point of the insistence on Jesus' heritage stretching neatly back to Abraham (in Matthew) or obscurely back to Adam (in Luke)? Of course, when you look into those individual lists of Matthew and Luke, there are plenty of historical omissions – so the genealogies cannot be intended to constitute a strict kind of linear pedigree. They are trying to say something else. That "something else", I would suggest, is a theological point. They are trying to say something significant, theologically, about Jesus. The Gospels of Matthew and Luke, composed after Mark's early account, add emphases or incidents or use different ways of describing the same or similar events in order to say something specific to their contemporaries.

It is commonly thought that Matthew wrote primarily for a Jewish readership while Luke was more concerned with communicating to non-Jews. Matthew certainly emphasises Jesus' pedigree as Son of Abraham, Son of David and answer to Israel's exile. In a sense, Matthew does the readers' exegetical work for them. He serves up his genealogy in selected groups of "fourteen" generations, and then, at its conclusion, summarises Israel's history via patriarchs, monarchy and exile: "Thus there were fourteen generations in all from Abraham to David, fourteen from David to the exile to Babylon, and fourteen from the exile to the Christ" (Matthew 1:17). Luke, on the other hand, seems less interested in the Jewish concern for a Messiah proceeding from the royal line of David – after all, he neglects the descent from David to Messiah via Solomon and goes instead for a descent via another son of David, Nathan. Beyond that shift, we are provoked to consider his selective listing of precursors of Jesus back to Adam, "the son of God" (Luke 3:37). As you finish reading Luke's genealogy, that phrase is left ringing in your ears. What did Luke mean by it?

There are many suggestions as to the various purposes lying behind Matthew's and Luke's constructions of genealogy. I will briefly mention a couple of possibilities here that I find attractive. With regard to Matthew, could it be that he is seeking, via his genealogy, to answer the question "How is Jesus the Son of God?" in a way that avoids an adoptionist view of Jesus as recruited to divinity? After all, if you only have Mark's Gospel in front of you, it would be very easy to conclude that at his baptism, Jesus was "adopted" by the heavenly Father as his Son. The Father declared (made?) Jesus his Son there at the Jordan riverside. Mark does not mention Christ's pre-existence (as divine Son), nor his virgin birth – not his birth at all in fact – nor in the most reliable, earliest manuscripts does he give any account of the bodily appearances of the resurrected Jesus. We know that there were early Christian groups that seemed to have made some such kind of adoptionist conclusion from their appreciation of Mark's Gospel. The Ebionites (a Jewish-Christian sect) and the later "Dynamic Monarchianists" of the second and third centuries claimed that Jesus was adopted as Son of God at his baptism. The Nag Hammadi documents have yielded, amongst other texts, the *Second Treatise of the Great Seth*. This mid-second century treatise insisted that "Jesus" and "Christ" were two different entities. At his baptism, the human Jesus received the heavenly Christ who indwelt him and empowered him for ministry before leaving him at some point prior to his crucifixion. Irenaeus specifically records that some such groups used Mark's Gospel to the near exclusion of the other three.[4]

Back to Matthew! Is this Gospel compiler trying to clarify that Jesus certainly is Son of God – but not in an adoptionist sense? The clue to this thought lies in Matthew's allusion to four special women as he develops his genealogy. Such reference is in itself an unusual procedure within a patriarchal frame of reference.[5] The four women concerned – Tamar, Rahab, Ruth and Uriah's wife (Bathsheba) – raised delicate issues for Jews about the ancestry of the expected

[4] *Irenaeus Against Heresies*, Kessenger Publishing [e-book], vol 3, chap 11, part 7, p 29.

[5] See my fuller investigation of Matthew's genealogy from a cultural perspective in Bill Musk, *Touching the Soul of Islam*, Monarch: Oxford (2004), pp 53–55.

Messiah. In each case (less perhaps with Ruth on one count), there were questions about their origins (as outside the people of Israel) and serious questions about their involvement in shameful sexual activities. Jewish tradition sought to uncover and relate the fate of each of these women. All four of them came to occupy an important place in later Jewish speculation – speculation that became strongly polemical. The Pharisees tended to expect a Davidic Messiah, but that meant that they had to accept or explain a somewhat contaminated line via David to Messiah – contaminated because of the involvement of these women. The Sadducees and Essenes tended to support the idea of a Levitical Messiah, and one of the strong arguments on which they capitalised in their polemics against the Pharisees was that these four women constituted an unacceptable blot on the Davidic ancestry.

Perhaps Matthew, in naming these four women so prominently – so shockingly – in his genealogy, is seeking to show that, in fact, in every respect the Pharisaic expectation of the Messiah as David's "son" had been fulfilled in Jesus of Nazareth. The compiler of Matthew's Gospel is certainly familiar with Jewish Rabbinic thinking. He serves up the body of his Gospel around five blocks of teaching that balance the words of Jesus with those of the great Moses, former teacher of Israel. Perhaps Matthew is saying via his genealogy: "No! Jesus wasn't adopted as Son or Messiah at his baptism! Look at the details of his genealogy as I summarise them. He fits perfectly with the 'Messiah' that so many of the Rabbis have been expecting. He is truly Messiah, truly David's Son!" If that is so, the Gospel writer conveys the additional implication that God is not put off from his purposes via Messiah through the inclusion of foreigners or women in the messy pre-history to his earthly appearing. God is gracious in embracing of all humanity in his giving of Jewish Messiah. What an implication!

And Luke? Luke inserts his genealogy in the middle of an account (Mark's?) of Jesus' baptism. His editorial action is obviously provoked by his recording of the voice that comes from heaven at Jesus' baptism: " 'You are my Son, whom I love; with you I am well pleased'." (Luke 3:22) Jesus as "Son of God" – just declared from heaven at the baptism – becomes the theme and goal of Luke's genealogy. Luke traces Jesus' heritage back through Adam, "the son of God" (Luke 3:37).

Again we note that Luke does not speak of Jesus as Son of God because he was pre-existent (that great theme will come, of course, only with the Gospel-writer John) nor because of any physical relationship between Father and Son. Rather, he declares him "Son of God" through a long line of Old Testament patriarchs and post-biblical historical figures. This genealogy, as we have already noted, ignores the royal line of Judah and focuses instead on Nathan, David's third son. It proceeds through unknown names to Shealtiel and Zerubbabel and then through more unknown names to Joseph.

The significant name is that of Nathan. We know that in late Old Testament times there was an important clan in Judah that traced its descent from Nathan (Zechariah 12:12). There also came to exist a Jewish tradition that brought together the identities of the two Nathans of the book of 2 Samuel – Nathan the third son of David, and Nathan the outstanding prophet of David's reign. This double "Nathan" especially came to figure in polemics between the priestly Hasmoneans and their opponents during the rulership of the later Maccabees, in the inter-testamental period. The Hasmoneans accused the "royal line" supporters of taint because of the Ammonite ancestry of Rehoboam through his mother, Naamah, the Ammonitess, wife of Solomon. The anti-Hasmoneans tried to evade the charge by declaring that Messiah would descend from David not via Solomon but via Nathan.

Was Luke picking up something of this "background noise" in his declaration of Jesus as Son of God in the sense of his being Messiah via Nathan's lineage – the prophetic line? Luke certainly has a strong emphasis on the prophetic ministry of Jesus. He presents Jesus' ministry in large part as a prophetic ministry. From its very inception Jesus opens up the identification: " 'I tell you the truth . . . no prophet is accepted in his home town'." (Luke 4:24) After the resurrection, the risen Christ hears two of his disillusioned disciples rueing the failure of his ministry as they walk together towards Emmaus: " 'He was a prophet, powerful in word and deed before God and all the people'." (Luke 24:19) Jesus comes across in Luke's writings as the eschatological[6] prophet, the Moses-prophet. In Peter's speech at the temple after the healing of the crippled beggar, Jesus is explicitly presented in such terms: "For Moses said, 'The Lord your God will raise up for you a prophet like me from among your own people; you must listen to everything he tells you'." (Acts 3:22)

[6] Eschatology has to do with the end-times, the bringing to judgement before God of the human race.

Was Luke aware of the Jewish identification of the Davidic Nathan with the prophet of the same name and did he play on that identification in the way his account of Jesus' life is constructed? What is more, through an emphasis upon Nathan as providing the line of descent from royal David, Luke is able to insist on Jesus as Messiah without opening himself to any charge from a gentile Roman readership that he was promoting in his Gospel a view of Jesus as a royal-political Messiah. He cannot be accused of playing the "Jewish" card in a world of nervous, Roman, imperial overlords.

I don't know how far such considerations concerning the genealogies recorded by Matthew and Luke are true in themselves or convincing in their suggestiveness. They certainly provoke a lot of reflection upon the text – they force the reader to ask: "Why is the Gospel-writer presenting Jesus Christ like this?" What is important, it seems to me, is for us to accept the possibility that some such processes of reasoning or editing lay behind why Luke interrupted his account of the baptism of Jesus to insert his particular "take" on Jesus' genealogy, and why Matthew precedes his whole document with his own provocatively-constructed alternative. Both Matthew and Luke were "doing theology" in putting together their accounts in such ways.

What I am asking is whether an equivalent grappling with the holy text of Islam might be allowed? The text is a given, for sure. No one is quibbling about that. But in the bringing down of that text, the experience and history and purpose of its human reciter – Prophet Muḥammad – form part of the equation. In his experience, in certain circumstances, there is a dialogue going on, and "for such a time as this" the angel passes on particular revelation. Such grappling with the qur'ânic text requires the foregoing of an uncritical hermeneutic of certainty. Without some such discussion, the Qur'ân remains beyond reasonable critiquing and consequently an instrument easily held hostage to the literalist interpretations of the Islamists.

Tariq Ramadan would appear to constitute one Muslim commentator who thinks along such lines. Forced, perhaps, by his participation as part of a Muslim minority in a post-modern Europe to think through his faith in a quite radical manner, Ramadan aspires to lead Western Muslims towards a faithful-but-enlightened approach to the Qur'ân:

> Certain verses (actually a minority) leave no scope for interpretation, or at least only a very narrow one. But the great majority demand real interpretive effort, and that on several levels: the meaning of the words, the general meaning of the instruction, the context in which it was revealed, the universal aspect of the principle (and consequently the temporal aspect of the manner of its application), its logical setting within the global meaning of the Qur'anic message and the Prophetic traditions (*Sunna*), and so on.[7]

Grappling with the holy text of Islam is nothing new, really. It is just that it can look very suspect unless one has the kind of credentials of a Tariq Ramadan. Does he remain at liberty to provide an alternative-to-the-literalist approach only because he lives in Switzerland?

We need to move to the final section of this book: "certain believing amid uncertainty." Is it possible to come to a position where one might live a confident life of faith, yet be immersed in or surrounded by uncertainty? Is it possible for convinced Muslims or Christians to escape the certainty trap? We begin our exploration of such questions with a consideration of Muslims of Ramadan's ilk who have sought, in different ways, to answer the Islamists.

[7] Tariq Ramadan, *Western Muslims and the Future of Islam*, Oxford University Press: Oxford (2004), p 22.

Certain believing amid uncertainty

Chapter 11

Answering the Islamists

AS we have seen, for the most part, Muslim political leaders and religious clerics have viewed the Islamists primarily as a security problem. Silencing them has been the main goal of such authority figures. Their common response has been to lock the Islamists away, or execute them. A few Muslims have, of course, tried to have a different voice.

Maḥmûd Muḥammad Tâhâ proposed a fascinating re-reading of the Qur'ân. He said, in effect, that the verses given by God to Muḥammad while the prophet was struggling to survive in Mecca constituted the original or "best" conveyance of God's word and will. The material sent down to Prophet Muḥammad after he had managed to escape to Medina amounted to a concession. People were evidently not ready for God's best, so God gave them his second-best. Out of the Medinan *tanzîl* came all the material on which the Islamists (especially) base their claims to literal obedience to God's word. The interesting thing to note here is that Tâhâ's reconstruction came to be stated in the context of political changes in the Sudan that were being fuelled by an Islamist approach to the reading of the Qur'ân and to the ordering of society. In a real sense, then, Tâhâ's work constitutes at least a counterpoint, if not a direct response to, the Islamist perspective. As we have sadly noted, Tâhâ paid with his life for his reconstructionist views.

Other Muslims have stood back from their inherited, literalist view of the Qur'ân and have sought to propose other readings of it. We will mention a few such theologians here, representative of radically different approaches. Each theologian concerned was stimulated to rethink his reading of the Qur'ân by having to come to terms with the real-life context in which he found himself.

RE-READING THE QUR'ÂN – AN IRANIAN CONTRIBUTION

In Iran in the years 1965–1977, a significant re-reading of the Qur'ân took place in the mind of 'Alî Shari'ati. This gentleman was born in Mazinan, Iran, in 1933 and educated in Mashhad, where he grew to know fellow students from poor backgrounds. Their poverty made a lasting impression upon him. After high school, teachers' training college and university studies in Mashhad, Shariʿati travelled abroad to undertake postgraduate studies in Paris. There, Shariʿati got to grips with the analytical and critical school of French sociology. He emerged from his doctoral studies with a strong understanding of the Western sociological approaches to analysing society. He also emerged with a deep conviction that Western models were totally inappropriate for coming to terms with a culture that was rooted in Islam. He returned to Iran in 1964 and worked hard to come up with a re-reading of the Qur'ân that would appeal to the impoverished masses of his tyrannically-ruled nation. Shariʿati helped to establish a centre for religious debate in Tehran and frequently travelled there from Mashhad to lecture. His talks were delivered to thousands of enthusiastic students and then distributed throughout the country via mimeographed copies. His first book quickly sold 60,000 copies. Shariʿati paid a high price for his original thinking and his popularity, however, and ended his life in exile in England. It is possible that his death there resulted from murder.

Shariʿati's aim was to find within Islam a valid, indigenous worldview that would be vigorous enough to counter the two options then on offer from the West, namely capitalism and communism. He saw both those options as humanistic and, consequently, spiritually bankrupt:

> We are clearly standing on the frontier between two eras – one where both Western civilization and communist ideology have failed to liberate humanity, drawing it instead into disaster and causing the new spirit to recoil in disillusionment; and one where humanity in search of deliverance will try a new road and take a new direction, and will liberate its essential nature. Over this dark and dispirited world, it will set a holy lamp like a new sun; by its light, the man alienated from himself will perceive anew his primordial nature, rediscover himself, and see clearly the path of salvation.[1]

Shariʿati felt that he could discover a radically different, and original, worldview within Islam – indeed, from within the Qur'ân. Shariʿati's target audience comprised the "followers" of Islam, the masses, people like those he had grown to know in Mashhad. In his

[1] In ʿAlî Shariʿati, *Marxism and Other Western Fallacies*, translated by R Campbell, Mizan Press: Berkeley (1980), p 95.

view, Prophet Muḥammad's vindication and authentication came because at a critical point in his life the masses heeded his words and followed him in exodus (*hijra*). The final sura of the Qur'ân (one of the earliest, chronologically) provides a major point of departure for Shari'ati's philosophy:

> Say: I seek refuge with the Lord and Cherisher of Mankind [*al-nâs*], The King (or Ruler) of Mankind [*al-nâs*], The God (or judge) of Mankind [*al-nâs*], – From the mischief of the Whisperer (of Evil), who withdraws (after his whisper), – (The same) who whispers into the hearts of Mankind [*al-nâs*], – Among Jinns and among men [*al-nâs*]. (Sura 114)

For Shari'ati, the qur'ânic address is being made to *al-nâs*, "the people." The Prophet is sent to *al-nâs* who are accountable for their deeds – in short, the whole responsibility for society and history is borne by *al-nâs*. The Qur'ân, he declared, begins in the name of God and ends in the name of the people.

Shari'ati longed for, and worked towards, a people, a mass, who would be aware of injustice and alienation, and critical of the manipulative ideologies currently being exported by the West to other nations. He wanted ordinary believers to realise their rich heritage as Muslims and awaken to their responsibility for carrying the Islamic vision of *tawḥîd*[2] into reality in an Iran gone wrong. The vanguard of that re-invigorated people was to be composed of the youth: students and other young Muslims. Shari'ati's Islam was that of the Muslim freedom fighter as distinct from the reactionary Islamism promulgated by the ulema.[3] Shari'ati sought to formulate a radical Islamic ideology as a first and most important step towards effecting social change:

> . . . the object of ideologizing Islam was to raise one's own consciousness but also to impart intellectual and social enlightenment to the masses. An Islamic ideology which could raise the consciousness of the people, he asserted, would create a liberating movement . . .[4]

The Islamic vision of *tawḥîd*, or wholeness, in which all of life is viewed from a spiritual perspective, was, in Shari'ati's thinking, the wellspring for a worldview different from capitalism or communism. In that worldview, humankind has a defined and wholesome place

[2] *tawḥîd* conveys a sense of "unity" in the oneness of God and, by implication, the potential holism of all creation in realising its theocentric nature.

[3] The body of Muslim doctors of sacred law and theology.

[4] Quoted by Ali Rahnema in *An Islamic Utopian: a Political Biography of Ali Shari'ati*, IB Tauris: London (1998), p 288.

as a created being who is appointed vice-regent on earth by his creator. Shari'ati sought a return to early Shî'ism, the system that existed before the Umayyads plunged Islam into decadence and tyranny. He contrasted that earlier "'Alid Shî'ism" (from 'Alî, the son-in-law of Prophet Muḥammad and the first *Imâm*) with "Safavid Shî'ism" (from the Safavids, whose Persian Empire existed from AD 1499 to 1736). It was a comparison between pure, original Islam and the diluted, institutionalised Islam of the Safavids. The Shî'ism of 'Alî represented an oppositional force challenging the ruling system and its repressive institutions. Safavid Shî'ism represented official state religion in which the incumbent clergy had become members of the ruling class defending the status quo. In Shari'ati's view, the Safavid type of Islam was inherited and embellished by the Pahlavis. It became, under them, an instrument of political enslavement *par excellence*.

By his exegesis of the positive qualities of "'Alid Shî'ism", Shari'ati dissociated himself from the contemporary, institutionalised, official Islam hated by idealistic Iranians, especially the youth. He also infused original Shî'a concepts with new meaning and force. So, for example, "prayer" in his reference to it carried political overtones, implying positive action. The annual *'Âshûrâ'* ceremonies emphasised the idea of fighting and dying for a just cause rather than simply a commemoration of the martyrdom of Husayn. The strongly motivational Shî'a concept of the imamate he interpreted as a concept of revolutionary leadership. He exegeted the Iranian idea of *intizar*, or "longing" for the Twelfth Imam, as a revolutionary posture defying the status quo. His approach proved very attractive to significant sections of Iranian society.

Although Shari'ati's interpretation of *tawḥîd* and his stirring of the masses against the Shah came to be totally and cruelly eclipsed by the thinking and role of Imam Khomeini, it would be hard to overstate the significance of Shari'ati's contribution to the groundswell of opposition to the Pahlavi regime. He offered an alternative, validly Shî'a, view that derived its construct and its authority from the Qur'ân. He demonstrated a radically different hermeneutical process from both the orthodox and the revolutionary clerics.

RE-READING THE QUR'ÂN – AN EGYPTIAN TALE

For the most part, open questioning of the received interpretation of the qur'ânic text has hardly been possible within the Islamic world. Tâhâ Ḥusayn (AD 1889–1973), for example, is often celebrated as the doyen of Arabic literature and one of the most significant figures of recent Egyptian cultural and intellectual history. His writings, however, often enraged the many religious conservatives of his day. His poetry and novels reflected a strong discontentment with his own experience of being educated in an Islamic school and at the ultra-conservative al-Azhar university. He waged many battles for enlightenment, for respect for reason and thought, and for women's emancipation. His book *Pre-Islamic Poetry* (published 1926 on his return from postgraduate studies in Paris) is typical of Ḥusayn's provocative literature. He adopted a Western scientific methodology in dealing with his subject and came up with a highly controversial text. In *Pre-Islamic Poetry*, Ḥusayn questioned the authenticity of the entire body of pre-Islamic poetry. He suggested that the material was actually composed after the Qur'ân had been revealed to Muḥammad. A late date for such poetry challenged traditional assumptions about how the Qur'ân fitted into Arabic literary history. The suggestion that Muslims possibly fabricated the poetry of the pagan Arabs after the revelation of the Qur'ân in order to make the latter look spectacular constituted a sensational provocation. Even more provocatively, Ḥusayn argued that the qur'ânic story of Abraham's arrival in Mecca with his wife Hagar and infant son Ishmael was really an oral narrative that pre-dated the giving of the Qur'ân.

The dispute caused by Ḥusayn's book reached the Egyptian Parliament where its author was accused of insulting Islam. The public attorney, however, decided not to prosecute Ḥusayn, concluding that Ḥusayn was innocent of any criminal intention against Islam. Ḥusayn was, nonetheless, forced to re-write his book, omitting the story of Abraham and Hagar bringing Ishmael to Mecca. The new edition had a new name: *Pre-Islamic Literature*.[5] Perhaps Tâhâ Ḥusayn got off with such a lenient punishment because he was primarily an author of literature, not a theologian.

[5] Tâhâ Ḥusayn, *Pre-Islamic Poetry* (in Arabic), Dar al-Ma'arif: Cairo (1926) and Tâhâ Ḥusayn, *Pre-Islamic Literature* (in Arabic), Dar al-Ma'arif: Cairo (1927).

Twenty years later a young scholar named Muḥammad Aḥmad Khalafallah presented his PhD thesis to the examining board in the Department of Arabic at Cairo University. It was entitled "The Art of Narration in the Qur'ân." Khalafallah explored using a literary approach in order to find meaning in the Qur'ân. The core of his thesis consisted in making a clear distinction between history and story within the Qur'ân. The university rejected his thesis and declared that such an approach when studying the holy text casts doubt on the authenticity and divinity of the Qur'ân. The university dismissed Khalafallah, transferring him to a non-teaching position within the Ministry of Education. Khalafallah's professor (Amîn al-Khulî) was forbidden to teach or supervise theses in Islamic studies. Khalafallah wrote an alternative thesis in order to obtain his degree.

At least Ḥusayn and Khalafallah were permitted to remain within the worlds of literature and education, within Egypt, after their respective experiences of castigation and rehabilitation. Nasr Abû Zaid found no equivalent possibility of remaining either within the university where he worked, nor even within his homeland, once the kind of thinking that he was doing became known. Abû Zaid wrote his Master's thesis on the concept of metaphor as it had come to be applied to Arabic rhetoric by the rationalist Mu'tazilâ. His thesis was later published as *The Trend of Rational Exegesis of the Qur'an.*[6] The departure point for Abû Zaid's thinking on this matter came in Sura 3:7 – the point in the Qur'ân in which, as we have seen, the unambiguous verses (*ayât muḥkamât*) confront the ambiguous verses (*ayât mutashâbiḥât*). There is no argument within Islam that ambiguous verses are to be interpreted in the light of unambiguous verses. Abû Zaid discerned that the Mu'tazilâ and their critics each brought different worldviews to their understanding of this text. What the Mu'tazila considered unambiguous, their opponents considered ambiguous, and vice versa. Abû Zaid concluded that each side attempted to bring the Qur'ân in line with its own *a priori* philosophical or theological beliefs. This raised a question for him of how the meaning of a text could be so easily manipulated. For his PhD research, Abû Zaid examined the hermeneutics of the Qur'ân as expressed in the thinking of Ibn al-

[6] Nasr Hamid Abû Zaid, *The Trend of Rational Exegesis of the Qur'an: A Study of the Mu'tazilite's Concept of Qur'anic Metaphor*, The Arabic Cultural Centre: Beirut (1982).

'Arabî, an Andalusian Ṣûfî theologian.[7] Abû Zaid proposed to study the hermeneutics of the Qur'ân from a mystical (Ṣûfî) perspective. Abû Zaid's conclusion, borne out of his academic research, was that all interpretation of text (the Qur'ân included) is informed by contemporary socio-political and cultural factors. Ibn al-'Arabî, he noted, wanted to ensure that Islam was an open-ended faith, reconciled with Christianity, Judaism and other religions. He therefore attempted to collect various facets of thought from Christianity, Judaism, Islam and other faiths adhered to within his society and integrate them into a unified Islamic system. His goal was to deduce a "religion of comprehensive love".[8]

As an Egyptian living in the 1960s and 1970s, Abû Zaid felt that he could see a similar process of working-out of the meaning of Islam in his own day. In the 1960s, the dominant religious discourse in Egypt presented Islam as the religion of social justice, urging its followers to fight imperialism and Zionism. In the 1970s, with the open door economic policy and peace with Israel, Islam became the religion that guarded private property and urged Muslims to make peace with the Israelis. Abû Zaid took another look at the Qur'ân.

His third book came from this investigation. It was entitled *The Concept of the Text: a Reinvestigation of Classical Qur'anic Disciplines*.[9] At its heart lay the conviction that before dealing with questions of interpretation, one must first define the nature of the text, plus examine the rules governing the study of that text. How did the various *mushafs* (books in which the Qur'ân is written) circulating among Prophet Muḥammad's followers at the time of his death eventuate in the standardised text in the standardised dialect that emanated from the editorial work commissioned by 'Uthmân, the third caliph?

No text comes free from historical context. As text, the Qur'ân is no exception to this reality. It is therefore a proper subject for interpretative study. Indeed, throughout its history, the Qur'ân has been subjected to the constructs of various schools of interpretation.

[7] The title of Abû Zaid's PhD thesis was *The Hermeneutics of the Quran by Muhyi al-Dîn Ibn al-'Arabi'*. Al-'Arabî's own great treatise was entitled *al-Futuhât al-Makkah* or *The Meccan Revelation*. Al-'Arabî died in Syria in AD 1279. Abû Zaid's thesis was later published as *The Philosophy of Hermeneutics*, The Arabic Cultural Centre: Beirut (1983).

[8] Abû Zaid quotes Ibn 'Arabî thus in Abû Zaid (2004), *op. cit.*, p 58.

[9] *Mafhûm al-Nass; Dirasah fî 'Ulûm al-Qur'ân*, Egyptian Public Organisation for Books: Cairo (1990).

Abû Zaid set out to investigate these within their historical contexts. As a result of his study, he argued for a human dimension to the Qur'ân in which the text needs to be interpreted by taking into account the cultural context in which it evolved. He also came to the personal conclusion that the text needs to be understood metaphorically rather than literally. His critical analysis of modern Islamic discourse was published in 1992,[10] and Abû Zaid's troubles exploded into the open.

On the basis of his prodigious output of scholarly material, Abû Zaid applied in May, 1992 for a professorship at the University of Cairo – until then he had held the humble post of lecturer in that academic institution. An advisory committee not only refused to recommend his promotion but actually accused Abû Zaid of

Figure 25

The Egyptian Supreme Court's decision on Abû Zaid's "apostasy"

	Reason given for upholding the conviction
1	Describing certain things mentioned in the Qur'ân, such as the throne of God, angels, devils, jinn, paradise, and hell, as myths of the past.
2	Calling the Qur'ân a cultural product, thereby denying its pre-existence in the preserved Tablet.
3	Calling the Qur'ân a linguistic text. [The implication is that the Prophet lied about receiving revelations directly from God]
4	Calling the qur'ânic sciences a "reactionary heritage," and saying that the *sharî'a* is the cause of Muslims' backwardness and decline.
5	Saying that a belief in the supernatural reflects a mind submerged in myth.
6	Calling Islam an Arabic religion, thus denying its universality.
7	Asserting that the final version of the Qur'ân was established in the Qurayshî idiom in order to assert the supremacy of the Quraysh tribe.
8	Denying the authenticity of the *sunna*.
9	Calling for emancipation from the authority of religious texts.
10	Contending that submitting to religious text is a form of slavery.

[10] Published as *Naqd al-Khitab al-Dînî* or *Critique of Islamic Discourse*, Cairo (1992).

producing material that was "against Islam".[11] Within weeks, Abû Zaid was pronounced an apostate (*murtad*) from the pulpits of various mosques. That pronunciation was eventually upheld at the Court of Appeal in Cairo in 1995. Abû Zaid had no choice but to flee for his life with his wife to the Netherlands where he now teaches as a professor of Arabic and Islamic Studies at Leiden University.[12] In 1996, in Abû Zaid's absence, the Egyptian Supreme Court upheld the Appeal Court's finding. Ten reasons were given for upholding the conviction (see figure 25).[13]

The politics of the interpretation of the Qur'ân – almost yesterday – claimed another victim!

RE-READING THE QUR'ÂN – AN ALGERIAN IN FRANCE

Some Islamic scholars, living outside the Muslim context, have managed to raise the hermeneutical issue with less overt restraint. Mohammed Arkoun, French academician of Algerian origin, is Emeritus Professor of the History of Islamic Thought at the Sorbonne. A modernist and critical voice in the contemporary world, he has been associated with several European initiatives to rethink and reshape the relationship between Europe, Islam and the Mediterranean world. His success in shaping Western scholarship on Islam on the one hand is mirrored on the other by a highly critical suspicion of his secularist approach within traditional Islamic intellectual circles. "Understanding Islam" means, for Arkoun, analysing the way in which the "Qur'ânic fact" became transcendentalised. He is interested in how the Qur'ân came to be accepted as a foundation for divine law and proclaimed as a universal truth – and why certain interpretations of the revelational fact ultimately prevailed, whereas alternative understandings disappeared from history. Arkoun's

[11] The voice of Dr 'Abd al-Sabur Shahin – professor in the College of Dâr al-'Ulûm and a fundamentalist preacher at the Amr ibn al-'Âṣ mosque in Old Cairo – came to dominate the committee's findings. There are complicated, historical reasons for his personal dislike of Abû Zaid. Perhaps most significant is the fact that Abû Zaid, in the introduction to his book *Critique of Islamic Discourse*, drew attention to the relationship between political Islamist discourse in Egypt and an economic scandal brought about by Islamic investment companies that had replaced Westernised banks in the country. In 1988 many people lost their savings in a huge public scandal involving these banks. The banks included one with which Shahin was associated!

[12] A full account of Abû Zaid's experience may be found in Nasr Abu Zaid with Esther R. Nelson, *Voice of an Exile: Reflections on Islam*, Praeger: Westport, Connecticut (2004).

[13] *Ibid.*, pp 9–10. The words in the figure are verbatim.

conclusion is that Islam belongs to the contested field of meaning and legitimacy, in which state power always seeks to reduce it to a single set of symbols. The unity and uniformity of Islam, in that case, derives from its historical role as a legitimising ideology for political power-holders. In his recent book, *The Unthought in Contemporary Islamic Thought*,[14] Arkoun proposes that the entire development of Muslim thought, from the qur'ânic worldview to the range of contemporary discourses (including that of the Islamists), be subjected to critical analysis. That analysis, he hopes, will engender a discussion as to how Islamic studies and thought can be brought to the level of the fertile criticisms witnessed in European scholarship and historical development since the seventeenth century. He opens his volume with two chapters designed to "problematise" the larger category of revelation by concentrating on the example of the Qur'ân. Arkoun proposes a programme of research aimed at constructing a new field for the comparative study of revelation as a historic, linguistic, cultural and anthropological articulation of thought, common to Christianity, Judaism and Islam:

> My purpose . . . is to reverse the approach of Revelation from the dogmatic theological systems developed by competing, opposed, self-promoting ethno-cultural groups during the Middle Ages, to the critical, deconstructive analysis of social sciences applied to the rich topic of religious phenomena.[15]

Arkoun wants to liberate reason from the grip of dogmatic postulates, but it is obvious that he can only pursue this daring exercise within the freedom and safety of a European academic institution.

RE-READING THE QUR'ÂN – A PAKISTANI IN AMERICA

Fazlur Rahman Malak (AD 1911–1988) – of Pakistani origins – is probably the most well known of recent Muslim theologians who have queried the "received" interpretation of the Qur'ân. Rahman came from a Pakistani family steeped in traditional Islamic learning. He balanced that rich background with studies under H.A.R. Gibb at Oxford where he was exposed to Western critical thinking. In the early 1960s, Rahman was appointed by President Ayub Khan to the

[14] Mohammed Arkoun, *The Unthought in Contemporary Islamic Thought*, Saqi Books: London (2002).

[15] *Ibid.*, p 30.

post of Director of the Central Institute for Islamic Research in Pakistan with a view to establishing a reformist syllabus for Islamic tertiary education in the country. Rahman sought to build a religiously-committed but critical scholarship in Pakistan that would be on a par with Western academies of excellence. He proceeded by looking at the basic tools of Islamic intellectual inquiry – namely, the Qur'ân, the *sunna*, *ijtihâd*, and *ijma'*. As Rahman's period of tenure (AD 1962–1968) progressed, the Pakistani ulema strongly rejected his approach to Qur'ân interpretation and there were large demonstrations against him. Rahman moved to the United States of America in order to pursue his vision of an Islamic modernity that could stand up to Western modernity. From 1969 until his death he held the post of Professor of Islamic Thought at the University of Chicago.

Early in his intellectual career Rahman grew angry at the scholastic rigidity of qur'ânic studies in the Muslim world. He commented that it "is notorious how frequently Muslims themselves, let alone Westerners, have mutilated the Qur'ân by projecting their own points of view or that of their 'schools of thought' on the text".[16] Rahman rejected the idea of the uncreatedness of the Qur'ân and asserted an active role for Prophet Muḥammad in the process of "sending down". If revelation descended upon Muḥammad's heart, as the Qur'ân asserts, then the man must have been heartily involved. Moreover, Prophet Muḥammad could not help but be involved as a person living in a specific context. The Qur'ân was thus the word of God and also the word of Muḥammad. The completed text amounts to a response to early stages of the Islamic community that were historically recorded. It consists of moral, religious and social pronouncements that were designed to answer specific problems that arose during those early stages. Most qur'ânic responses to questions or problems are, according to Rahman, "stated in terms of an explicit or semiexplicit *ratio legis*"[17] designed to address concrete issues.[18] Through an examination of the original, localised occasions for revelation, one can come to understand the rationale

[16] Fazlur Rahman, *Major Themes of the Qur'ân*, Bibliotheca Islamica: Minneapolis (1980), p 16.

[17] *Ratio legis* or "reasoning of law"; the underlying principle or basis of a law.

[18] Fazlur Rahman, *Islam and Modernity: Transformation of an Intellectual Tradition*, University of Chicago Press: Chicago (1982), pp 5–6. Rahman objects to the position taken by most Qur'ân commentators that although an injunction might have been occasioned by a certain situation, it is nevertheless universal in its general application.

for the answers that are given, and then deduce some general laws from those answers. Rahman accepts the potential universality of a qur'ânic injunction, but allows it only in terms of principle – not in terms of the literal wording.[19] He thus seeks to uphold qur'ânic core values while moving away from a literalist view of the text.

One of Rahman's main concerns was to elicit from his reading of the Qur'ân a reformist programme of action. He came to the conclusion that the "central concern of the Qur'an is the conduct of man".[20] The revelation focuses on the behaviour of human beings in this world. God exists in the mind of the believer – if (s)he has had a religious and moral experience – to control his or her behaviour. The key human response to this purpose of the Qur'ân should be a sense of *taqwâ*, or deep God-consciousness:

> The Qur'ân calls itself "guidance for mankind" (*hudan li'l-nâs*) and by the same term designates earlier revealed documents. Its central moral concept for man is *taqwâ*, which is usually translated as "piety" or "God-fearingness" but which in the various Qur'ânic contexts may be defined as "a mental state of responsibility from which an agent's actions proceed but which recognizes that the criterion of judgment upon them lies outside him". The whole business of the Qur'ân appears to be centered on the attempt to induce such a state in man.[21]

Such a sense of *taqwâ* contrasts strongly with secularism and provides a transcendent morality that should govern human interrelating. It contrasts strongly with the erosion of an inner sense of responsibility that Rahman observed to be producing increasingly chaotic societies in the West.

Rahman sought to live, himself, by such a vision of *taqwâ* or God-consciousness. He wrote irenically during a period when Western suspicion of Palestinian "terrorists" and other Muslims was growing, trying to mend broken fences between Muslims, Christians and Jews. He attempted to demonstrate from the Qur'ân that, throughout his life, Prophet Muḥammad evidenced a spiritual communion with earlier prophets – including especially those of Jewish and Christian heritage. This communion finds focus in the commitment of former prophets from Abraham to Jesus to a rigorous monotheism. As non-deviant monotheists, claimed Rahman, they were actually *ḥunafâ'* (plural of *ḥanîf*) – not just "People of the Book" but

[19] *Ibid.*, p 17.
[20] *Ibid.*, p 14.
[21] *Ibid.*, p 155.

purists, submitters before the one God – and Prophet Muḥammad was proud to align himself with them:

> "For me, I have set my face, firmly and truly, towards Him Who created the heavens and the earth, and never shall I give partners to Allah." (Sura 6:79)

In Sura 6:79, the Arabic clearly says: 'I have set my face as a *ḥanîf* towards Him . . .'

Rahman's revisionism takes seriously the separation of the early Islamic *umma'* or brotherhood from the pagan, Jewish and Christian communities surrounding it, but not to the extent that Muslim theologians have traditionally insisted upon:

> Important developments do take place in Madina but they do not consist in the Qur'ân abandoning Moses and Jesus to Jews and Christians and linking the Muslim community directly and exclusively with Abraham.[22]

Rahman seeks to retain the positive connection – the continuity aspect – between Islam and the other monotheistic faiths, thus giving grounds for a contemporary rapprochement between Muslims, Christians and Jews. His assertion flies in the face of the orthodox emphasis on the discontinuity that increasingly emerged during Prophet Muḥammad's years in Medina. There, it is usually asserted, Muḥammad substantially distanced himself from the Christians and especially from the Jews. Rahman's hermeneutic serves a reconciliatory end. Rahman's experience suggests that, until now, a Muslim theologian might only be able to make such overtures of reconciliation – on such grounds – from privileged security in North America.

RE-READING THE QUR'ÂN – LIBERATION FROM APARTHEID

Farid Esack grew up in Bonteheuwel, a coloured township on the Cape Flats in South Africa. His family was forcibly moved there under the Group Areas Act. Esack had Christian neighbours on both sides of the family home and recalls regular encounters with a kind debt collector who was a Jew plus the presence in his primary school of a Baha'i girl. For Esack, the "religious Other" was not the

[22] Rahman (1980) *op. cit.*, p 144.

dominating concept of his early intellectual formation as a Muslim. Rather that role was played by apartheid, by oppression, by injustice. In the townships, folk from various religious communities maintained their religious separateness (in worship and so on), but they all found themselves as one over against their common oppressors.

Esack's maturing thought as a Muslim liberation theologian reflects his early background. He seeks to develop from a study of the Qur'ân a "hermeneutic of liberation" that both attacks injustice and accepts to do so in concert with the religious Other. Esack derives six hermeneutical keys from the Qur'ân that he feels find validity in a society characterised by oppression and in which the struggle for justice and freedom needs to take place as an inter-religious striving (see figure 26).

Like Fazlur Rahman, Farid Esack focuses on the qur'ânic term *taqwâ*.[23] The word conveys the idea of heeding the voice of one's conscience in the consciousness that one is ultimately accountable to God. Esack quotes several examples of the significant occurrence of this term within the Qur'ân, for example Sura 49:13:

Figure 26

Esack's hermeneutical keys for a theology of liberation

Qur'ânic term	Meaning	Esack's explanation
taqwâ	an awareness of the presence of God	protecting the interpreter from him or herself
tawḥîd	the unity of God	an undivided God for an undivided humanity
al-nâs	the people	the people's understanding must rule
al-mutaḍ'afûn fî'l-arḍ	the marginalised	bias to the vantage-point of the dis-empowered, marginalised
'adl and *qist*	justice	life through the eyes of justice
jihâd	struggle	"struggle" as praxis and a path to understanding

[23] The Arabic root of this word carries the meanings "to ward off", "to guard against", "to heed", "to preserve".

> O mankind! We created you from a single (pair) of a male and a female, and made you into nations and tribes, that ye may know each other (not that ye may despise (each other). Verily the most honoured of you in the sight of Allah is (he who is) the most righteous of you.[24] And Allah has full knowledge and is well acquainted (with all things).

The Qur'ân underlines the requirement for a community of individuals deeply imbued with *taqwâ* to carry on the prophet's calling of society to transformation and liberation. The challenge for Muslims under apartheid, suggests Esack, is that of remaining true to themselves and to their commitment to God. In the struggle for liberation, not everything goes! The seekers of liberation are still subject to God's standards and requirements regarding their belief and behaviour.

Esack's second hermeneutical key – *tawḥîd*, or the unity of God – came to carry strong overtones for Muslims under apartheid who sought to return sovereignty of the nation to God. A "*tawḥîdi* society" was commonly proposed by many Muslims as their goal for South Africa. Esack seeks to emphasise that the significance of this key lies in continuing to allow different approaches to the Qur'ân (philosophical, spiritual, juristic or political) validity in their own right lest the merely political view dominate and marginalise other approaches.

Esack sees the divine trust placed in the hands of humankind (Sura 33:72), plus humanity's viceregency for God on earth (Sura 2:30) as indicative of God's openness to all of humanity, not just his servants. This comprises his third hermeneutical key. He insists that the Qur'ân be interpreted in a way that gives support to the interests of the people as a whole. Such a view very much complemented the aspirations of the great majority of oppressed "people" under apartheid, but for Esack it also constitutes a continuing critique of any Islamic society in which a privileged minority of humanity comes to dominate the majority.

Esack suggests that the Qur'ân singles out a particular section of humankind – the marginalised – and seeks to promote their cause. He outlines the qur'ânic account of the disempowered in their different statuses: Muslim, *kafir* or unbelieving, and those of both groups. Prophet Muḥammad and his followers, of course, knew the experience of operating from a place of powerlessness, especially

[24] "most righteous of you" is *atqâkum* or "most deeply conscious of God among you".

during the Meccan period. Much is made by Esack of Sura 28, where a preferential option is made for the marginalised in unambiguous terms, despite their rejection of God. Verses four to eight of this sura came to be quoted at most rallies of most Islamist organisations in South Africa during the uprisings of the 1980s:

> Truly Pharaoh elated himself in the land and broke up its people into sections, depressing a small group among them: their sons he slew, but he kept alive their females: for he was indeed a maker of mischief. And We wished to be Gracious to those who were being depressed in the land, to make them leaders (in Faith) and make them heirs, To establish a firm place for them in the land, and to show Pharaoh, Haman, and their hosts, at their hands, the very things against which they were taking precautions. So We sent this inspiration to the mother of Moses: "Suckle (thy child), but when thou hast fears about him, cast him into the river, but fear not nor grieve: for We shall restore him to thee, and We shall make him one of Our messengers." Then the people of Pharaoh picked him up (from the river): (It was intended) that (Moses) should be to them an adversary and a cause of sorrow: for Pharaoh and Haman and (all) their hosts were men of sin.

In this passage, the promise of liberation is held out despite the absence of any commitment by the enslaved people to faith in God and belief in his prophets. The word *mustadʿafûn* was applied to all the oppressed people of South Africa, irrespective of their religious background. Esack suggests that what should be recognised in the making of such an application is that in the struggle in South Africa, the huge majority of the "oppressed" or "marginalised" belonged in fact to the religious Other. It was mostly Christian people who constituted the bulk of the *mustadʿafûn.*

Esack presents a model of *ʿadl* and *qist* (justice) based on *tawḥîd* as his next hermeneutical key. He derives his thinking about justice from a consideration of various qur'ânic texts, for example Sura 55:1–10. Justice, he avows, needs to be upheld as the only appropriate basis of socio-economic life. Qur'ânic verses about justice probably comprised the major inspiration for Muslim resistance to apartheid in South Africa. The Qur'ân proves itself to be strongly against oppression. So, suggests Esack, continuing contexts of injustice – such as gender inequality – need just as strongly to be opposed, if Muslims are to treat the Qur'ân's concerns with integrity.

Jihâd as "struggle and praxis" forms Esack's final hermeneutical key. In the anti-apartheid years, it was the centrality of justice rather than the establishment of Islam as a religious system that became the objective of *jihâd*:

> In the midst of an ongoing experience of suffering and resistance, on the one hand, and a commitment to praxis as an expression of faith, on the other, a clear implication is made that both faith and understanding take shape in the concrete programmes of resistance against suffering and dehumanization.[25]

The centrality of justice in calls to *jihâd* meant that, within South Africa during the uprisings against apartheid, there was an expectation that *jihâd* was something undertaken alongside others, of different faiths and convictions, against an oppressing force. *Jihâd* was, in this sense, open to the religious Other.

Esack promotes a liberation theology that stands as much for a freeing of Muslim minds from static Islamic theological categories as for a freedom for all oppressed South Africans from their struggles under apartheid. His theology is inherently pluralistic and open to the "religious Other", to use his phrase. He turns the tables on those Muslim leaders who would constrict interpretation of the Qur'ân to their own, limited categories. He sees the "word of God" as something far too dynamic, far too liberating to be tied down by a frozen few:

> It was and remains inevitable that this word of God that has pitched its tent in the midst of history would be affected by the storms, rain, wind and, yes, the sunshine, surrounding it. The word has regularly become contested terrain as various entities staked claims to its ownership. For Muslims in South Africa during the 1980s, much of the controversy of these claims revolved around the question of space for the religious Other. The progressive Islamists argued fervently that faith and *taqwa* enabled them to access the text. They ignored the clerics, and insisted that the word also had space for all the marginalized. The word of God also excludes; but the excluded were now seen to be those who, despite possessing the correct formulae of faith, had made themselves unworthy of the description *muslim* by their participation in the structures of oppression.[26]

The Islamic case demonstrates the very real difficulty – for Muslims – of answering the Islamists where the latter are in the political or popular ascendant, or of finding a secure environment from within which to pursue an understanding of the Qur'ân as the "word of God" from other than a literalist, dogmatic perspective. The Islamic case also demonstrates the possibility, in some circumstances, of saying something radically different or of pursuing or promoting

[25] Farid Esack, *Qur'ân, Liberation and Pluralism: An Islamic Perspective of Interreligious Solidarity against Oppression*, Oneworld: Oxford (1997), p 108.

[26] *Ibid.*, p 111.

precisely such an alternative understanding. We have mentioned a few male, Muslim theologians here. Others also exist. Those others include women! Amina Wadud, Azizah al-Hibri and Riffat Hassan, for example, have each deliberately focused on the delicate subject of qur'ânic hermeneutics in their attempt to make space for a different reading of the original religious text – a reading not controlled by male interpreters of the divine will.[27] The struggle is not over yet! Indeed, it has barely begun!

[27] See Amina Wadud, *Qur'an and Woman: Rereading the Sacred Text from a Woman's Perspective*, Oxford University Press: Oxford (1999); Azizah al-Hibri, *Women and Islam*, Elsevier: London (1982); Riffat Hassan, "An Islamic Perspective" in Karen Lebacqz & David Sinacore-guinn (eds.), *Sexuality: A Reader*, Pilgrim Press: Cleveland (1999). Christian Troll includes the following Muslims as advocates of what he calls "progressive thinking" in contemporary Islam: Mohamed Arkoun, Abdul Karim Soroush, Nasr Hamid Abu Zaid, Abdou Filali-Ansary, Abdelmajid Charfi, Farid Esack, Ebrahim Moosa, Asghar Ali Engineer, Abdullah an-Naim, Amina Wadud, Fatima Mernissi, Leila Babès, Khaled Abou el Fadl, Nurcholish Madjid, Farish Noor and Ömer Özsoy. In "Progressive Thinking in Contemporary Islam" in *Encounter*, no 317–318 (January–February, 2007), p 9.

Chapter 12

Beware the uncertainty trap!

PERHAPS now we might return to our interrogation of a Christian fundamentalist view of the Bible in order to proceed, as this chapter develops, to its opposite! At heart, Christian fundamentalism constitutes a particular tradition of interpretation. That tradition, mostly within evangelicalism, has been strongly concerned with defending the integrity of the Bible, plus its theological and moral authority, in the context of a world increasingly reifying scientific reasoning and personal lifestyle choice. Marsden has helpfully summarised what he discerns as the broad sweep of the history of Christian fundamentalism as it has found expression in the United States of America (figure 27).[1]

In the 1920s, proponents of a Christian fundamentalist perspective reached national prominence. Such proponents vehemently opposed liberalism within theology and rued the cultural changes in society that tended to be endorsed by modernism. Millenarians stood at the centre of the fundamentalist coalition of this period, but premillennarianism per se was not the organising principle of their cause. *The Fundamentals*, published in twelve paperback volumes from 1910 to 1915, served as the well-resourced voice of this militantly anti-modernist group of Protestant evangelicals. In the decade from 1920, conservative evangelical councils were dominated by fundamentalists who had in their sights the scourge of liberal theology, the teaching of evolution, and the menace of Communism. The fundamentalists of this period, however, embarrassed themselves into ridicule and isolation through the infamous "Monkey Trial" at Dayton, Tennessee.[2]

After the Second World War, Billy Graham provided a strong focus for many evangelicals within the United States of America.

[1] Adapted boxes pp 234–235, 222w from *Fundamentalism and American Culture* (2nd edition) by George M. Marsden (1983); by permission of Oxford University Press, Inc.

[2] In 1925, John Scopes tested a law in Tennessee that banned the teaching of Darwinism in any public school. William Jennings Bryan prosecuted. Although Scope was found guilty of teaching evolution, Bryan himself was humiliated on the witness stand where he was badgered into confessing his agreement with Archbishop Ussher's chronology of creation.

Figure 27

George Marsden on the history of fundamentalism in the USA

Period	Constituency	Trends
"evangelicalism" in the nineteenth century	a broad coalition including most major Protestant denominations and new revivalist groups	vast cultural changes 1870–1920 lead to a crisis within the evangelical coalition resulting in a split between theological liberals and conservatives
"fundamentalism" in the 1920s	emergence of militant wing of conservatives from major denominations and revivalists calling themselves "fundamentalist"; opposed to liberal teaching in churches and unbiblical cultural mores	by mid 1920s the fundamentalists gain national prominence, but then dramatically decline; premillennial dispensationalists come to dominate the movement
"fundamentalism" in the 1930s	fundamentalists tend to leave the mainline Protestant denominations (especially those associated with the ecumenical Federal/National Council of Churches); also remain separate from the holiness movement and from Pentecostalism	such separatists differentiate themselves from the many conservatives remaining within the mainline denominations; most fundamentalists are Baptists and most are dispensationalists
"new evangelicalism" and "fundamentalism" in the period 1950s to 1970s	"new evangelicals" (eventually just "evangelicals") form the core of a broad coalition mostly cohering around Billy Graham; other streams are found in the charismatic and Pentecostal movements. "fundamentalists" – predominantly separatist Baptist dispensationalists – see Billy Graham as increasingly compromised through his willingness to work ecumenically	the term "fundamentalist" is used as a specific self-designation by premillennial dispensationalists who break with Billy Graham.

Period	Constituency	Trends
"fundamentalistic evangelicalism" in the late 1970s to the early twenty-first century	the Religious Right, including "fundamentalistic" militants deriving from separatist fundamentalist groups and from almost the whole spectrum of evangelicals, plus some Catholics and	the Religious Right emerges as a national movement with conspicuous southern leadership: Jerry Falwell, Pat Robertson, James Robinson and so on

Sometimes referred to as "new evangelicals", these Protestant Christians were united in a primary concern for evangelism. Other "streams" of evangelicalism finding prominence in this period were the Pentecostal and charismatic movements. Many of the leaders at the core of the "new evangelical" wave were (like Billy Graham himself) fundamentalist by background in terms of their theological roots. Gradually, the urgent requirement for evangelism led such evangelicals to work with Christians from other Protestant streams and even with Christians from non-Protestant denominations. This was a step too far for more militant fundamentalists who broke with Billy Graham over his "compromises". The abandoners of Graham – predominantly separatist Baptist dispensationalists – took to themselves the term "fundamentalist". They nearly all subscribed to a premillennial dispensationalist perspective.

From the mid-1970s, when the Religious Right as a politically active movement took the United States of America by storm,[3] it gave voice to leaders at its core whose backgrounds lay in the separatist fundamentalist groupings within the country. People like Jerry Falwell and Tim and Beverley LaHaye came to have disproportionately strong voices in representing what Marsden calls "fundamentalistic evangelicalism".

Here is my point in briefly rehearsing the development of a fundamentalist stream of biblical interpretation within the United States of America. The biblical hermeneutic represented by contemporary fundamentalistic evangelicals, and indeed by those speaking out of a fundamentalist perspective from earlier periods, is in my view neither the most natural nor the most faithful.

It is not the most natural in that it too easily withdraws from the immediate historical or textual context to make sweeping generalisations that "fit in" with a certain view of how history or prophecy

[3] See chapter 2, above.

are to be perceived. The result feels a bit like a mainstream Christian equivalent of the proof-texting done by Jehovah's Witnesses. In the detail of particular verses, moreover, an intellectually honest approach needs to come to terms with the problem of "mistakes" or inconsistencies in the text, instead of glossing over them.[4]

It is not the most faithful in that it ignores verses that do not agree with its proposals and often proceeds by relying on single verses or paragraphs that do.[5] It functions without acknowledgement that the Bible contains different kinds of writing and, most spectacularly, insists on interpreting apocalyptic literature as predictions of actual events to come. This faithlessness can lead to frightening scenarios, as Victoria Clark described vis à vis her conversation with Pastor Cohen in Jerusalem, or as Grace Halsell unearthed in her investigation of Christian Zionists like Jerry Falwell. One might fairly conclude, with Barr:

> Few can doubt what many observers have noted: that the continuance of religious fundamentalism, and of the attitudes associated with it, may have great importance in determining whether or not mankind is to be destroyed through nuclear warfare![6]

[4] This is not a major issue for me in this chapter, but intellectual honesty has to constitute a *sine qua non* of biblical reflection. At the beginning of Mark's Gospel, the author attributes the whole of his quotation from the Old Testament in verses 2 and 3 to Isaiah. In fact, the first part of his quotation is not from Isaiah, but from Malachi 3:1 or possibly from Exodus 23:20. One might argue that Isaiah is named to summarise the contribution of both prophets (Isaiah and Malachi) because his book begins the section called "Latter Prophets" in the Hebrew Bible (see Figure 16 above). In Mark 2:25–26, Jesus is quoted as talking about what David did "in the days of Abiathar the high priest". In fact, they were the days of Abiathar's father, Abimelech, as high priest (1 Samuel 21:1–6; 1 Kings 2:26–27). Abiathar did not become high priest until the reign of David (1 Samuel 22:20–23). Jesus mentions the wrong name: perhaps the more prominent one comes into his mind rather than the more accurate? Or Mark wrote it down wrongly? Matthew and Luke do not name the priest concerned (Matthew 12:1–8; Luke 6:1–5). In Matthew 23:35, Jesus is quoted as mentioning "the blood of Zechariah son of Berekiah" when he is probably referring to "Zechariah son of Jehoiada" (2 Chronicles 24:20–21). Zechariah 1:1 refers to its author as "Zechariah son of Berekiah." There is, however, no biblical evidence of his death as a martyr, plus the temple was in ruins by his time. The one biblical martyr named Zechariah is the son of Jehoiada, whose story appears near the end of Chronicles. Reference to that Zechariah makes sense: Abel (Genesis 4:8) is the first victim of murder in the Bible, and the prophet Zechariah is the final victim of murder in the Hebrew Bible in which the books of Chronicles stand last (again, see Figure 16). Some uncertainty about the patronymic of Zechariah son of Berekiah (Zechariah 1:1) is excusable inasmuch as he is referred to as the son of Iddo in Ezra 5:1, when Iddo was actually his grandfather. Some interpreters identify Zechariah with Zechariah son of Baruch, killed in AD 70 shortly before the fall of the temple in Jerusalem (Josephus, *The Wars of the Jews*, book 4, chap 5, para 4). Again, Luke in his recounting of Jesus' words omits the name of the father (Luke 11:51).

[5] Probably, most significantly, the "thousand year" reign mentioned in Revelation 20.

[6] James Barr, *Escaping from Fundamentalism*, SCM: London (1984), p x.

No wonder Joanne Harris puts such cynical words into the mouth of Guy Le Merle in her book *Holy Fools*. Set in an abbey at St Marie-de-la-Mer in seventeenth century France, Harris explores the themes of faith, disbelief, self-delusion and cruelty. In her novel, Le Merle takes on different characters in order to avoid arrest for previous crimes – and in order to advance his own power and prestige through clever deceit. He reappears in the story as a priest, adviser to the young, innocent yet fanatical, incumbent abbess of the abbey in which the book's main character, Juliette, has won acceptance as Soeur Auguste:

> "Time for a quote, I think. Seneca, perhaps? *It is a rocky road that leads to the heights of greatness*? No. I don't think this company is quite ready for Seneca. Deuteronomy, then. *Thou shalt become an astonishment, a proverb and a byword among all nations*. Of course, the wonderful thing about the Bible is that there's a quote to justify anything, even lechery, incest and the slaying of infants!"[7]

Such cynicism "outside" the church is, I think, increasingly matched by a hesitation from within the church about the nature or authority of the Bible. It is as if contemporary Christians, like contemporary Muslims, have also had the rug pulled from under them by the fundamentalists – this time the Christian ones. The fundamentalists look as if they are saying the "right" things in terms of their allegiance to the Bible as God's word. They are certainly Bible-focused. They also have a clear and neat view of how the Bible relates to life and especially to contemporary world events. The *Scofield Reference Bible* describes the different "dispensations" of world history while Hal Lyndsey's *The Late Great Planet Earth* gives a roadmap of the end of the world. The widely-read, 12-volume *Left Behind* series, by Tim LaHaye and Jerry B. Jenkins, offers a fictional account of the seven-year period associated with the end-time rapture and tribulation. The worldview of the Christian fundamentalists, however, seems not only unacceptably literalist, but also exceedingly dangerous in a world in which some of that world's most powerful politicians, who succeed each other in putting a finger on the nuclear button, subscribe to the fundamentalists' route for reaching Armageddon.

Evangelicals (and other non-fundamentalist-but-committed Christians) find themselves today between a rock and a hard place. They want to affirm a confidence in the Bible, but not accept

[7] Joanne Harris, *Holy Fools*. Black Swan: London (2003), p 114.

a fundamentalist appropriation of scripture's authority. They want to live in obedience to God's word, yet relate compassionately to the post-Christians and non-Christians of the contemporary Western world. At the same time, they want to be radically Christian, not compromised by the prevailing culture's suspicion or rejection of any confession of adherence to a religious meta-narrative. They want to avoid the uncertainty trap as much as the certainty trap!

The delicacy of trying to live such a *via media* is reflected in my own experience, in the years that I have lived in the United Kingdom since returning from the Middle East.

THE UNCERTAINTY TRAP!

My family returned from Egypt to Britain in 1986, with me hopefully having developed a more humble heart. I soon realised that I had come back to live within a culture in which any kind of expression of certainty had become highly suspect.

At present, I am vicar of a multi-cultural parish in London. The church congregation reflects the demography of the area and the people are warm and friendly and positively embracing of diversity. What got me thinking, recently, was my reaction to something said by a colleague in the course of his sermon.

I don't think anyone noticed me wincing – but wincing I was! My colleague was preaching his heart out. As usual, this gifted young man delivered his oration without any notes to hand. He was well into his sermon, building on his theme, when he made a quick reference to a further passage of scripture – a passage not under consideration that morning. That passage supported the burden of his sermon. He apologised to the congregation that there was not time to look at the verses in detail. "Just trust me," he pronounced, "I am a minister." That was when I winced. Not because I thought that he was wrong in making reference to the particular passage concerned. Nor because I disagreed with his summary of what that further passage conveyed. I winced because he asked people to accept something on his say-so. I don't think that "ministers of the Word" can do that any more. I'm not sure that they ever should have done, previously. Today, certainly, people are very suspicious of being asked to swallow something simply because it is offered to them by an authority figure. Indeed, any demand by an authority figure that folk accept without question what that person is suggesting becomes in itself counter-productive. The act of demanding is a turn-off. I have winced at more speakers than just my colleague.

My wincing episode brought to a head some questions that have occupied me since returning home from the Middle East. What goes on in church members' minds when they hear me preach? Or even when they hear the Bible being read? My preaching will be peppered with affirmations like "The Bible says . . ." or "Jesus comments in Matthew . . ." At any public reading of Scripture in our church, the reader will declare, "This is the word of the Lord" to which everyone responds, "Thanks be to God." In sermons and lessons and worship songs, the words of Scripture are appealed to and declared. What do members of the congregation really think about that?

My conclusion is that for most of the time, most people think, "This is Bill's opinion of what the Bible says." We in the West today are all participants in a post-modern, individualistic approach to allowing (or not allowing) others' "truths" to impinge upon our own lives. And I am happy for my congregation's reticence about what I say the Bible says, in a way. One of my main aims as a pastor and teacher is to help people cultivate "filters" in situations where an authority figure (like myself) is trying to tell people what they should be believing. I want them to employ filters that ask, "Is this true?" "Is the Holy Spirit saying this?" "Is this God speaking to me now?" However, what is happening as I preach, I think, is not the application of that kind of conscious filter, but of a more subtle one, one strongly embedded in contemporary British culture. It is a filter that says, "Well, that is just one individual's (Bill's) opinion and it is only that – one particular opinion."

For some in the congregation of course, the reticence is far deeper. Any acknowledgement of the Bible as "the word of the Lord" is only made with some pretty strong mental reservations. Old Testament is harder to swallow than New Testament. Passages that seem to imply that God is quite happy with ethnic cleansing or with the second-class status of women are acknowledged as "the word of the Lord" only with considerable reluctance. For such folk the hesitation finds expression in a genuine questioning – "Is this really the word of the Lord?" or "In what sense can this be the word of the Lord?" And, probably supremely, "Could this ever be the word of the Lord for me?"

Whether the filter is of the "Well, that is only Bill's opinion" type or whether it is of the "Well, that surely cannot be the word of the Lord" type, the attitude of the hearer is one of doubt or hesitation. The authority of Scripture is accepted only delicately or grudgingly, if accepted at all. The prevailing perspective is what one might call a "hermeneutic of suspicion". It is a perspective that prevails in our secular-humanist culture. It is a perspective, I think, that increasingly pervades the church in Britain, even where lip-service is given to an opposite hermeneutic of certainty.

Not British, but a retired bishop in the Episcopal Church of the United States of America, John Shelby Spong has been a vocal proponent of modernist, Western attempts to free the Bible from the clutches of what is seen by many Christian theologians as a mindless literalism. In his book *Rescuing the Bible from Fundamentalism*, Spong calls for acceptance of a paradigm-shift in the contemporary Christian's approach to Scripture. His contention is that context has shifted so much (from the biblical world to the modern world) that demythologising or "bringing up to date" will not go far enough. Abandonment is the name of his game. The reader can no longer take the Bible at face value – its story makes "no sense" nowadays. Spong's call, therefore, is for an open recognition of the pointlessness of taking the Bible as recording "fact" and for an embracing of a brave new world in Bible study. That new world consists primarily in suspicion about literalness. Historical incarnation, cross and resurrection, for example, are in this view to be held lightly. Those unbelievable "events" constitute the conviction of primitive believers expressed in simplistic narratives. The only thing they invite today is incredulity. So forget them! It is the story behind them that is significant:

> In a human life [that of Jesus] God has been met and known, even in a human life that was once a helpless infant. In a human life the limits of finitude have been broken, including the ultimate barrier of death. That is the story we have to tell. It is, I believe, a story that men and women are eager to hear. It is a pity that this truth cannot be heard until the Bible is freed from the hands of those who are in fact destroying Christianity with their literalistic claims even though in their naïveté they believe themselves to be serving the Bible faithfully.[8]

[8] John Shelby Spong, *Rescuing the Bible from Fundamentalism*, HarperCollins: San Francisco (1991), p 226.

Perhaps John Spong is more openly honest than most of us, especially those of us who consider ourselves evangelical or orthodox. He cannot as a modern (Western) man, accept the biblical text at face value. He will not, as a twenty-first century North American, buy into a non-questioning of passages that seemingly devalue women or homosexuals or non-believers. His resolution as a person who loves the Bible is to look behind the passages for a meaning or message that can be retrieved and received once it has been divested of culture-bound misrepresentation.

The thinking of John Spong resonates with much that has come from the mind and pen of Wilfred Cantwell Smith. This renowned, Canadian Islamicist has done his re-thinking about the nature of "religion" out of an encounter with Islam on the world stage. Cantwell Smith mulled long and hard over a discovery he made concerning the mistranslation of the verb *âmana* in the Qur'ân as "believe" in English (and its related noun *îmân* as "belief"). Over a research period of eight years he came to conclude that in the Bible also, the category of "believing" (deriving from the Latin *credo*) was mistakenly perceived in the modern world:

> The Islamic and Christian world-views used to be the conceptual frameworks, the intellectual systems, patterns, within which thinking was carried on, and within which faith and infidelity were conceived and articulated. These coherent systems of ideas had not been something at which men looked, but through which they looked – at the world, at themselves, at their neighbours. Or, changing the metaphor, and speaking of Western Christendom, may we not assert the following: that what had been taken for granted, and had formed the basis for the superstructure on which our particular drama was mounted, was brought out into the open, for critical intellectual scrutiny, and therefore could no longer serve as presuppositional base on which our faith, and our whole religious and indeed social life, could rest. When that happened, we unwittingly shifted our categories. (And that 'unwittingly' is crucial). We diverted our attention from the meaningful question of faith (the question of what one does, given the symbol-system) to the modern question of belief (the question of whether to have that particular symbol-system or not).[9]

Cantwell Smith's innovative conclusion came to be that the two faith communities (Muslim and Christian) diverge in belief but converge in faith.

[9] Wilfred Cantwell Smith, *On Understanding Islam: Selected Studies*, Mouton Publishers: The Hague (1981), pp 278–279.

Cantwell Smith's re-thinking in effect "relativises" religions – indeed, sidelines them really. He has little time for "religion" as such. His focus is on faith or the inherent experience of the religious by people from different backgrounds, and the relationship between that inner life of faith and the outer life of the tradition concerned. To declare that one religious expression has "the Truth" to be shared and received by all, he finds quaint, distasteful and irreverent:

> It is an impoverishment of life, but an impoverishment also of theology, not to take seriously God's mission to us all through all traditions, all his servants everywhere. In a way, this constitutes the central point of my presentation here: that it is not only intellectually, and morally, wrong, to fail to recognize God's mission to other people through their traditions; and nowadays, through those traditions and those other people, to us. More than simply wrong, theologically one may say that it is blasphemous.[10]

John Hick characterises Cantwell Smith's experiment in re-conceptualisation as opening up vast issues concerning, for example, the relationship between faith and truth and the cultural traditions (see figure 28).

Cantwell Smith looks for an end to "religion" as traditionally conceived out of hope that the true end of religion – namely God – might become the overarching referent of "faith", in whichever community that "faith" might be engendered.

In respect of a hermeneutic of suspicion, then, that hermeneutic is pretty strongly in place at the beginning of the twenty-first century. In

Figure 28

John Hick on Cantwell Smith

	Effect of re-conceptualisation
1	No longer to consider religions as socio-theological entities; so that the question "Which of these is the true religion?" no longer applies.
2	To focus instead on the area of inner personal faith and experience; so that the experiential, not the cognitive, aspect of human functioning is foundational.
3	To leave behind the illusion that different religious traditions are monolithic; so concentrating on the rich and detailed variety between and within traditions.

[10] Wilfred Cantwell Smith, "Mission, Dialogue, and God's Will for Us", in *International Review of Mission*, vol 78, no 307 (1988), p 367.

my local congregation, it provides a major filter for many people in their listening for or to "the Word of the Lord". It is increasingly the conviction of some theologians in the Western world that the Bible has to be radically "reviewed" in order for it to become at all meaningful to post-modern people, Christian and non-Christian. On the world stage, any interpretation of a faith that is prescriptive and universalistic in its truth-claims is treated increasingly with hesitation and distaste. The uncertainty trap is well-nigh closed here in the West.

How might today's Western Christians find a way out of the "uncertainty trap"? How might the authority of the Bible come to be recovered within a context where a hermeneutic of suspicion holds sway? I have a few suggestions to make.

ESCAPING THE UNCERTAINTY TRAP

My conclusion, with regard to my much-appreciated, current congregation and their receiving of "the Word of the Lord" is that the only way through the filter of "suspicion" is by the Holy Spirit's independent operation in the life of each hearer or receiver. Paul reminisces in his first letter to the Christians at Thessalonica that "our gospel came to you not simply with words, but also with power, with the Holy Spirit and with conviction" (1 Thessalonians 1:5). In a contemporary society overdosed on rationalism and consumerism, on non-commitment and disengagement, God the Holy Spirit must himself authenticate the word in people's hearts and lives. Without God himself sharpening and re-negotiating our worship, all we Christians are in danger of doing, it seems to me, is replicating what happens (during Sunday!) on the terraces of Old Trafford and elsewhere – offering a communal, liturgical, but wholly human experience. John Tiller writes wistfully of the need for a sense of the numinous to be at the heart of Christian worship in our kind of culture:

> Even, or perhaps especially, in a materialistic society men and women are seeking a sense of the transcendent power and majesty of God, an awareness of the beauty of holiness in worship, and a response to the magnetic call of the eternal realm. Such religious needs are often met in acts of worship where music and colour and drama and ritual are employed with great effect.[11]

[11] John Tiller with Mark Birchall, *The Gospel Community and its Leadership*, Marshall Pickering: Basingstoke (1987), p 148.

If God were to authenticate his word by acting miraculously in our midst, perhaps we might take his word more seriously. I realise I am speaking as an Anglican here. Many contemporary churches (including some Anglican churches!) do experience considerable "power" manifestations on a regular basis as part of their worship experience. In those situations, the other side of the coin needs careful attention – who, in the midst of such power encounters, is defining what church members should or should not believe, or how they should or should not behave? For revitalised Anglicans and others, divine authenticating of the preached word would not necessarily equate with agreement concerning all that the "preacher" is saying or all that the church leadership is promoting as divinely authorised. A few miracles in our midst, however, might make us tremble, might help us begin to honour God for whom he is worth – to offer him "worthship". In an awe-filled context, God's word might carry a re-negotiated authority.

My prayer for my congregation and myself each Sunday is the prayer of morning "Preparation" in the Anglican rite of *Common Worship*:

> O Lord, open our lips
> *and our mouth shall proclaim your praise.*
> Give us the joy of your saving help
> *and sustain us with your life-giving Spirit.*

Or, in other words:

> God, please gatecrash the filters!

With regard to Bishop Spong's agnosticism concerning the biblical record, I want to affirm my conviction that in the Bible we are still given in the twenty-first century "all things necessary for eternal salvation through faith in Jesus Christ."[12] For me, the Bible comprises, above all, a divinely given revelation centred on Jesus Christ and the salvation he brings. What purports in it to be historical – like virgin birth or cross and resurrection – therefore needs to be taken very seriously, even if it challenges our current categories of what might be "possible". Christianity, unlike Hinduism for example, is centred in real events in the time/space continuum. It is nothing if not factual in its essential reference. At the same time, I do not buy into a locating of Scripture's authority in scientifically inerrant words

[12] Anglican Ordinal, as for example in the presentation of deacons and priests.

and I do not think that the Bible can be interpreted fairly without taking seriously its historical and cultural contexts. I have learned to respect deeply the Orthodox language of "condescension" (Egypt's Copts endeavour to express "incarnation" thus in an Islamic milieu) – God condescended to use imperfect human forms of communication to get across his divine message for humanity. The message is normative, supra-cultural; the medium has historical and cultural contexts that need unwrapping. It seems to me that Spong takes a wrong path in venting his frustration that "how the Bible expresses itself" is a long way from twenty-first century scientifically mature humanity. In rescuing the Bible from fundamentalism – a positive goal – he ends up rejecting the essential message because the packaging is too remote for him and his North American peers.

If only John Spong could have listened to the contemporary world church (mostly southern and non-White) with their insights into the integrity of Scripture. Just to learn a little of the reliability (not unreliability) of material handed down by word of mouth in oral cultures helps give a refreshing confidence in the material finding its way to and through Ezra for the Old Testament or brought together via *Q*[13] or Mark or Matthew or Luke and so on for the New Testament. It is no coincidence that Muslims today refer to someone who has memorised the Qur'ân – a text the same length as the New Testament – as a *ḥâfiẓ* or "guardian". Oral transmission equates to safe transmission! Just to experience a little of living in an honour/shame culture brings alive much of the early material in Genesis, helps one live a little more easily with some of the "excessive" killings of the Old Testament, and maybe interprets more insightfully what was going on when Jesus died on a Roman cross, honouring his absenting Father while despising the enveloping shame.[14] Perhaps a period of residence in a strongly hierarchical culture would help John Spong and most of us Westerners "see" the Christ event as modelling something more to do with vertical relationships (Christ obeying his Father) than horizontal relationships (Christ loving the world). John Spong is strong on "love" but weak on "obedience" in his theologising – yet it must be significant that in none of the proclamation speeches in Acts does Luke record any

[13] The "Q document" (*Q* for German *Quelle* meaning "source") is a postulated, lost textual source for the Gospels of Matthew and Luke.

[14] See my *Touching the Soul of Islam*, p 216 on the theme of rivalry, and pp 110–113 on a view of the crucifixion from within an honour/shame perspective.

talk about *agâpé* ("divine love"). For these and other insights into the medium or packaging, and hence into the message wrapped within them, Spong and I need to become indebted to the living Christian tradition – the church worldwide – and also to those of other faiths whose cultural heritage is far nearer the biblical form than our own. That way, we might get to infer something more powerfully close to what God was condescending to say instead of turning our back on it all as "primitive" or "naïve" or "unscientific".

I have huge respect for Cantwell Smith's knowledge of Islam and consequent wrestling with inter-faith issues. I find myself attracted to his differentiation between "belief" and "faith" as offering hope for serious understanding and trust across the religious traditions. At the same time, I consider his charge of making exclusive truth-claims as being tantamount to blasphemy difficult to hear.

I have been immensely helped by another theologian and church leader who also immersed himself in an Asian context for most of his life. Bishop Lesslie Newbigin returned to Britain in the late twentieth century seeing British culture with adopted Indian eyes. He exposed (for me) the unstated but all-pervasive secular-humanist lens through which we Westerners tend to view the world.[15] This is a lens not recognised as being present among those who grow up seeing through it! Perhaps I should quickly confess that David Tracy appears to be an exception to this rule. In his study of hermeneutics, religion and hope, he unmasks the underlying – and false – certainties of *both* fundamentalist and secular readings of life:

> The difference between fundamentalist readings and secularist readings seems startling. But these are surface differences of answers, not of fundamental hermeneutical approaches . . . The certainty of contemporary positivist and empiricist critiques of religion is well matched by the literalism and fundamentalism of religious dogmatists in all traditions.[16]

The uncertainty trap can be just as blindly coercive as the certainty trap! Both the secular humanist and the religiously fundamentalist see, unknowingly, through lenses that are similar in hermeneutical terms. Tracy mirrors Newbigin's point exactly in his perception of this reality. Muslims, among others, tend to see clearly the powerful effect in the West of the "secular humanist certainty" while not perhaps acknowledging the similar hermeneutic at work in their own religious experience. We seem to be talking, in societal or worldview

[15] Lesslie Newbigin, *The Gospel in a Pluralist Society*, SPCK: London (1989).
[16] Tracy, *op. cit.*, p 101.

terms, of beams and motes! The question is, which is which? I for one returned to the United Kingdom with an awareness that my "sight" had come to be affected by my living among Christians and Muslims in the Middle East, but with few tools to analyse why I was feeling so discomforted at "home".

Newbigin also carefully unpacked (for me) the result – for a view of the Bible's authority – of an uncritical acceptance within theological studies of a Cartesian approach to the problem of knowing. Descartes looked for "certainty" in a world of reason that was not seduced by a supposed reality beyond itself. Reason – human reason – was to be the sole guide in getting at the "facts". The Age of Reason, or Enlightenment, noisily exploded open the possibility of wide-ranging research and study. It also (silently) imposed its own intrinsic worldview upon the methodology to be utilised in such work. The study of the Bible in modern universities, for example, has become dominated by the application of reason as arbiter over revelation in determining the "facts" of what is being looked at. The historical-critical method, while helpful in focusing upon contexts in which biblical writings arise, becomes unhelpful once it becomes a judge of what might be considered true (that Jesus of Nazareth lived, for example) or untrue (that Jesus performed miracles, for example). The presuppositions of "the reigning plausibility structure" of contemporary society have so invaded the historical-critical method, suggests Newbigin, that they blind the "liberal" theologian to the possibility that the Christian story might be evaluating him as much as he is evaluating it. What if the miracles of Jesus really did happen? What would that say about human hubris that, *a priori*, denies their possibility?

Today, of course, the Cartesian model of reasoning is disintegrating within a post-modernist world. Within that brave, newer world, reason itself is relativised so that something may be "true" for me while its opposite may be "true" for you. The Age of Reason is finding itself swallowed up by an age of deconstructionism. Current chaos theories, the conviction that an observer affects the experiments being observed, the possibility of conceiving light as both waves and particles – the world that entertains such thoughts is rapidly undermining the possibility of achieving a commonly-agreed "certainty" through purely rational effort.

Newbigin sees contemporary secular humanists as pluralist with regard to "values" and particularist with regard to "facts". In our worldview, a variety of values may be chosen or discarded by individuals at will, but empirical facts still largely provide the continuing bedrock of human knowing. The Bible, of course, comes in the "value" category, so people (including church-going believers) may take it or leave it. Newbigin suggests that "dogma" in its original sense of "seeming to be the case" (seeming to be "fact") is a healthy, counter-cultural irritant to a worldview that has subsumed Gospel "facts" such as incarnation, miracle, or resurrection under the "values" aspect of reality.[17] Christian "faith" is based on recorded "fact", declarations by eyewitnesses and others of what they confessed to be *factum*, something "done" by God. Buying into the factual story – by the eyewitnesses or by ourselves – is for sure a subjective faith-matter, but the historicity of the Gospel-claims is the starting-point for such trusting confidence:

> Here we have the most radical attack possible on the assumptions of modernity. To state the situation straightforwardly, this attack can hardly fail to rouse the same kind of anger in contemporary society as it did among those who heard [the] words of Jesus. Perhaps nowhere is this anger more deep today than among those Christians who have sought (with the truly admirable intention of making the gospel acceptable to the modern world) to commend Christianity as a tenable belief within the liberal assumptions of modern society.[18]

Lamin Sanneh complements Newbigin's assertions with his assurance that the historic foundations of the Christian faith are well able

[17] Lesslie Newbigin, *Proper confidence: faith, doubt and certainty in Christian discipleship*, Eerdmans: Grand Rapids (1995), p 55.

[18] *Ibid.*, pp 68–69. Wittgenstein embodies the logical thinking behind a Western worldview no longer at ease with what had previously been accepted as "factual" or certain. Interestingly, he uses language similar to Newbigin's, but with an opposite application, in his consideration of propositions: "From its *seeming* to me – or to everyone – to be so, doesn't follow that it *is* so. What we can ask is whether it can make sense to doubt it." In Ludwig Wittgenstein (ed. G.E.M. Anscombe and G.H. von Wright; trans. Denis Paul and G.E.M. Anscombe), *On Certainty*, Blackwell: Oxford (1977), p 2e. Similarly, in the world of Western scientific thought, "certainty" (or causal determinism) has been strongly undermined by chaos theories and revisions of the concept of time. See Ilya Prigogine's original contribution to such debate from the perspective of a physicist in *The End of Certainty*, The Free Press: New York, 1997. For Westerners, issues of "value" now impinge on scientific "knowing" so that any kind of rational "certainty" is made that much more remote. Newbigin, free from the confines of a "suspicious" Western worldview, in effect asks whether the core history of Jesus Christ can be doubted simply for the reason that it is extraordinary. The post-modern, Western worldview says, "Yes, it can" and resets that "history" in the "values" category. Other contemporary worldviews allow the extraordinary as part of their "factual" categorisation and see the record about Jesus Christ as reflecting objective truth. Newbigin wants to retain the possibility of "certainty" with regard to Christian believing but avers that proper "certainty" cannot be the certainty of Descartes. He places the locus of confidence "not in the competence of our own knowing, but in the faithfulness and reliability of the one who is known" (1995, *op. cit.*, p 67). He suggests that such "certainty" constitutes, "not a claim to possess final truth but to be on the way that leads to the fullness of truth." (*Ibid.*, p 67).

to "stand on their own two feet" in the public arena. Sanneh stands aghast at the post-modern attitude that concludes that:

> since there are so many religions with a claim to truth, no one religion matters in the end, thus allowing us to ransack religions to suit our personal tastes.'[19]

Rather, let the facts speak for themselves and let God be God – if he is – in the public domain!

Figure 29

Dogma: yes, but . . .

1	Dogma must be kept free of any kind of human coercion.
2	Dogma is not defended by domesticating it within the reigning plausibility structure (e.g. by trying scientifically to "prove" the reality of resurrection). It is not proven in that sense, but witnessed to.
3	Dogma is offered as "it seems to be the case" in humility.
4	Dogma is not a set of presuppositions; it is a story about a divine Person set in eternity/history.

Newbigin is careful in his promotion of "dogma" to warn against four potential underminings of his argument for its validity (figure 29). "Dogma", in Newbigin's careful sense, is offered against suspicion, bearing witness to a story. Such offering may confidently be made in a public manner. If truth lies within it, then it is up to the Person about whom it speaks to underline that truth, *contra* suspicion. This approach to springing the uncertainty trap shifts responsibility for determining "truth" away from mere human reason, and places it elsewhere:

> The important thing is not how we formulate a doctrine of biblical authority but how we allow the bible to function in our daily lives. We grow into a knowledge of God by allowing the biblical story to awaken our imagination and to challenge and stimulate our thinking and acting.[20]

Perhaps there are ways, then, out of the uncertainty trap for contemporary Western Christians. Are there ways, for both Christians and Muslims, out of the opposite snare – the "certainty trap"? The final chapters of this book consider this question.

[19] Lamin Sanneh, "Muhammad's Significance for Christians: Biography, History and Faith". In *Piety and Power: Muslims and Christians in West Africa*, Maryknoll, Orbis: New York (1996), p 48.

[20] Newbigin (1995), *op. cit.*, p 91.

Chapter 13

Escaping the certainty trap!

DESIDERIUS ERASMUS of Rotterdam got into serious trouble in AD 1516! That was the year when he produced his edition of the Greek New Testament along with his own translation of it into Latin, plus some annotations. The greatest outcry was against his omission from the Greek text of 1 John 5:7 (a touchstone verse for Trinitarian theology)[1] on the grounds that he could find no evidence of the verse in any Greek manuscript (including Codex Vaticanus in Rome) that he had managed to consult.[2] He also questioned the authenticity of other New Testament passages, such as Mark 16:9–20 and John 7:53–8:11. The translation into Latin that he made caused further disquiet. Firstly, people had to come to terms with the fact that here was a *second* translation into Latin, sitting alongside the ancient Vulgate. Secondly, readers had to come to terms with how Erasmus chose to translate some Greek words into Latin. Most significant among these was his rendering of the Greek word *logos* in John 1:1: "In the beginning was the *???*". Instead of the Latin *verbum* meaning "word", Erasmus chose to use the Latin *sermo*, meaning "conversation". His rendering of the beginning of John's Gospel thus read: "In the beginning was the conversation . . ." Erasmus felt that *sermo* or conversation more accurately expressed the richness of the Greek term *logos*.

Erasmus' translation of *logos* as "conversation" is very helpful, it seems to me, in moving us away from a literalist interpretation of the nature of the Bible towards one in which the Bible better reflects the

[1] 1 John 5:7 begins in all texts: "For there are three that testify:". Most texts then proceed to verse 8: "the Spirit, the water and the blood; and the three are in agreement" (New International Version). The larger rendering of verses 7 and 8 reads: "For there are three that bear record in heaven, the Father, the Word, and the Holy Ghost: and these three are one. And there are three that bear witness in earth, the Spirit, and the water, and the blood: and these three agree in one" (Authorised Version).

[2] Erasmus rashly proclaimed that if he were to find so much as one Greek text containing the "Three Witnesses" (of 1 John 5:7) he would include it in his next edition. Of course, such a manuscript was quickly produced. Many suspect it as having been produced specifically for the occasion. It is today known as "minuscule 61" and is housed at Trinity College, Dublin. It is dated to the 16th century. Erasmus duly included the verse in the third edition of his *Novum Instrumentum omne, diligenter ab Erasmo Rot. Recognitum et Emendatum*.

purpose for which it appears to have been created. That purpose was to bear witness to "*the* Word" himself, or to allow "*the* Word" through scripture to speak to us. Karl Barth expresses it thus in his section of *Church Dogmatics* that explores the doctrine of the word of God:

> The Word of God is God Himself in Holy Scripture. For God once spoke as Lord to Moses and the prophets, to the Evangelists and apostles. And now through their written word He speaks as the same Lord to His church. Scripture is holy and the Word of God, because by the Holy Spirit it became and will become to the Church a witness to divine revelation.[3]

Barth's focus upon the living *logos* or "Word" being the author or voice of scripture happily reflects for me the Semitic perspective of "truth" being conceived in personal terms. Apart from the deliberate personification of "wisdom" in various Old Testament books, Jesus' declaration about being himself "the way, the truth, the life" carries an aura of relationship – of "conversation" – about it. Even today in the Middle East, if you ask directions of, say, an Egyptian (more likely in a non-urban context), he will rise and declare, "I am the way," and will lead you to your destination. My son-in-law, on reaching this point in his review of my text, reminded me of our joint experience in downtown Cairo, Egypt. My wife and I had returned to that country to visit friends and colleagues, taking with us our daughters and associated spouses and children. During a visit to Khan al-Khalili in Cairo in order to buy presents, we were escorted all round the bazaar, round the university, round the university hospital(!) by an Egyptian who had asked us what we were looking to buy. We had told him and he spent the next hour or more taking us (or, truthfully, failing to take us) to where we wanted to go. For that hour or so, during a hot dusty day in downtown Cairo (an urban context, no less), our Egyptian acquaintance became "the way" for us.

When Jesus declared, "I am the truth", he was not pointing to some selection of presuppositions or some deposit of words. He was saying that he lives the truth. Going with him constitutes going with the truth. Truth, in that perspective, is about relationship with the divine. Christian discipleship, one might say, constitutes learning to hear the voice of God, supremely, but not exclusively – and certainly

[3] Karl Barth (trans. G.T. Thomson & Harold Knight), *Church Dogmatics, Vol 1, The Doctrine of the Word of God*, T. & T. Clark: Edinburgh (1956), p 457.

not presuppositionally – through Scripture. The Bible constitutes the record, if you like, of the invitation to "go with Jesus." In that kind of context, "inerrancy" has not so much to do with the preservation of a text free from mistakes, as with an assurance that going with the One to whom the Bible bears witness will certainly not lead us into error.

Newbigin makes the cogent point that Protestant "fundamentalism", just as much as "liberalism", is a child of the Enlightenment. In seeking to reassert the authority of the Bible in the modern world, Christian fundamentalists have often pursued an unhelpful methodology:

> I am referring to a kind of fundamentalism which seeks to affirm the factual, objective truth of every statement in the Bible and which thinks that if any single factual error were to be admitted, biblical authority would collapse. Human judgement would replace the word of God. The unavoidable existence of discrepancies in matters of fact to be found in the Bible was sometimes countered by the statement that the original text (now lost to us) was without error.[4]

Newbigin suggests that this kind of "defence" of biblical integrity actually leads to absurdity. It arises, he proposes, from a false view of biblical authority that has come to be imposed upon the Bible by minds shaped by the Enlightenment:

> The doctrine of verbal inerrancy is a direct denial of the way in which God has chosen to make himself known to us as the Father of our Lord Jesus Christ.[5]

Why is Newbigin so strong in his assertion? Surely it is because the doctrine of verbal inerrancy is a human construct for supposedly measuring faithfulness or consistency or accuracy or certainty. We all recognise that, in fact, Jesus did not himself make the Father known via infallible, unrevisable, propositional statements. He chose rather to limit himself to coming and being with some friends in community and through his life with them to convey what he had been given to convey. Actions and speech consistently provoked others to draw their own conclusions out of their encounters with him. Truth, by this accounting, is not imposed, nor is it squandered as a kind of commodity. It is personal in essence. Knowing Jesus – encountering the Truth – is the starting-point and key for living in

[4] Newbigin, (1995), *op. cit.*, p 85.
[5] *Ibid.*, p 89.

the truth. We, today, meet Jesus in and through Scripture. Our knowing proceeds by faith. It is not based on logically demonstrable certainties but proceeds from trust in the One who is encountered in the Bible. As Barr reflects:

> God informs us not by imparting to us direct communications of absolute truth, but by bringing us face to face with narratives, laws, precepts, songs and hymns, letters and teachings and works of the imagination, through which a deeply adequate and authoritative insight into his nature and works is made accessible.[6]

The point of the text is to lead us to know the One to whom it bears witness, the One of whom it speaks in such a variety of ways. The Bible, therefore, owns authority because of the authority of the God who speaks through it. Again, "conversation" proves a good word -– there is a "ring of truth" about the voice that engages with humankind through the text of the Bible.

Perhaps here a brief comparison between Islamic and Christian views of "Word of God" may prove beneficial (see figure 30).

Islam knows an eternal Word "sent down" in God's mercy. Christianity knows an eternal Word "come down" in self-emptying humility. The Qur'ân purports to be that eternal book made

Figure 30

Revelation as portrayed in Islam and Christianity

Islam	**Christianity**
eternal speech ("**Word**") in heaven	eternal person ("**Word**") in heaven
↓	↓
sent down via dictation (*tanzîl*)	comes down via incarnation
↓	↓
recited Word on earth as **Qur'ân**	Word as flesh on earth as **Jesus Christ**
+	+
witness of Muḥammad	witness of disciples
↓	↓
recorded in **Traditions** (*ḥadîth*)	recorded in **Gospels**
+	+
exegesis of Qur'ân	implications of Gospels
↓	↓
explained in **Commentaries** (*tafsîr*)	explained in **Epistles**
	↓
	exegeted in commentaries

[6] James Barr, *op. cit.*, p 125.

accessible to Arabic-attuned, human ears. The Bible constitutes a witness by Spirit-attuned ears to the personal Word who lived in our midst as Jesus Christ. In passing, we may note the barrenness of trying to compare Qur'ân with Bible or Gospels. The appropriate comparison, as we have indicated, is between "sent down" Word (Qur'ân) and "come down" Word (Jesus Christ).

Even given the differences expressed in the above comparison between "Word of God" as it finds expression in Islam and Christianity, Kenneth Cragg still insists on some element of "conversation" within both faiths:

> This paradox of a decisively closed Canon meant as an ever-used Scripture, which obtains in respect of both Bible and Qur'an, means that it both regulates by its fixity and anticipates in its meanings. It both enshrines and expects. Its command is over minds on which it must depend if its authority is to avail.[7]

Tariq Ramadan makes an equivalent point, referring specifically in his case to the Qur'ân:

> It is a text, revealed at a given moment in history, in a certain context, and presented to the intelligence of women and men of faith. It must be said over and over again that the Revelation of a Book, of a Text, would have no meaning if intelligence, human reason capable of grasping its meaning, were not taken for granted. There can be no revealed Text unless there is human intellect up to the task of reading and interpreting it.[8]

Without some kind of conversation between given "word" (of either variety) and recipient community, the divine word would carry little weight.

Within the history of Christian reflection on the text of the Bible, "conversation" has meant a lot more than in the Islamic case. The giving of the word of God has been initiated through incarnation. The divine word, indeed the divine person, has come to be expressed through limited human reality. In coming to earth as a man, Christ took on in his flesh real human limitations. Similarly, the resultant written record of his sojourn on earth is a record put together in human words through which God speaks his divine word. In Christian considering of the Bible, then, the significance of context for the meaning of any passage under review has long been accepted. Long accepted also has been the fact that any text has a

[7] Kenneth Cragg, *The Weight in the Word. Prophethood: Biblical and Quranic*, Sussex Academic Press: Brighton (1999), p 141.

[8] Ramadan, *op. cit.* (2004), p 20.

pretext – the four Gospels, for example, are not simply straight "biography"; they are proclamations of "Good News" clearly devised for specific audiences by composers or compilers with a potent purpose. Why were they served up in such a way? How did they come to be presented in such a manner? What was the *sitz in lieben* of the community that threw up each particular composition? Historical, textual and many other genres of "criticism" have come to be pursued in an attempt to answer such questions. Answering those "critical" questions helps us get to the point of the word or passage or book concerned.

Mark's Gospel comprises a key text for theologians asking those kind of questions because that Gospel, supremely, disrupts the oral life world of the pre-synoptic traditions. Previously, words had been inseparable from persons. The earliest New Testament documents were letters written by the apostle Paul.[9] Paul often refers in those letters to the equivalence of word and deed. He calls his hearers to be imitators of himself in receiving and acting on the epistles he is sending to them. Mark, however, acts as an interpreter of the tradition that reaches him, selecting and reproducing certain elements of that tradition, putting them together to tell the story of a special life. Mark deliberately produces a narrative structure that is designed to carry the tale he wants to tell. We, as Mark's current readers, are enticed by his editorial creativity to ask, "Why did he include this or exclude that, or say such-and-such in such a manner?" There is an incipient openness in Christian exegesis – because of the very nature of the material itself – to the possibility of interrogating the text in a manner strongly denied (officially and historically) within Islam.

Sometimes such incipient openness in the Christian exegetical tradition leads to the espousing of unhelpful (unfaithful) perspectives.

[9] Incidentally, it is partly because of this fact that some Muslim polemicists have accused Paul of distorting the "gospel" that Jesus brought. The infamous and spurious *Gospel of Barnabas* makes this point specifically. In its preamble, the author of the "Gospel" introduces himself as "Barnabas, apostle of Jesus the Nazarene, called Christ." He declares that he is writing this Gospel because many of his contemporaries "being deceived of Satan, under pretence of piety, are preaching most impious doctrine, calling Jesus son of God, repudiating the circumcision ordained of God for ever, and permitting every unclean meat: among whom also Paul hath been deceived . . ." See Lonsdale and Laura Ragg, *The Gospel of Barnabas*, Clarendon Press: Oxford (1907). Muhammad 'Ata ur-Rahim pursues this line of thought concerning the apostle Paul. He claims, for example, that "Paul deviated further and further from the teaching Jesus had embodied, and laid more and more emphasis on the figure of Christ whom he claimed had appeared to him in visions." In Muhammad 'Ata ur-Rahim, *Jesus – a Prophet of Islam*, MWH: London (1977), p 68. Nietzsche also proposed that Paul was the first Christian and the inventor of Christianity.

Figure 31

Christian theologians between extremes

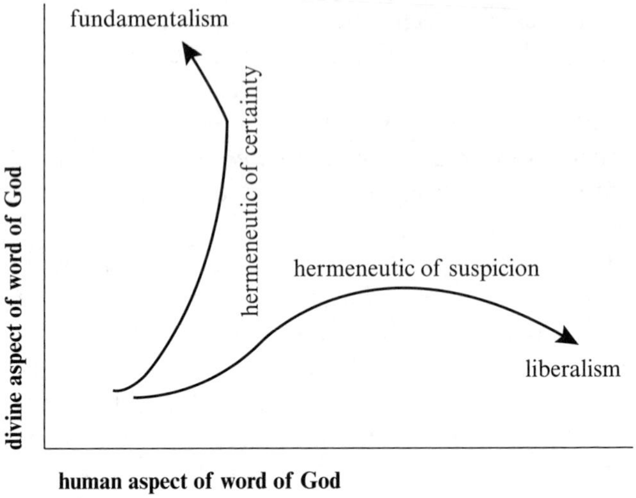

It is evident that Christian theologians may be described as occupying positions somewhere along an axis between extreme "liberal" and extreme "conservative" in their view of the text of the Bible (see figure 31). We have looked mostly at the extreme conservative or fundamentalist response in this book, with just a brief reference in chapter 12 to an opposite end-of-the-axis, liberal response.

Perhaps one might say that an extreme liberal approach chooses to concentrate almost exclusively on the details of the human aspect of "word of God". Its interest in the textual or contextual dynamics leads to serious background research concerning the text, but tends to obscure any recognition of the Word of God himself within those fragile human words. In other words, liberals easily miss the wood for the trees! Their openness only to consideration of the human aspect of the formation of the Bible leads inexorably to a hermeneutic of suspicion.

At the other end of the axis, perhaps one might say that an extreme conservative view of scripture is so interested in its hearing of the divine Word that its listening is untempered by human elements in the biblical equation. Fundamentalists easily become deaf to context or different styles of speech and writing. They remain uninformed by some of the culturally-coloured ways in which (for example) relationships between men and women, masters and slaves or visions of God are described. In other words, fundamentalists easily miss the trees for the wood! Their openness only to consideration of the divine aspect of the formation of the Bible leads inexorably to a hermeneutic of certainty.

A faith that derives from incarnation must, it seems to me, allow both elements fair play in the formulating of a view about the authority of the Bible. The Bible is God's word expressed through the minds and pens of human beings. Human words are able to bear God's truth. And they can sustain proper analysis and investigation. At the same time, the "truth" that they convey is not an end in itself; it is not composed of a list of propositions. It consists, rather, in a witness to a person. Christ is Word made flesh. For that reason, the New Testament has priority (abrogating authority even) over the Old Testament. The New Testament describes the fulfilment (not the establishment) in Christ of the Old Testament covenant. In Christ, the law is radicalised – he lives according to its spirit. In Christ, much of the law is relativised – it finds focus no longer, for example, in limited promises of seed and land to one people. Equally, there need be no problem with having four, as opposed to one, recountings of the life of Christ:

> Each gospel consists *both* of certain sayings and doings of the historical Jesus and of the interpretation that has been put upon these by the evangelist . . . If a doctrine of the authority of scripture is to be meaningful, it must be primarily the gospels as we have them, and not some historical (and usually debatable) reconstruction that goes behind the text, that is authoritative for the community of faith. This means that to regard each gospel as inspired and authoritative entails according inspired and authoritative status to each gospel's interpretation of Jesus.[10]

The biblical text needs to be taken "literally", both in the sense of respecting the literary categories of scripture and in the sense of taking seriously the historical character of the Bible story. But the biblical text does not need to be taken "literalistically", as if poetic imagination or apocalyptic dreaming function in the same way as historical reportage. A real event, such as the creation of the world by a sovereign God, may be described poetically or symbolically in the Bible. The very fact of its being described does not warrant an insistence that the poetic description of creation is necessarily a

[10] R.W.L. Moberly, "Proclaiming Christ Crucified" in *Anvil* (1988), vol 5, no 1, p 45.

scientifically accurate record of the event. Equally, the poetic or symbolic language used in Hebrew to describe the fact of creation does not permit the conclusion that the event being thus poetically portrayed did not occur in a phenomenological sense. You cannot claim that "creation" was just an image in a poet's mind and did not really happen.

What am I trying to say? In the context of a hermeneutic of suspicion, such as that which widely prevails in the Christian church in Britain today, a lot of hard work remains to be done in order to retrieve a sense of engaging with the divine when contemplating the Bible. The Bible is not simply text in a manuscript kind of sense. It is a truthful word. It is a text-bearing-witness-to the divine Word of God. As "holy" book, the Bible engenders a conversation between contemporary reader and the One to whom it bears witness. How can we have a conversation with God without losing some of our human pride, without becoming more open to what he might be saying to us?

In the context of a hermeneutic of certainty, such as that which widely prevails in certain segments of the Christian community in Britain and North America today, a lot of hard work remains to be done in order to free the text of the Bible from a seemingly faithful but actually dangerous manipulation of that text. The Bible must not be used in a proof-text manner to give support to other agendas. As human record, the Bible invites intellectual integrity and honesty in our handling of it. Scrutinising the medium constitutes part of the means of reaching to its core so that God's authentic voice can be heard through it.

Within the Christian community, such hard work – on both counts – can, more or less, freely be done. I say "more or less" because I am aware that within Western academic institutions, the study of theology has been largely captured and held to ransom by a prevailing humanist or liberal approach to text-appreciation. In such places of learning, it is often difficult for non-liberal theologians to command a serious hearing. Equally, I am aware that, in the United States at least, it is increasingly difficult for committed Christians (especially from an evangelical background) to posit difficult questions of the Bible. All too often, any querying of a culturally embedded, fundamentalist line runs the risk of ridicule and disempowerment. Tony Campolo, for example, bemoans his being labelled as an "agent of the antichrist" by right-wing, fellow evangelicals because of his belief that justice requires that Palestinians as much as Israelis have a right to a homeland of their own.[11] Nevertheless, despite the difficulties mooted here at each end of the Christian theological spectrum, people of that faith are at least permitted to ask the questions and present their different perspectives.

Is there an equivalent permission for Muslims to query and renegotiate their faith at the beginning of the third millennium? The answer has, by and large, to be a resounding "No!" My contention at the conclusion of this book is that the events of 9/11 and 7/7, plus other dramatic actions of contemporary, radical Islamists, require the Muslim community to somehow change that "No" to a "Yes" – and quickly!

[11] Campolo, *op. cit.*, p 222.

Chapter 14

A straight path less certain?

THE challenge for the Muslim community, especially at a time when it finds itself under microscopic scrutiny for its literalist view of the Qur'ân, is for its power-holders to allow some hard thinking to be done about that literalist perspective. There are, as we have discovered, precedents in the history of Muslim reflection upon the Qur'ân that might prove helpful or provocative in such reconsideration. One of the earliest precedents, not yet mentioned, occurred during the battle of Siffin (AD 657) when the supporters of Mu'âwiya (died AD 680) requested that hostilities be halted and that their argument with 'Alî ibn Abû Ṭâlib (died AD 661) be settled by resorting to the Qur'ân as arbitrator. 'Alî allegedly responded with the following, wistful reflection:

> When Mu'awiyah invited me to the Qur'an for a decision, I could not turn my face away from the Book of Allah. The Mighty and Glorious Allah declared that 'if you dispute about anything, refer it to Allah and His Apostle'. [However,] this is the Qur'an, written in straight lines, between two boards [of its binding]; it does not speak with a tongue; it needs interpreters and interpreters are people.[1]

Interpreters are needed, and interpreters are people. How is meaning that is faithful to the text and yet relevant to the contemporary world to be arrived at? An open-ended view of exegesis and a less antagonistic defensiveness about the application of a historico-critical method to explaining the text of the Qur'ân might constitute positive starting-points for distilling and re-stating original meaning. Somehow, contemporary Muslims must redefine the nature of the "word" by which their fellow Muslims – Islamists – claim to be living and killing. And they must do so openly, in the public arena. Ed Husain admits the folly of allowing the Islamist groups, in the United Kingdom for example, to do all the public talking:

[1] Cited in Abu'l-Hasan Sayyed Muhammad al-Razi (comp.; Askari Jafery trans.), *Peak of Eloquence: Nahjul Balaghah – Sermons, Letters and Sayings of Imam Ali (A.S.)*, Islamic Seminary for World Shia Muslim Organizations: Bombay (1979), p 248.

> Islamist groups organized conferences, the media gave them vast amounts of airtime, and they began to be seen as 'mainstream' Islam. I, a spiritually oriented, moderate, mainstream Muslim, like millions of others, had nothing to say. We did not advocate suicide bombings, challenge the governments of countries, threaten to hijack – why should we make the news?[2]

The volatile and unpredictable world that we humans have managed to construct at the beginning of the twenty-first century is a world offering little certainty. The litany of extremist, Islamist atrocities grows and, in growing, discloses that the Islamist agenda *is* making more sense to more Muslims as the months and years pass. Muslim perpetrators of terrorist acts now come from, and act within, many societies of the world. Think of the bombers of the British consulate in Istanbul, the Jewish cultural centre in Casablanca, the nightclub in Bali, the foreigners' compound in Riyadh, the American consulate in Karachi, the railway station in Madrid and the transportation system in London. All these terrorists have been persuaded of the legitimacy of their actions and have perpetrated their murderous expressions of *jihâd* since 9/11 and the declaration of war on terror. As Jason Burke, Observer journalist and specialist on the *al-Qaida* movement, discerns:

> The vast bulk of the world's . . . Muslims remain moderate, if resentful and "conflicted". But the truth is that al Qaeda makes sense to many more people today than ten years ago. A previously fairly restricted discourse which is full of hate, prejudice and myth and which, in its extreme form, legitimises atrocious acts and enables young men to transgress against all their own social norms and kill themselves and innocent civilians, is spreading . . .[3]

The year 2006 saw the democratic election of a Palestinian government dominated by ḤAMAS[4] and the denting of Israel's pride in her armed forces by Ḥizballah[5] guerrillas in southern Lebanon. Most Muslims sympathise with, or applaud, both circumstances, even though ḤAMAS and Ḥizballah represent the extreme Islamist wing of contemporary Islam.

[2] Ed Husain, *The Islamist*, Penguin Books: London (2007), p 214.

[3] Jason Burke, "Al Qaeda after Madrid" in *Prospect*, June (2004).

[4] ḤAMAS or *Ḥarakat al-Muqâwama al-Islâmiyya*: Islamic Resistance Movement. ḤAMAS was originally formed in 1987 as the military arm of the Palestinian branch of the Muslim Brotherhood.

[5] Ḥizballah: Party of God. This radical Shî'a group was formed in Lebanon in the early 1980s.

The growing litany of extremist, Islamist atrocities plus the recent international stance of groups like ḤAMAS and Ḥizballah, is mirrored by, and in many ways is a partial result of, another kind of violence that marks our contemporary world. India's oppression of Muslims in Kashmir, the ethnic cleansing of Muslims in Bosnia and Kosovo,[6] the Russian domination of Chechnya, the unwillingness of the United States of America for so many years to hold Israel to account for illegal occupation of parts of Palestine, the Gulf war and the Iraq war – all contribute towards a strong persecution complex that many Muslims justifiably feel. Perhaps such feeling explains the relatively muted voice of British Muslims, for example, after the atrocities associated with 9/11. The perception of wider society in Britain at the time certainly was that British Muslims did not condemn the murderous acts unreservedly or sufficiently.[7] In the Muslims' view, however, it appeared obvious that 9/11 was connected to other events on the world stage that preceded it – events that had largely gone uncondemned and unchecked within the international community. Surely no Western leader can be in doubt any longer that the two kinds of violence are connected. Iraq constitutes the current hotspot where both kinds of violence meet head-on. There, Western armies try to facilitate the development of a Western-style democracy, amidst the reluctance of large sections of the indigenous population. There, the Islamists successfully recruit wave after wave of *jihâdîs* from around the Muslim world to wreak unspeakable horror in the lives of foreign troops and contractors as well as innocent Iraqi civilians. Successive polls since 2001 (9/11) document a gradual increase in the proportion of British Muslims who have shifted from understanding of to support for more extremist, Islamist initiatives on the world scene and within the United Kingdom. We live in disturbing times!

One cannot challenge the Muslim community to rethink its literalism with regard to the Qur'ân or its sympathy towards an aggressively Islamist political agenda, without asking that Western politicians find another way to engage with Muslims over issues of national and international justice. Such a reciprocal call is especially urgent in that, as we have seen, Muslims view the foreign policy of

[6] NATO did eventually, and fairly, intervene on this issue, though Muslims around the world saw the intervention as a long time overdue.

[7] Lady Thatcher, for example, voiced this perception in an interview with *The Times* in September 2001.

the United States of America as strongly religiously motivated. Western nations have a responsibility for helping to make possible a rethink by Muslims of their hermeneutic of certainty. As Sardar rightly observes:

> The war on terror, in fact, cannot be a war at all. It has to be a reasoned engagement with the politics of tradition. If Islam has been construed as the problem, then Islam is also the essential ingredient in the solution.[8]

At the same time, and especially in the British context after the London bombings of July 2005, there lies strong potential for a willingness by British Muslims at least towards rethinking their hermeneutic of certainty. They live in a country in which the majority of the British people oppose their government's involvement in the White House's war on terror, and especially the use of military force to bring about the humiliation of Saddam Hussein in Iraq. In March 2003, the largest public demonstration in British history took place. Between 1½ and 2 million people marched through London on the eve of the war on Iraq. The event was co-organised by the Islamist (yes, Islamist!) Muslim Association of Britain (an affiliate of the Muslim Council of Britain) and the Stop the War Coalition. The majority of marchers may not have understood or agreed with the particular grievances or goals of the Muslim Association of Britain, but those Islamists – and Muslims in general in Britain – certainly discovered that they were not alone in their opposition to the proposed war on Iraq. Millions of ordinary Britons were in sympathy with them.

British Muslims also live in a country in which Christian leaders, especially, have worked hard over several decades to engage and include Muslims in national, regional and local public life. Many expressions of understanding and solidarity by British Christians towards British Muslims since 7/7 have been humbly and gratefully received.

The world of British Islam has been strongly shaken from within by the London bombings. It is obvious, though needing to be restated in this concluding chapter, that the majority of literalist Muslims – fundamentalist Muslims or Islamists even – are not militant in their personal stance nor supporting of the use of terror by their co-religionists. Some Muslims have responded to the involvement of young British Muslims in unspeakable acts of terror by

[8] Sardar (2005), *op. cit.*, p 12.

denying that Islam bears any responsibility for those acts. Others have chosen to blame their traditional rivals (the Wahhâbis or Salâfis or whoever) for the atrocities, refusing to allow any corporate responsibility to fall on their own shoulders. Others, such as Ziauddin Sardar or Najah Kadhim, director of the International Forum for Islamic Dialogue, have boldly admitted that the terrorists are products of an Islamic worldview and that their specific views on *jihâd* are part of a stream of interpretation that has a history within Islam. Their call to fellow Muslims today is to recognise that reality and vigorously address it:

> If Muslims do not take on the challenge, they cede the initiative to those who have misconceived the problem and accepted a military strategy that is no solution. And that will make us all prey to more violence.[9]

Recent Presidents of the United States of America, supremely, have opted for a military solution to the problem of "Muslim terrorism". Certainly until 9/11, and probably until 7/7, there had been a distancing of most British (and European) politicians and public opinion leaders from what Fred Halliday identifies as "strategic anti-Muslimism".[10] This attitude he observes as originating in the United States and being related to issues such as oil supplies, nuclear weapons and terrorism. He suggests that it dates from the 1970s and was fed by the OPEC price rises, the Islamic Revolution in Iran (which came to involve US diplomatic personnel in Tehran in the drawn-out hostages crisis), the bombing of the World Trade Centre in 1993 and – since the time of Halliday's writing, we might add – the tragedy of 9/11. Although such a kind of "strategic anti-Muslimism" has existed in European political circles, by and large a different type of anti-Muslimism has tended to dominate there.

Halliday identifies this other anti-Muslimism as "populist". It has emerged, he suggests, in the context of issues relating to the presence of Muslims in Western societies – issues such as assimilation, integration, race, veiling and so on. It constitutes, in his view, part of a general anti-immigrant attitude that has developed in Western

[9] Sardar (2005), *op. cit.*, p 12. See also Najah Kadhim's comments, here quoted by Sardar: "The best way to fight the Kharijite tradition is with the humanistic and rationalistic traditions of Islam. This is how they were defeated in Islamic history. This is how we will defeat them now."

[10] Fred Halliday, *Islam and the Myth of Confrontation. Religion and Politics in the Middle East*, I.B. Tauris: New York (1995). Halliday suggests that "anti-Muslimism" encompasses racist, xenophobic and stereotypical elements.

Europe since the 1980s, and which has found expression in some cases in the programmes of right wing and racist politicians.[11] Something of what Halliday is suggesting seems to be encapsulated in the identifying – by the Runnymede Trust in 1997 – of a general, British attitude of "Islamophobia." Such Islamophobia was discovered by the Trust to be made up of seven major aspects (see figure 32) endemic in British society.[12]

A further report, published by the Commission on British Muslims and Islamophobia in 2004, accused British public bodies of "institutionalised Islamophobia" and claimed that the problem was growing worse, not better.[13] Further support for Halliday's pinpointing of populist as opposed to strategic anti-Muslimism in the United Kingdom might be deduced from events in the north of the country that narrowly preceded 9/11 and which came to be strongly overshadowed by that tragedy. In May, June and July of 2001, there were "riots" in Bradford, Burnley and Oldham in which mostly South Asian men of either Bangladeshi (in Oldham) or Pakistani

Figure 32

"Islamophobia" defined

	Feature
1	Muslim cultures are seen as monolithic.
2	Muslim cultures are seen as substantially different from other cultures.
3	Islam is perceived as implacably threatening.
4	Muslims are seen as using their faith to political or military advantage.
5	Muslim criticism of Western cultures and societies is rejected out of hand.
6	The fear of Islam is mixed with racist hostility to immigration.
7	Islamophobia is assumed to be natural and unproblematic.

[11] See the helpful article by Wasif Ahadid and Sjoerd van Koningsveld, "The Negative Image of Islam and Muslims in the West". In W.A.R. Shadid and P.S. van Koningsveld (eds.), *Religious Freedom and the Neutrality of the State: the Position of Islam in the European Union*, Peeters: Leuven (2002), pp 174–194.

[12] The summary concerning Islamophobia may be found in Tahir Abbas, "British South Asian Muslims: before and after September 11" in Tahir Abbas (ed.), *op. cit.*, p 12.

[13] Robin Richardson (ed.), *Islamophobia: Issues, Challenges and Action*, A report by the Commission on British Muslims and Islamophobia, Trentham Books: Stoke-on-Trent (2004).

origin reacted strongly to mobilisations by the neo-fascist British National Party. Such serious public disturbances, mirrored by lesser disorders in Leeds and Stoke-on-Trent, did not erupt in a vacuum. They emerged out of a long, developing, pre-history:

> The spread of unrest was linked to an increase in racial violence, long-standing mistrust of and disillusionment with the police, the overt and taunting presence of the BNP and other far-right groups, and the entrenched poverty and unemployment that existed within the cities.[14]

The official response to such disturbances has been twofold. At a local level the criminal justice system came down hard on the "protesters", especially in the case of those arrested for the Bradford riots. At a national level, there developed a focus on community cohesion, social capital and policy prescriptions based upon them.[15] From the perspective of the British Muslim communities concerned, the twofold response to the rioting might easily be construed as expressing further, populist anti-Muslimism.

Riots in "the north" during 2001 pale to insignificance (in the popular mind) when compared with terrorist acts on the transportation network in the heart of Britain's capital during the summer of 2005. There is a real danger that after 7/7 and the identification of *British* Muslims as suicide bombers, the "strategic" type of anti-Muslimism will come to be overlaid on the "populist" type already finding expression within British society.

Despite such intimations of potential worsening of relations between Muslims and non-Muslims within Britain, it is my conviction that the current climate in this country after 7/7 provides a unique opportunity for the questioning of unhelpful certainty. That questioning needs to take place in the political sphere, within the Muslim community and within the Christian community.

[14] Paul Bagguley and Yasmin Hussain, "Flying the Flag for England? Citizenship, Religion and Cultural Identity among British Pakistani Muslims," in Tahir Abbas (ed.), *op. cit.*, p 209.

[15] The investigations into the rioting produced official reports. The Denham Report (*Building Cohesive Communities*) arose from a ministerial Group on Public Order coordinated by the Home Office. The Cantle Report (*Community Cohesion*) was produced by an "independent" Community Cohesion Review Team. The Ritchie Report, funded by the Home Office, focused on Oldham. The *Report of the Burnley Task Force* was commissioned locally. See *ibid.*, pp 210–213.

LESS CONVINCED POLITICIANS?

A questioning of certainty needs to take place in the political sphere, in the realisation that politics and religion are intimately connected – certainly in the eyes of Muslims, if not in the eyes of British secular humanists. William Dalrymple's cryptic commentary, in the wake of 7/7, needs to be heard at least by Premiers Blair and Brown, if not by President Bush:

> Bush has fulfilled Bin Laden's every hope. Through the invasion of secular Ba'athist Iraq, the abuses in Abu Ghraib, the mass murders in Falluja, America – with Britain's obedient assistance – has turned Iraq into a jihadist playground while alienating all moderate Muslim opinion in the Islamic heartlands and, crucially, in the west.[16]

The identification of an "axis of evil" and the decision, at least within the American administration, to pursue the neutralising of that axis, only serves to reinforce the sense of alienation and injustice that many Muslims around the world currently feel. The choreographing of the route to regime change within Iraq has become a precedent through which other tensions between the "Christian" West and the Muslim world are assessed. The stunning victory of ḤAMAS in elections democratically seen through by Palestinians in 2006 has to serve as a reminder that Palestinians are adamant about their right to self-determination. Their espousal of an extremist alternative to the corruption ridden Fatah movement both makes the Middle East peace process more difficult to manage and underlines the reality that addressing this particular historical issue of international injustice must engage the positive attention of powerful Western nations quickly. Attitudes are becoming increasingly entrenched in "extreme" modes. Solving the Palestinian/Israeli issue is a far surer way to protect America and the West from Islamist suicide attackers than ratcheting up a possible pursuit of "evil" in more countries than Afghanistan and Iraq. Similarly, the international confrontation with Iran over the latter's nuclear programme proceeds from a Western assumption that Iran must be seeking to develop a nuclear weapon in order to attack Israel, and an Iranian presupposition that the West's dominating role in opposing her "peaceful", nuclear programme derives from the West's subservience to a pro-Zionist lobby in Christian America.

[16] William Dalrymple, "A largely bourgeois endeavour" in *The Guardian*, 20th July (2005).

In too many "political" confrontations between "Christian" Western nations and Muslim nations, political leaders refuse to step back from their own rhetoric to consider whether, perhaps, they have potentially misread the situation. The unleashing of military and political violence in the name of combating terror is quickly seen through in those parts of the world on the receiving end of the violence. In so many cases, at the moment, "those parts of the world" comprise Muslim nations and peoples.

LESS CONVINCED MUSLIMS?

A questioning of certainty needs to take place within the Muslim community in the realm especially of Qur'ân appreciation, where a literal-only interpretation is widely upheld:

> When the Qur'an, for example, says God sits on His throne, He sits on His throne, period. No discussion can be entertained on the nature of the throne or its purpose. Nothing can be read metaphorically or symbolically.[17]

Ziauddin Sardar has for many years constituted a somewhat lone (maverick?) voice within the Islamic *umma* calling for just such a questioning of certainty. His reflection on 9/11, in which his family nearly lost two close relatives, is offered as much to a Muslim readership as to anyone else:

> Literalism. Literally taken. When metaphors are taken literally, should it surprise us that they lead to madness? It was hardly a revelation to me that Osama bin Laden was behind all this. It was the glint in his eyes, all those years ago, when I first caught sight of him in that fateful meeting of Mujahidin groups in Peshawar. The insistent refrain at that meeting was 'impossible'. Nothing could be negotiated. Everything was impossible. To make the Word flesh one must have the power of God. The literalists had assumed that impossible power. They had ceased to ask the fundamental questions of existence: 'Who are we?' 'Why are we?' 'Where are we going?' 'What is the purpose of humanity?' Their literalism provided ready-made answers to everything. It was impossible for them to do otherwise.[18]

Nasr Abû Zaid writes passionately in the same tone, urging freedom of thinking upon faithful Muslims in today's world while demand-

[17] Ziauddin Sardar, (2004), *op. cit.*, p 145. Sardar is here commenting on the style of Qur'ân appreciation that modern students at Medina University inherit from Ibn Taymîyya. Everything has to be interpreted literally.

[18] *Ibid.*, p 334.

ing political freedom within contemporary Islamic societies for faithful Muslims to pursue such freedom of thought:

> We need an untrammelled exploration of our religious heritage. This is the first prerequisite for a religious renewal. We must lift the embargo on freedom of thought. The area of the renewal should be unlimited. There is no room for safe doctrinal havens in Islamic teaching, sacrosanct and closed to critical research. Such safe doctrinal havens constrain the process of renewal. They represent censorship, and this has no place in the history of Islamic thinking.[19]

Some British, Muslim, authors of fiction have recently tried to vindicate or promote a more questioning approach to the Qur'ân. Through their novels, they have presented themselves as interrogators of the fundamental questions of existence. Nadeem Aslam, for example, crafts an engaging account of a Pakistani family trying to work out its identity as "Muslim" and "British" in *Maps for Lost Lovers*. The story is set in a Pakistani community in an unnamed, northern English town. The main characters of the novel are Shamas, a former poet, and his wife Kaukab. There is a crisis in the family due to the disappearance (presumed murdered) of Shamas' brother, Jugnu, and his lover, Chanda. Chanda has been previously married and divorced. She and Jugnu have fallen in love and moved in together, living next door to Shamas and Kaukab. Chanda's two brothers are strongly suspected of being involved in the disappearance of Jugnu and Chanda – indeed, on a visit to Pakistan the siblings boast of their murdering the couple, their motive having been to preserve their family's honour.

It gradually transpires in the novel that Shamas and Kaukab's own sons and daughter have also "disappeared" from a traditional, Pakistani, Muslim approach to life as embodied especially, and with considerable pathos, in their mother Kaukab. Even Shamas himself seems to have lost his way. On the surface he appears to be a Muslim of standing within the community, as director of the Community Relations Council, but beneath the surface he lives a life that would shame his wife if only she knew about it. Kaukab lives "by the book" as much as she can, a faithful Muslim, operating in a "little Pakistan", protected by her non-understanding of English and her non-meeting with white people.

[19] Nasr Abû Zaid in *Al-Ahram* (2002), quoted in Troll, *op. cit.*, p 8.

The clash of worlds between Kaukab and her children, Charag, Ujala and Mah-Jabin, finds its dénouement in a family get-together in the parents' home. Charag arrives with his white wife and son. Charag brings along a magazine with a photograph of one of his successful works of art. It is a painting of himself, naked, surrounded by butterflies and other insects and animals. In the self-portrait he has an uncircumcised penis. His mother cannot understand why he would paint such a "false" picture of himself and is deeply offended on God's behalf. Mah-Jabin, the daughter, keeps silent about most of her life far away in London. She is in her late twenties, living on her own after divorcing the first cousin she had gone to Pakistan to marry at sixteen years of age. She is refusing to cooperate with her mother in finding a replacement husband. Ujala, the younger son, is present at the gathering under sufferance, still angry at the memory of his mother poisoning him with bromide as prescribed by a local Muslim cleric when Kaukab had complained, years ago, of her younger son's teenage rebelliousness. At the get-together, Ujala eventually lets rip at his mother. He pushes her to admit that she thinks that the murder of Jugnu and Chanda is deserved because of their sinfulness in cohabiting. He recites a long list of deficiencies that he discerns in Islam, contradicting his mother's insistence that Islam has brought dignity to millions of people around the world. She eventually asks him how he dare speak so strongly and bitterly about what Islam means. The second generation, British Muslim lad answers:

> "I've read the Koran, in English, unlike you who just chant it in Arabic without knowing what the words mean, hour after hour, day in day out, like chewing gum for the brain."[20]

Ujala reads his faith with his eyes open, and finds some aspects wanting. And he is not afraid of saying so! Aslam's book has many related themes concerning exile and cruelty, love and self-sacrifice. In an interview with a British newspaper, Aslam revealed that *Maps for Lost Lovers* constituted, in part, his response to the events of 9/11. He declared that he was inspired through it to "condemn the small-scale September 11s that go on every day."

Hanif Kureishi, another well-known, contemporary, British, Muslim author and screen-writer, tried to raise the "questioning" aspect of being a Muslim in his second novel, *The Black Album*. His

[20] Nadeem Aslam, *Maps for Lost Lovers*, Faber and Faber: London (2004), p 322.

story centres around Shahid, a young Muslim who comes to London to study after the death of his father. In London, he finds himself drawn into two opposing worlds. In the room next to his own in his rented accommodation lives Riaz, a convinced Islamist who leads a small cell of radicalised male and female youths. To some considerable degree, Shahid is attracted to what these fellow-Muslims stand for in their solidarity with poor Muslims in various parts of the capital who are being subjected to racial discrimination and abuse. At the same time, he falls in love with a college lecturer named Deedee Osgood. She epitomises free-thinking and free-living liberal humanism and he learns to live a life of questionable ethical irresponsibility with her. The two contradictory worlds come together in the aftermath of the publication of Salman Rushdie's *The Satanic Verses*. The Islamist group seeks to hold a book-burning protest within the college where Shahid studies and in which Deedee lectures. Deedee responds by shopping the protestors to the police. They, in turn, seek to destroy her home. Shahid has to choose where his loyalties, and his heart, really lie.

At one point in the novel, Deedee and Shahid are discussing the Islamist cell with which he has become involved:

> She was looking at him. "But don't they scare you?"
> "Who?"
> "Your friends?"
> "Why should they?"
> "They're devoid of doubt."[21]

Without doubt, religious certainty within Islam at the beginning of the twenty-first century will damage that faith's expression in others' eyes and will rob its own constituents of the possibility of asking questions that urgently need to be asked from within the household of faith.

Perhaps authors of fiction can more easily make the case for a less entrenched literalism than can contemporary Muslim theologians. Most theologians who have dared to critique received, hermeneutical norms have either been forced to flee their homelands or have only been accorded the liberty to think creatively about Qur'ân interpretation because they live in the West. Such circumstances

[21] Hanif Kureishi, *The Black Album*, Faber and Faber: London (1995), p 110. For a real-life, insider account of arrogant "doubtlessness", see Ed Hussain's confessions of a former student leader within *Hizb ut-Tahrir* on London campuses in *The Islamist*, Penguin Books: London (2007).

notwithstanding, the theological work that such men and women have begun offers real hope for an unspringing of the certainty trap, if only their voice can be dispassionately heard.

LESS CONVINCED CHRISTIANS?

A similar or equivalent questioning needs to take place within "end-of-the-axis" traditions of Christian appreciation of the Bible:

> Every time we turn the Word of God into an infallible biblical word of man or the biblical word of man into an infallible Word of God we resist that which we ought never to resist, i.e., the truth of the miracle that here fallible men speak the Word of God in fallible human words – and we therefore resist the sovereignty of grace, in which God Himself became man in Christ, to glorify Himself in His humanity.[22]

Barth's neo-orthodox recovery of the authority of Christian Scripture from a liberal denigration of it should inspire contemporary evangelicals to wrestle with difficult questions arising from the captivity of a biblical hermeneutic to a strongly literalist, fundamentalist perspective. Again, I need to highlight that not all Christians who would accept the labels "fundamentalist" or "literalist" would ascribe to the more extreme views of influential, American, evangelical spokespersons for a "biblical perspective" on contemporary world events. Nevertheless, the significant role played by such spokespersons begs of the wider evangelical community a serious consideration of what constitutes "the word of God". Is that concept primarily focused in the person of Christ (the *Logos*) with an inspired, verbalised (and written) text pointing to him? Or is it focused upon a literally-given, divinely-authored text that stands completely on its own – a kind of "absolute transcript" of God's mind whereby the Bible might be understood to be "a Book dropped out of heaven"?[23] Does that phrase remind you of anything? What might make up a faithful, contemporary, evangelical conviction about the authority of Scripture without allowing an intentional or accidental reifying, let alone deifying, of a text?

In such consideration of what precisely constitutes the "word of God", a proper doubting would appear to be a critical necessity. Indeed, there can be no ideal kind of certainty that does not admit

[22] Barth, *op. cit.*, p 529.

[23] Words of Rev George S. Bishop in the early twentieth century, giving his definition of biblical inerrancy, as quoted by Marsden in (2006) *op. cit.*, p 122.

of doubt. To imagine that there can be leads either to irrational literalism or to unrestrained scepticism, even nihilism:

> The confidence proper to a Christian is not the confidence of one who claims possession of demonstrable and indubitable knowledge. It is the confidence of one who has heard and answered the call that comes from the God through whom and for whom all things were made: "Follow me".[24]

Yet the fact of the matter is that the admission of doubt or hesitation is almost universally forsworn in contemporary political and religious ideologies. Hasn't the majority of the British nation waited with baited breath, but in vain, for its Prime Minister to admit that he was wrong about going to war against Iraq? We all secretly know that it will be body bags, ballot boxes and budget deficits, rather than reservations about the conflict possibly being unjust, that will eventually undermine the "war on terror". Would not a recognition by Wahhâbîs in Saudi Arabia of the extremes to which they have gone to control certainty – in terms of what God wants in their society – mark a brave first step away from "the pathologically reductive brand of Islam"[25] that currently characterises them? Would that such admission might breathe a refreshing, liberating possibility for Muslims of all descriptions to freely apply themselves to working out what "submission" might faithfully mean in the contemporary world. How long do we have to endure before those Christian leaders and spokespersons in America who have publicly labelled Islam as "wicked" or accused Prophet Muḥammad of being "a terrorist" or "a paedophile" publicly declare their sorrow for such blasphemous (in Muslims' eyes) and falsely-loaded claims? How many more deaths will result from the drawing of cartoons in a world in which proponents of the "freedom of the press" will not self-regulate according to the sensitivities of a neighbour and in which some Muslims feels so insecurely defensive about their faith that violent expressions of anger are deemed necessary to undo the shame cast upon them? What a long time it takes for us human beings to learn not to judge the "worst" of someone else's history or personality or intention by the "best" of ours!

An acknowledgment by all of us religious believers that a battle for meaning is currently raging within our own separate faiths might help us to be somewhat more guarded in our quick claims to certainty:

[24] Newbigin (1995), *op. cit.*, p 105.
[25] Sardar (2004), *op. cit.*, p 135.

> In the light of the worldwide neoconservative resurgence, an insistence on the plurality of ways within every great religion is an ethical and religious responsibility. No thunderings from the Ayatollah Khomeini to his fellow Muslims, no preremptory decrees from the 'Holy Office' to Roman Catholics, no threats from Reverend Falwell to his fellow Protestants, and no terror tactics by Rabbi Kehane directed at his fellow Jews should be allowed to destroy such an insistence.[26]

For the most part, sadly, we humans do not dare to consider that we might be only partly accurate in our perception of temporal or eternal matters. Maybe, for all of us, the wake-up calls of 9/11 or 7/7 will reintroduce an essential element of wistful questioning into our respective certainties, whether they are political or religious in nature. Meanwhile we might all acknowledge with sorrow our responsibility – especially those of us who claim to be in touch with God – in bringing our world to such a critical state at the beginning of the third millennium:

> Whoever comes to speak in favour of religion and its possibilities of enlightenment and emancipation does not come with clean hands nor with a clear conscience.[27]

Kyrie eleison – Lord have mercy!

Security in believing, it seems to me, comes not by hedging that faith about and seeking to protect it. Rather it comes through the risk of allowing it to stand in its own right, open to critique and rejection by others. God alone knows what of Islam or Christianity, your life or mine, truly or closely or vaguely resembles reality as he knows it. And, according to both faiths, he reserves ultimate judgment about such matters to himself. Certainty, certainly, remains solely with the creator and judge of us all. The "certainty trap" is a dead end of our own making.

For Christians – and I can only speak here as a Christian – there can really be no excuse for tripping the certainty trap. Why? Because Jesus Christ modelled an approach to living and believing that managed to include uncertainty as an element of faithfulness. Jesus was prepared to say to his heavenly Father: "not my will but yours be done". Jesus endured the humiliation of having his motives impugned and his mission hijacked, misinterpreted, foreclosed by those around him who thought that they knew God's mind better

[26] Tracy, *op. cit.*, p 95.
[27] *Ibid.*, p 85.

than he did. Jesus ultimately lived through overwhelming doubt as to what his whole life and ministry amounted to: "Why?" he screamed at God from the cross. Uncertainty did not equate with unfaithfulness in Jesus' life, and it need not in ours.

In the apocalyptic visions of the apostle John, recorded at the end of the New Testament, there features a wonderful cameo in which the old man finds himself "in the Spirit" and looking at a scene in heaven. In focus is a throne. Within earshot is a sound of great lamentation because no one can be found who is worthy to move the scene forward. A scroll needs opening but no one in heaven or on earth or under the earth – that includes all of *us*! – has the inherent holiness to break the seals which protect it nor to glimpse the writing that the scroll contains. The apostle finds himself weeping also. He – just like all of us – is totally unworthy to help here. He may have been a disciple of Jesus. He may have suffered for his faith. He may have composed in his Gospel one of the most amazing contributions to the New Testament. But John cannot be certain of himself now, before the throne in heaven. He weeps, as all others around him weep. At that point, the tearful apostle is directed to look again. Through his tears he glimpses an almost unbelievable sight:

> Then I saw a Lamb, looking as if it had been slain,
> standing in the centre of the throne. (Revelation 5:6)

His vision is of a personification of weakness, frailty, death, or in our language here, uncertainty. Yet his vision is at the same time a representation of strength, life and absolute certainty. In the slain/standing Lamb is found the only being who can move the scene forward. In the dead/alive Lamb is portrayed the one who alone can break open the seals and pronounce fully the writing contained within the scroll. Life – everlasting life – arises out of this Lamb's death. Strength, incredible strength to conquer all evil, all falsehood, arises out of this Lamb's weakness. Truth, or absolute certainty, proceeds from this Lamb's submission to others' "truth", others' false certainty. Jesus Christ, the Lamb of God, the Lion of the tribe of Judah, avoids the certainty trap through trust in and obedience to his heavenly Father. What an appropriate song fills the heavens:

> You are worthy to take the scroll and to open its seals,
> because you were slain,
> and with your blood you purchased men for God
> from every tribe and language and people and nation. (Revelation 5:9)

We need to close our exploration of where true "certainty" might lie with this song ringing in our ears and with prayers for mercy and cleansing issuing from our proud hearts.

Our Lord! Condemn us not if we forget or fall into error;
Our Lord! Lay not on us a burden like that which
Thou didst lay on those before us;
Our Lord! Lay not on us a burden greater than we have strength to bear.
Blot out our sins, and grant us forgiveness.
Have mercy on us.
Thou art our Protector.[28]

Almighty God,
unto whom all hearts be open, all desires known,
and from whom no secrets are hid:
Cleanse the thoughts of our hearts by the inspiration of
thy Holy Spirit,
that we may perfectly love thee, and worthily magnify thy holy Name;
through Christ our Lord.[29]

[28] From Sura 2:286.

[29] The "Collect for Purity" taken from the service of holy communion, *The Book of Common Prayer*, Church Book Room Press: London (n.d.), p 237.

Appendices

Appendix 1

Transliteration

A CONSIDERABLE number of non-English terms appear throughout this book. Italics have been used to indicate that a word is a transliteration, and does not appear as an English word in standard dictionaries. Some proper nouns have not been transliterated strictly, in order to ease reading. A glossary of all italicised transliterations is given in Appendix 3.

Most of the terms employed occur in Arabic. A standard form of transliteration, set out in figure 33, has been used to render all Arabic expressions in English. A few words, such as "Qur'ân" and "*ḥadîth*", which do feature in some English dictionaries, are transliterated in this text.

A short list, explaining some of the more significant, historical, Muslim names and movements, is also given at the end of the glossary in Appendix 3.

Figure 33

Transliteration and pronunciation of Arabic alphabet

Arabic name	*Sign used*	English pronunciation where unclear
hamza	'	glottal stop, as "a" in "apple"
âlif	*a*	
bâ'	*b*	
tâ'	*t*	
thâ'	*th*	as in "think"
jîm	*j*	
ḥâ'	*ḥ*	(aspirated)
khâ'	*kh*	as in German "*nacht*"
dâl	*d*	
dhâl	*dh*	as in "this"
râ'	*r*	
zâ'	*z*	
sîn	*s*	
shîn	*sh*	as in "shoe"
ṣâd	*ṣ*	(velarised)

Figure 33 (*cont.*)

Arabic name	***Sign used***	**English pronunciation where unclear**
ḍâd	*ḍ*	(velarised)
ṭâ'	*ṭ*	(velarised)
ẓâ'	*ẓ*	(velarised)
'ayn	ʿ	voiced counterpart of *ḥâ'*
ghayn	*gh*	similar to throaty French "*r*"
fâ'	*f*	
qâf	*q*	(uvular) as "k", not "kw"
kâf	*k*	(palatal)
lâm	*l*	
mîm	*m*	
nûn	*n*	
hâ'	*h*	
wâw	*w*	
yâ'	*y*	
âlif yâ	*ay*	(diphthong)
âlif wâw	*aw*	(diphthong)
tâ' marbûṭa	*a*	*a*
unmarked (short) vowels:	*a*	as in "had"
	i	as in "sit"
	u	as in "fruit"
vowels with a circumflex	*â*	as in "aah"
above are long:	*î*	as in "eee"
	û	as in "ooo"

Appendix 2

An introductory bibliography

Abbas, Tahir (ed.). *Muslim Britain: Communities under Pressure*. Zed Books: London, 2005.

'Alî ibn Abî Ṭalib *Nahjul Balagha: Sermons, Letters and Sayings of Hazrat Ali* (trans. Syed Mohammed Askari Jafery). 2 vols., Golshan Printing House: Tehran (c. 1975). Reprint of Hyderabad edition of 1965.

Ali, Tariq. *The Clash of Fundamentalisms. Crusades, Jihads and Modernity*. Verso: London, 2002.

Andrae, Tor. *Mohammed: The Man and his Faith* (trans. Theophil Menzel). George Allen & Unwin: London, 1936.

Aslam, Nadeem. *Maps for Lost Lovers*. Faber and Faber: London 2004.

Armstrong, Karen. *Muhammad: A Western Attempt to Understand Islam*. Victor Gollancz Ltd: London, 1991.

'Ata ur-Rahim, Muhammad. *Jesus – a Prophet of Islam*. MWH: London, 1977.

Ateek, Naim. *Justice and Only Justice: A Palestinian Theology of Liberation*. Orbis Books: Maryknoll, New York, 2001.

Barr, James. *Escaping from Fundamentalism*. SCM: London, 1984.

Barth, Karl (trans. G.T. Thomson & Harold Knight). *Church Dogmatics. Vol 1, The Doctrine of the Word of God*. T. & T. Clark: Edinburgh, 1956.

Barton, John (ed.). *The Cambridge Companion to Biblical Interpretation*. Cambridge University Press: Cambridge, 1998.

Bayḍâwî, 'Abd Allah ibn 'Umar. *Baiḍâwî's Commentary on Sûrah 12 of the Qur'ân* (text, accompanied by an interpretative rendering and notes by A.F.L. Beeston). Clarendon Press: Oxford, 1963.

Bebbington, David W. *The Dominance of Evangelicalism: The Age of Spurgeon and Moody*. Inter-Varsity Press: Leicester, 2005.

Bell, Richard. *A Commentary on the Qur'ân* (eds. C. Edmund Bosworth & M.E.J. Richardson). 2 vols, University of Manchester: Manchester, 1991.

al-Bukhârî, Muḥammad bin Ismâ'îl bin al-Mughîrah (Khan, Muhammad Muhsin, trans). *Al-Ṣaḥîḥ*. Vols 1–9. Kazi Publications: Chicago, 1977–79.

Burton, John. *The Collection of the Qur'ân*. Cambridge University Press: Cambridge, 1977.

Caetani, Leone. "Uthman and the Recension of the Koran." In *The Moslem World*, vol. 5 (1915), pp 380–390.

Campolo, Tony. *Speaking My Mind*. W Publishing Group: Nashville, 2004.

Cantwell Smith, Wilfred. *The Meaning and End of Religion*. SPCK: London, 1963.

Cantwell Smith, Wilfred. *On Understanding Islam: Selected Studies*. Mouton: The Hague, 1981.

Cantwell Smith, Wilfred "Mission, Dialogue, and God's Will for Us". In *International Review of Mission*, vol. 78, no. 307 (1988), pp 360–374.

Cantwell Smith, Wilfred *What is Scripture? A Comparative Approach*. Fortress Press: Minneapolis, 1989.

Carson, Donald A. *When Jesus Confronts the World: An Exposition of Matthew 8–10*. Inter-Varsity Press: Leicester, 1987.

Carson, Donald A. and Woodbridge, John D. (eds.). *Scripture and Truth*. Inter-Varsity Press: Leicester, 1983.

Clark, Victoria. *Holy Fire: The Battle for Christ's Tomb*. Macmillan: London, 2005.

Cragg, Kenneth. *Islam and the Muslim*. The Open University Press: Milton Keynes, 1978.

Cragg, Kenneth. *Muhammad in the Qur'an: The Task and the Text*. Melisende: London, 2001.

Cragg, Kenneth. *The Call of the Minaret*. Oxford University Press: New York, 1964.

Cragg, Kenneth. *The Mind of the Qur'ân*. George Allen & Unwin: London, 1973.

Cragg, Kenneth. *The Weight in the Word. Prophethood: Biblical and Quranic*. Sussex Academic Press: Brighton, 1999.

Dashti, 'Ali (trans. F.R.C. Bagley). *Twenty Three Years: A Study of the Prophetic Career of Mohammad*. Mazda Publishers: Costa Mesa, 1994.

Esack, Farid. *Qur'ân, Liberation and Pluralism: An Islamic Perspective of Interreligious Solidarity against Oppression*. Oneworld: Oxford, 1997.

Gätje, Helmut (trans. Alford T. Welch). *The Qur'ân and its exegesis: selected texts with classical and modern Muslim interpretations*. Oneworld: Oxford, 1997.

Gilchrist, John. *Jam' al-Quran: The Codification of the Qur'an Text*. TMFMT: Warley, 1989.

Goldingay, John. *Models for Interpretation of Scripture*. Eerdmans: Grand Rapids, 1995.

Guillaume, A. *The Life of Muhammad*. A Translation of Ibn Ishaq's *Sirât Rasûl Allah*. Oxford University Press: Oxford, 1978 (first edition 1955).

Haija, Rammy M. "The Armageddon Lobby: Dispensationalist Christian Zionism and the Shaping of US Policy towards Israel-Palestine." In *Holy Land Studies*, vol. 5, no. 1 (2006), pp 75–95.

Harris, Joanne. *Holy Fools*. Black Swan: London, 2003.

Havelaar, Henriette W. (ed.). *The Coptic Apocalypse of Peter: (Nag-Hammadi-Codex VII,3)*. Akademie Verlag: Berlin, 1999.

Hawting G.R. & Shareef, Abdul-Kader (eds.). *Approaches to the Qur'ân*. Routledge: London, 1993.

Helms, Randel. *Gospel Fictions*. Prometheus Books: New York, 1988.

Husain, Ed. *The Islamist*. Penguin Books: London, 2007.

Islam in Britain: The British Muslim Community in February 2005. The Institute for the Study of Islam and Christianity: Pewsey, 2005.

Jansen, Johannes J. G. *The Neglected Duty: the Creed of Sadat's Assassins and Islamic Resurgence in the Middle East*. MacMillan: New York, 1986.

Jeffery, Arthur (ed.). *Materials for the History of the Text of the Qur'an: The Old Codices*. AMS Press: New York, 1975.

Jeffery, Arthur. *The Qur'an as Scripture*. R.F. Moore: New York, 1952.

Kureishi, Hanif. *The Black Album*. Faber and Faber: London, 1995.

LaHaye, Tim and Jenkins, Jerry B. *Left Behind*. Tyndale House: Wheaton, 1995.

Lindsey, Hal. *The Late Great Planet Earth*. Zondervan: Grand Rapids, 1970.

Lindsey, Hal. *The Apocalypse Code*. Western Front: Palos Verdes, 1997.

Lings, Martin. *Muhammad: His Life Based on the Earliest Sources*. Unwin Paperbacks: London, 1986.

Magermans, A.H. *Index of Qur'ânic verses to the English part of Materials for the text of the Qur'ân, edited by Arthur Jeffery*. E.J. Brill: Leiden, 1951.

Manji, Irshad. *The Trouble with Islam*. Mainstream Publishing: Edinburgh, 2004.

Marsden, George M. *Fundamentalism and American Culture* (2nd edition). Oxford University Press: Oxford, 2006.

Marsden, George M. *Reforming Evangelicalism: Fuller Seminary and the New Evangelicalism*. Eerdmans: Grand Rapids, 1987.

Marsden, George M. *Understanding Fundamentalism and Evangelicalism*. Eerdmans: Grand Rapids, 1991.

Masood, Steven. *The Bible and the Qur'an*. OM Publishing: Carlisle, 2001.

McAuliffe, Jane Dammen, Barry D. Walfish & Joseph W. Goering (eds.). *With reverence for the word: medieval scriptural exegesis in Judaism, Christianity, and Islam*. Oxford University Press: Oxford, 2003.

McCurry, Don M. (ed.). *The Gospel and Islam: A 1978 Compendium*. MARC: Monrovia, 1979.

McDermott, G.R. *Can Evangelicals learn from world religions?* InterVarsity Press: Downers Grove, 2000.

Memon, Muhammad Umar. *Ibn Taimîya's Struggle against Popular Religion*. Mouton: The Hague, 1976.

Muslim, Imâm. (trans. 'Abdul Ḥamîd Siddiqi). *Ṣaḥîḥ*. Vols 1–4, Sh. Muhammad Ashraf: Lahore, 1976.

Mustansir, M. "The Qur'anic Story of Joseph: Plot, themes and Characters". In *Muslim World* (1986), vol. 76, pp 1–55.

Newbigin, Lesslie. *Proper Confidence: faith, doubt and certainty in Christian discipleship*. William B. Eerdmans: Grand Rapids, 1995.

Newbigin, Lesslie. *The Gospel in a Pluralist Society*. SPCK: London, 1989.

Noll, Mark A. *The Rise of Evangelicalism: The Age of Edwards, Whitefield and the Wesleys*. Inter-Varsity Press: Leicester, 2004.

Packer, J.I. *"Fundamentalism" and the Word of God*. Eerdmans: Grand Rapids, 1958.

Prigogine, Ilya. *The End of Certainty: Time, Chaos, and the New Laws of Nature*. The Free Press: New York, 1997.

Rahman, Fazlur. *Major Themes of the Qur'ân*. Bibliotheca Islamica: Minneapolis, 1980.

Ramadan, Tariq (trans. Saïd Amghar). *Islam, the West and the Challenges of Modernity*. The Islamic Foundation: Leicester, 2001.

Ramadan, Tariq. *Western Muslims and the Future of Islam*. Oxford University Press: Oxford, 2004.

Rippin, Andrew (ed.). *Approaches to the History of the Interpretation of the Qur'ân*. Clarendon Press: Oxford, 1988.

Rippin, Andrew (ed.). *The Qur'an: Formative Interpretation*. Ashgate Publishing Limited: Aldershot, 1999.

Sardar, Ziauddin. *Desperately Seeking Paradise*. Granta Books: London, 2004.

Scofield, Cyrus Ingerson. *Scofield Reference Bible*. Oxford University Press: New York, 1909.

Sell, Charles Edward. *The Historical Development of the Qur'án*. Marshall & Co: London (1923) as reprinted by People International: Tunbridge Wells (n.d.).

Shadid, W.A.R. and Koningsveld, P.S. van (eds.). *Religious Freedom and the Neutrality of the State: the Position of Islam in the European Union*. Peeters: Leuven, 2002.

Shariati, Ali (trans. Hamid Algar). *On the Sociology of Islam*. Mizan Press: Berkeley, 1979.

Sizer, Stephen. *Christian Zionism: Road-map to Armageddon?* Inter-Varsity Press: Leicester, 2004.

Spong, John Shelby. *Rescuing the Bible from Fundamentalism*. HarperCollins: San Francisco, 1991.

Spong, John Shelby. *Why Christianity Must Change Or Die*. HarperCollins: New York, 1998.

Sweetman, J.W. *Islam and Christian Theology*. Part Two, vol 2. Lutterworth Press: London, 1967.

Taji-Farouki, Suha (ed.). *Modern Muslim Intellectuals and the Qur'an*. Oxford University Press & The Institute of Ismaili Studies: Oxford, 2004.

Tracy, David. *Plurality and Ambiguity: Hermeneutics, Religion, Hope*. SCM Press Ltd.: London, 1988.

Troll, Christian W. "Progressive Thinking in Contemporary Islam". In *Encounter*, no. 317–318, January–February, 2007.

Wagner, Donald. *Anxious for Armageddon*. Herald Press: Scottsdale, 1995.

Waldman, Marilyn R. "New Approaches to Biblical Materials in the Qur'ân". In *Muslim World* (1985), vol. 75, pp 1–16.

Wansbrough, John. *Quranic Studies: Sources and Methods of Scriptural Interpretation*. Oxford University Press: Oxford, 1977.

Wansbrough, John. *The Sectarian Milieu: Content and Composition of Islamic Salvation History*. Oxford University Press: Oxford, 1978.

Watt, W. Montgomery. *Bell's Introduction to the Qur'ân*. Edinburgh University Press: Edinburgh, 1970.

Watt, W. Montgomery. *Muhammad at Mecca*. Oxford University Press: Karachi, 1953.

Watt, W. Montgomery. *Muhammad at Medina*. Oxford University Press: Karachi, 1956.
Watt, W. Montgomery. *Muhammad: Prophet and Statesman*. Oxford University Press: Oxford, 1961.
Wheeler, Brannon M. *Moses in the Quran and Islamic Exegesis*. RoutledgeCurzon: London, 2002.
Wiktorowicz, Quintan. *The Management of Islamic Activism: Salafis, the Muslim Brotherhood, and State Power in Jordan*. State University of New York Press: New York, 2001.
Williams, D.H. *Retrieving the Tradition & Renewing Evangelicalism*. William B. Eerdmans: Grand Rapids, 1999.
Wild, Stefan (ed.). *The Qur'an as text*. EJ Brill: Leiden, 1996.
Wittgenstein, Ludwig (ed. G.E.M. Anscombe and G.H. von Wright; trans. Denis Paul and G.E.M. Anscombe). *On Certainty*. Blackwell: Oxford, 1977.
Zakaria, Rafiq. *The Struggle Within Islam. The Conflict Between Religion and Politics*. Penguin Books: London, 1988.

Appendix 3
Glossary

SOME SIGNIFICANT TERMS USED IN THE TEXT

al-aḥruf al-sab'a: "the seven modes" of reading the Qur'ân.
'Alids: descendants of the Prophet's cousin 'Alî.
Anṣâr: "Helpers"; the Muslims in Medina who welcomed the émigrés from Mecca.
'aql: 'reason'.
al-Azhar: ancient university mosque in Cairo, Egypt.
aslama: "to submit".
âya: "sign" of God's work in nature; verse of the Qur'ân.
Badr: victorious battle fought by Prophet against Quraysh in AD 624 consolidating Muḥammad's power.
Codex Sinaiticus: a Greek manuscript of the Old and New Testaments, discovered by Constantine Tischendorf in St Catherine's monastery, Sinai in 1859, and now at St Petersburg. The New Testament portion is well preserved and includes *The Letter of Barnabas* and the *Shepherd of Hermas*. A manuscript from the mid-fourth century.
Codex Vaticanus: a Greek manuscript, the most important of all the manuscripts of the Bible. It was found in the Vatican Library at Rome. A manuscript from the first half of the fourth century.
Companions: the *aṣḥâb* or associates of the Prophet Muḥammad. The general view is that everyone who embraced Islam, saw the Prophet and accompanied him was a "Companion".
al-dîn: "religion"; religious practice in Islam.
al-Fâtiḥa: "Opener", opening sura of the Qur'ân.
fatwâ: legal opinion given by a jurist-theologian.
fiqh: "understanding"; applied law.
al-furqân: "the criterion" referring to Torah or Qur'ân.
Gush Emunîm: "Bloc of the Faithful"; fundamentalist Zionist group in Israel.
ḥadîth: (plural *aḥadîth*) "prophetic tradition"; a short account of some word or act of Muḥammad's. In its classic form it is passed on by one authority who has received it from another. The chain reaches back to an eyewitness.
ḥadîth qudsî: comprise sayings of the Prophet that are in fact direct words from God through him, recorded by those who heard them spoken. They do not form part of the Qur'ân. There are several collections of such *ḥadîth*. A two volume work, published in Cairo in 1969 by the commission for Qur'ân and *ḥadîth*, is entitled *al-Aḥadîth al-Qudsîyya*.

ḥajj: "setting out"; pilgrimage to Mecca and surrounding holy places.
hijra: "migration", hejira; date of Muḥammad's flight from Mecca on the fourth day of the first month of AD 622. The Islamic calendar commences from the beginning of this year.
ijtihâd: "exerting oneself"; individual initiative to reinterpret Islamic law or (in Shî'a Islam) to mediate it.
Iqra': "Recite"; title of Sura 96.
îmân: "faith"; in the sense of a formal declaration of belief in the six articles of the Muslim creed.
Injîl: "Gospel".
'Îsâ: Jesus; name used by Muslims.
islâm: "submission".
isnâd: chain of transmitters (of *ḥadîth*) going back to Companions of the Prophet.
jihâd: "a striving"; religious war of Muslims against unbelievers or apostates.
ka'ba: "a cube"; the cube-like building in the centre of the Sacred Mosque at Mecca. It contains the black stone.
kalâm Allâh: speech of God – the Qur'ân.
kalimât al-shahâda: "the word of testimony"; the confession: "I bear witness that there is no deity but God and that Muḥammad is his apostle."
al-Lât: feminine form of *Allâh*.
Logos: the divine "Word"; Greek.
al-Manât: goddess of fate.
mansûkh: verses in the Qur'ân that are abrogated.
al-Masîh: "the Christ".
matn: the substance of a *ḥadîth*, as distinct from its *isnâd*.
mawlânâ: from "protector"; official versed in Islamic theology, Pakistan.
Mishkât al-Masâbîh is a well-known book of Sunnî *ḥadîth*, used by Muslims in India. It was originally compiled by Imâm Ḥusayn al-Baghâwi (died AD 1116 or 1122), and entitled *Masâbihu'l-Sunna* or "Lamps of the Traditions". In AD 1336 Shaykh Walî al-Dîn al-Tabrîzî revised it, added on an extra chapter to each section, and called it *Mishkât al-Masâbîh* or "Niche for Lamps".
muftî: expert in Islamic law qualified to give legal opinions.
Muḥâjirûn: "Emigrants"; Muslims who transferred from Mecca to Medina with Muḥammad.
mujtahid: person qualified to exercise *ijtihâd*.
mu'min: "believer" or person of faith.
muslim: "a submitted person".
nabî (plural *anbîyâ*): "the called"; a prophet.
nâsikh: verses in the Qur'ân that abrogate other verses.
qara': "to recite".
qirâ'ât: "modes" of reading the Qur'ân.
Qur'ân: "Recitation" of Muḥammad.
Quraysh: The Arabian tribe of which Muḥammad was a part and to which the majority of Meccans belonged.

Rabb: "Lord".
al-Raḥmân: "the Merciful".
Ramaḍân: the fast during the ninth month of the Muslim calendar.
rasûl, (plural *rusul*): "messenger" who receives a Book from God and is sent on a mission.
Salâfî: from *salaf* "to precede". Those who adhere to the way of the forefathers of the faith to three generations of Muslims, usually ending with Aḥmad ibn Ḥanbal.
ṣalât: ritual or liturgical prayer, performed five times a day.
Septuagint: a Greek version of the Jewish Bible, including the apocrypha, produced in Alexandria in the 3rd and 2nd centuries BC.
shahâda: Muslim confession of faith in God and his apostle.
sharî'a: the "path" to be followed; the totality of the Islamic way of life.
shaykh: "sheikh"; Muslim religious leader, sometimes head of an order.
Shî'a: "followers"; followers of 'Alî, first cousin of Muḥammad and the husband of his daughter Fâṭima.
shirk: the cardinal sin of idolatry, of associating anyone or anything with God.
Ṣûfî: Sufi; a Muslim mystic, named after the early ascetics who wore garments of coarse wool (*ṣûf*).
sunna: "a path, manner of life"; the custom, especially of Muḥammad, transmitted via the *ḥadîth* literature.
Sunnî: those who accept the *sunna* and the historic succession of the caliphs, as opposed to the 'Alîds or Shî'as; the majority of the Muslim community.
sura: from *sûra*, "a row or series"; chapter of the Qur'ân.
tafsîr: "explaining", from the root *fassara* (literally "to explain") or *asfara* (literally "to break"); term used for exegesis or commentary, especially with regard to the Qur'ân.
taḥrîf: alteration or corruption of scripture.
tanzîl: movement of revelation in Islam; causing to "come down".
Taurât: "Torah" of Moses.
tawḥîd: "unity"; the oneness of God and, by implication, the holism of all creation in realising its theocentric nature.
Torah: the five books of Moses.
'ulamâ' (ulema): plural of *'âlim*, "knower"; learned ones who are custodians of Islamic teachings.
umma: the "community" of Islam; the whole of the brotherhood of Muslims.
al-'Uzzâ: goddess of east Mecca.
Vulgate: Latin version of the Bible prepared mainly by Jerome in the late 4th century.
waḥy: inspiration.
Yahweh: the Lord; the God who reveals himself to mankind; Hebrew.
Yasû'a: Jesus, name used by Christians.
Zabûr: "Psalms" of David.
zakât: "purification"; alms-giving, one of the five pillars.

SIGNIFICANT NAMES IN THE TEXT

Abû Bakr: 'Abd Allâh ibn Abî Quhâfa (died AD 634). An early convert and the first caliph or successor to Prophet Muḥammad.

Abû Hurayra: 'Abd al-Raḥman ibn Sakhr al-Azdi (died AD 678). He was a Ṣaḥâbi, and is the narrator of *ḥadîth* whose name is most quoted in their *isnads* by Sunnî Muslims.

'Â'isha: daughter of Abû Bakr and the favourite wife of Muḥammad. She died in Medina in AD 678 aged 67. Often referred to as *Ummu'l-mu'minîn* or "the mother of the believers".

Ibn al-'Arabi: Muhyi'l-Dîn (AD 1165–1240). Influential Ṣûfî master, born in Spain. He wrote many poems and other works, proposing a system of mystical knowledge.

al-Ash'arî: Abû'l-Ḥasan 'Alî Ismâ'îl (AD 873–935). At first he was a disciple of Abû 'Alî al-Jubbâ'î, the leader of the Mu'tazilî school in Basra. He later departed from that school to found his own which is named after him. The Ash'arî school has become the most representative in Sunnî Islam.

al-Banna: Ḥasan (AD 1906–1949). Founder of the Society of Muslim Brothers or Muslim Brotherhood in Egypt.

al-Bayḍâwî: 'Abd Allah ibn 'Umar (died AD 1286). He was a Shafi'î scholar and chief *qadi* of Shiraz. His most famous work is his commentary on the Qur'ân, called *Anwâr al-Tanzîl wa Asrâr al-Ta'wîl.*

al-Bukhârî: Muḥammad ibn 'Abd Allâh ibn Ismâ'îl (AD 810–870). Major collator of *ḥadîth* whose collection is approved as a work second only to the Qur'ân itself. It is entitled *al-Jâmi' al-Ṣaḥîḥ* but widely came to be referred to as *al-Ṣaḥîḥ al-Bukhârî.*

Abû Da'ûd: Abû Da'ûd Sulayman ibn al-Ash'ath (AD 817–888) studied *ḥadîth* under ibn Ḥanbal and produced his own collection entitled *Kitâb al-Sunan.* It is commonly referred to as *Sunan Abi Da'ûd.*

al-Ḍaḥḥâk: ibn Qays al-Shaybânî (died AD 746). He was a Kharijî leader.

Erasmus: Desiderius (AD 1466–1536). Dutch humanist and scholar and a significant Renaissance figure. He edited the Greek New Testament (AD 1516).

Fakhr al-Dîn al-Râzî: Abû 'Abd Allâh Muḥammad ibn 'Umar (AD 1149–1209). He wrote a comprehensive commentary on the Qur'ân, *al-Tafsîr al-Kabîr*. It is based on strict exegetical rules and alludes to different readings of the qur'ânic text.

al-Farisî: Abû 'Alî al-Ḥasan ibn 'Alî (AD 900–987). An outstanding grammarian.

al-Ghazâlî: Abû Ḥamîd Muḥammad ibn Muḥammad ibn Aḥmad (AD 1058–1111). Sunnî theologian who incorporated aspects of Sufism into orthodox Islam.

al-Ḥallâj: al-Ḥusayn ibn Mansûr. Preacher-mystic of Khurasan and Afghanistan; executed in Baghdad in AD 922.

Ḥanbal: Aḥmad ibn (AD 780–855). Celebrated theologian, jurist and scholar of *ḥadîth*. Founder of the Hanbalite school of Sunnî law, the most strict school. He was persecuted during the rule of al-Ma'mûn ibn Hârûn al-Rashîd for refusing to acknowledge that the Qur'ân was created (the view introduced by the Mu'tazila).

Ḥanîfa: Abû Ḥanîfa al-Nu'mân (AD 700–767). Founder of Hanifite school of Sunnî law.

Ḥusayn: al-. Second son of Fâṭima (daughter of Prophet Muḥammad) by her husband 'Alî, the fourth caliph. Slain at Karbalâ' by Yazîd who became seventh caliph.

Ibn 'Abbâs: 'Abd Allâh, son of 'Abbâs, an uncle of Prophet Muḥammad (AD 619–687). He is considered to be the most knowledgeable of the Companions of the Prophet in *tafsîr*.

Ibn Ḥazm al-Andalusî: Abû Muḥammad 'Alî ibn Aḥmad ibn Sa'îd ibn Ḥazm (AD 994–1064). Andalusian poet, historian, philosopher and theologian; a literalist in his interpretation of the Qur'ân.

Ibn Kathîr: (AD 1301–1372). He was taught by Ibn Taymîyya and wrote a famous commentary on the Qur'ân named *Tafsîr Ibn Kathîr*. His commentary linked certain *ḥadîth* to verses of the Qur'ân in order to explain the latter.

Ibn Mâjah: Ibn Mâjah Muḥammad ibn Yazîd (AD 819–886) recorded some *ḥadîth* not mentioned elsewhere in his *Kitâb al-Sunan*. Some of these *ḥadîth*, however, are considered invalid or weak.

Ibn Mas'ûd: 'Abd Allâh ibn Ghâfu. He was reputedly the sixth man to convert to Islam after Muḥammad started preaching in Mecca. One of the closest *ṣaḥaba* or Companions of the Prophet.

Irenaeus: (about AD 130–200). Originally from Asia and a student of Polycarp of Smyrna (modern Izmir), he became bishop of Lyons from about AD 178.

Khadîja: daughter of Khuwailid, a Qurayshi. After being widowed, she married Muḥammad becoming his first wife and first convert. She died in AD 619, aged 65 years.

Khomeini: Ruhollah (AD 1900–1989). Iranian Shî'a leader who was exiled to Turkey, Iraq and France from 1964. Returned to Iran in the Islamic Revolution of 1979 and led the "government of God" there until his death.

Kulaynî: Thiqat al-Islâm Muḥammad Ibn Ya'qûb Kulaynî (died AD 940). His arrangement of *ḥadîth*, known as the *Kâfî*, contains some 16,000 *ḥadîth* and is the best known amongst Shî'a Muslims.

al-Mahallî: Abû 'Alî Jalâl al-Dîn (AD 1389–1459). Egyptian scholar who, with Jalâl al-Dîn al-Suyûtî, produced *Tafsîr al-Jalâlayn* or *Commentary of the Two Jalals*.

al-Majlisi: Muḥammad Baqir. (died AD 1699). Author of *Bihar al-Anwâr* or *Seas of Lights*.

Mâlik: Abû 'Abd Allâh Mâlik ibn Anas (AD 716–796). Medinan founder of the Malikite school of Sunnî law.

al-Mawdûdî: Sayyid Abû'l-'Alâ (AD 1903–1979). He was one of the chief architects of contemporary Islamic resurgence. A journalist by training, he founded the *Jamâ'at-i Islâmi* or Islamic Party.

Muslim: Abû'l-Ḥasan Muslim Ibn al-Ḥajjâj (AD 817–875). Muslim is considered second only to al-Bukhârî in the science of the methodology of *ḥadîth*. His collection, *al-Jâmi' al-Ṣaḥîḥ*, is known as *al-Ṣaḥîḥ al-Muslim*.

Mu'âwiya: son of Abû Sufyân. He became sixth caliph and founder of the Umayyad dynasty.

al-Nawawî: Abû Zakarîya Yahya ibn Sharaf al-Nawawî (AD 1233–1278). Author of *Forty Ḥadîths* (actually 42) which collection of major traditions has been frequently published with commentaries in Cairo.

al-Nisâ'î: Abû 'Abd al-Raḥmân Aḥmad ibn Shu'aib al-Nasâ'î (AD 830–915) produced a collection of *ḥadîth* under the title *Kitâb al-Sunan*. It is popularly known as *Sunan al-Nisâ'î* and is third to al-Bukhârî in terms of containing the least weak *ḥadîth*.

Qutb: Sayyid (AD 1906–1966). Egyptian member of Muslim Brotherhood who was strongly influenced by Mawdûdî's writings. Became a promoter of *jihâd* as tool to bring in an Islamic state.

Shâfi'î: Muḥammad ibn Idrîs al-Shâfi'î (AD 767–820). Descendant of Prophet and founder of one of the four schools of Sunnî law.

Shâh Walî Allâh al-Dihlawî: Qutb al-Dîn Aḥmad ibn 'Abd al-Raḥîm (AD 1703–1762). Indian thinker who set forth principles of qur'ânic exegesis in his *al-Fawz al-Kabîr fî Usûl al-Tafsîr*. He also translated the Qur'ân into Persian.

al-Suddî: Ismâ'îl ibn 'Abd al-Raḥmân (died AD 745). Popular preacher in Kufa. His reputation as a transmitter of *ḥadîth* has been disputed but his exegesis of the Qur'ân is renowned with much of it included in Ṭabarî's *Tafsîr*.

al-Suyûtî: Abû'l-Fadl 'Abd al-Raḥmân (AD 1445–1505). An Egyptian scholar who memorised the whole Qur'ân by the age of eight years. Cooperated with Jalâl al-Dîn Mahallî on *Tafsîr al-Jalâlayn* or *Commentary of the Two Jalals*.

al-Ṭabarî: Abû Ja'far Muḥammad ibn Jarîr (AD 838–923). A Sunnî historian and theologian, he is probably the most important source for the early history of Islam. He also wrote a commentary on the Qur'ân entitled *Jâmi' al-Bayân fî Tafsîr al-Qurân*.

Ibn Taymîyya: Taqî al-Dîn Aḥmad (AD 1263–1328). He emerged as spokesman for the traditionalists (*Ahl al-Ḥadîth*) with a programme of renewed emphasis on the *sharî'a* (Islamic law) and a vindication of religious values. He spoke out strongly against the many forms of popular practices prevalent among his peers. Ibn Taimîyya's thoughts influenced the late eighteenth-century Wahhâbî movement.

Tertullian: Q. Septimus Florens (about AD 160–220). Legal background; based in Carthage. Later in life became a Montanist.

Tirmidhî: Abû 'Isâ Muḥammad ibn 'Îsâ al-Tirmidhî (AD 824–892). A student of al-Bukhârî, he arranged his collection of *ḥadîth* as *al-Jâmi' al-Ṣaḥîḥ*, later known as *Sunan al-Tirmidhî*. It comprises one of the six canonical *ḥadîth* compilations used in Sunnî Islam.

al-Turâbî: Ḥassan ʻAbd Allah (AD 1932-). Leader of the Sudanese Muslim Brotherhood in the early 1960s. A convinced Islamist, he was instrumental in institutionalising *sharîʻa* law in the north of the country.

ʻUmar: ibn al-Khaṭṭâb (died AD 644). Succeeded Abû Bakr as caliph.

ʻUthmân: son of ʻAffân; the third *khalîfa* of Islam (died AD 661). During his rule, a definitive text of the Qur'ân was determined and authorised, all other versions being destroyed.

Wahhâb: Muḥammad ibn ʻAbd al-Wahhâb (AD 1703–1787) was a native of Najd in Arabia, and founded the Unitarian, conservative movement named after him. The Wahhâbî view influenced the development of the Muslim Brotherhood in Egypt, and the *Jamâʻat-i Islâmî* or Islamic Organisation in Pakistan.

Waraqa: ibn Nawfal ibn Asad ibn ʻAbd al-ʻUzzâ. Cousin of Khadîja, a Christian.

Zaid ibn Thâbit ibn al-Ḍaḥḥâk (died AD 666). A native of Medina and a companion and amanuensis to Prophet Muḥammad.

al-Zamakhsharî: Abû'l Qâsim (AD 1075–1144). A Muʻtazilî theologian, renowned for his commentary on the Qur'ân entitled *al-Khashshâf ʻan Haqâ'iq al-Tanzîl.*

Index

7/7 xiii, xvii, xxv, xxix, 17, 219, 223–224, 226–227, 234
9/11 xxv, 32, 219, 221–222, 224–225, 230, 234

Abbas, Tahir xv, 14, 225–226, 241
Abbasid 4, 159
Abraham 80, 83, 92, 151, 164–165, 167, 179, 186–187
abrogation xxvi, 11–12, 38–40, 42–44, 46, 49, 55–57, 59–60, 63–64, 72–75
Abû Bakr: caliph 52, 143–144, 147, 249, 252
Abû Hurayra 13, 50, 161, 249
Abû Zaid, Nasr ix, 5, 152, 180–183, 192, 228
Adam 55, 61, 98, 104–105, 129, 161, 164–167, 169
adultery 16, 48–52, 62, 67
Afghanistan 4, 227, 249
Aḥzâb: Sura *al-* 51, 53–54, 145
Â'isha 53–54, 148, 249
Alam, M.Y. 151
alcohol 45–46, 71
ʿAlî: caliph 4, 52–53, 178, 220, 250
ʿAlid Shîʿism 178, 246, 248
Allah xiv, xv, 3, 5, 7, 9, 11, 13, 15–16, 18, 38, 41–48, 50–52, 54, 56–58, 74, 80–90, 92, 94–100, 102–104, 106–108, 142–143, 145, 154–157, 160–162, 187, 189, 220, 247
American Israel Public Affairs Committee 28
Anas bin Mâlik 45, 98, 100, 145,
Anṣâr 52
Anselm 125–127
apocrypha ix, 119, 130, 132–134, 138, 248
apostasy ix, 6, 11, 75, 182
Apostolic Fathers 137
Armageddon 20, 27–29, 31–32, 197, 242, 244, 260
Asad, Muhammad 157
Aslam, Nadeem 229–230, 241
Assumption of Moses: *The* 129
Assyria: Assyrians 116,
Athanasius: bishop 126
Augustine: bishop 125, 127
âyât muḥkamât 155–157, 180
âyât mutashâbiḥât 155–157, 180
ʿAzîz, al- 81–82, 84, 90–91

Babylonians 116
Baghdad xvi, 249
Banna, Ḥasan al- 19, 161, 249
Barlas, Asma 59
Barth, Karl 211, 232, 241
Bayḍâwî, al- 38, 79, 89, 90–92, 249
Begin, Menahem 29–30
Bible ix, xviii–xxv, xxvii–xxviii, 18, 20, 25–26, 31–32, 60–61, 69, 109, 112–113, 116–117, 123, 128, 131–134, 136–137, 139–140, 165, 193, 196–197, 199–201, 203–205, 207–209, 212–214, 216–218, 232, 243, 244, 246, 248
Black Album: *The* 230–231, 243
Blair, Tony xiii, 227
Book of Enoch 129
British National Party 226
Bukhârî, Muḥammad al- 9, 44–52, 57, 142–144, 145, 147, 241, 249, 251
Burton, John 146–148, 242
Bush: President George W. 21, 27–29, 227

Caetani, Leone 144–145, 241
Calvin, John 71
Campolo, Tony 23, 27, 32, 218, 241
Canaan xix, 85, 88, 93, 110
canonisation xxvii, 128, 142, 150
Cantwell Smith, Wilfred ix, 201–202, 206, 241, 242
Carchemish 116
Carter: President Jimmy 22, 27–28,
certainty xiv–xv,xvii, xix, xxii, xxiv–xxix, 3, 6, 15, 17, 19, 33, 49, 51, 153, 171–172, 198, 200, 206–208, 210, 212, 216–218, 221, 223, 226–228, 231–236, 243, 245
Christian Coalition 23, 24
Christian Zionism 27–28, 31, 242, 244
Christian Zionist Congress 30–31
Christianity xxiii, xxv–xxvi, xxviii–xxix, 21–23, 60, 125, 128, 135–136, 138–139, 150, 154, 181, 184, 200, 204, 208, 213–215, 234, 242, 243, 244
Chrysostomos, John 71
Church Dogmatics 211, 241
Clement of Rome 135, 137, 139
Codex Sinaiticus 119, 246
Codex Vaticanus 119, 210, 246
Commission on British Muslims and Islamophobia 225

Concept of the Text: *The* 181
Council of Carthage 140
Council of Laodicea 140
Cragg, Kenneth 32, 214, 242
Cur Deus Homo 125

Daniel 20, 26, 61, 111, 123, 131, 133
David 66, 104, 121, 123, 151, 164–167, 169–171, 196, 248
Dawkins, Richard xxvii
Dead Sea Scrolls 112
Decalogue 60–63, 70
Deobandi 4
Deuteronomy xix, xxi, 64, 130, 197
Dine, Tom 28
dispensationalist xviii, 25–29, 194–195, 242
dogma ix, xxviii, 208–209
Dutch Reformed Church xxi

Ebionites 138, 168
Ecclesiastical History 136
Egypt ix, xx, xxii, 6–9, 11, 15–16, 31, 56, 61, 81, 83, 85–88, 93, 110, 116, 126, 129, 138, 179–183, 198, 205, 211, 246, 249, 250, 251, 252
Ehrman, Bart D. 120
Erasmus 210, 249
Esack, Farid ix, 187–191, 242
Esther 111–112, 130–131, 133
euaggeliou See Gospel
eucharist 123–124, 126
European Economic Community xviii
Eusebius ix, 136–137
evangelical xvii–xviii, xxi, xxiii, 22–23, 25–26, 29, 32, 61, 193–195, 197, 201, 218–219, 232, 241, 243
Exodus 61, 110, 112, 130, 196
Ezra 128, 130–131, 196, 205

faith xiii, xv–xviii, xxii–xxviii, 3, 10, 14, 21, 33, 61, 69–70, 75–76, 87–88, 96, 101–102, 118, 128, 132, 158, 162, 171, 181, 187, 190–191, 197, 201–204, 206, 208, 213–214, 217, 219, 225, 231, 233–235, 241, 247, 248
Falwell, Jerry ix, xxiii, 22–25, 27–31, 195–196, 234
Faraj ix, 6–14, 56–57, 59
Fâṭima 142, 248
fatwâ 5, 11, 246
Fawz al-Kabîr: *al-* 40, 251
fundamentalism ix, xvii, xxiii, xxvi, 22, 27, 31–32, 141, 193–194, 196, 200, 205, 212, 216, 241, 243, 244
fundamentalist xiv, xvi–xviii, xxii–xxvi, xxviii–xxix, 5, 16, 21–24, 27, 29–33, 183, 193–195, 197–198, 206, 212, 216–218, 223, 232, 246

Gabriel 37, 95, 97, 142, 160, 161
genealogy 165–169, 171
Genesis xviii, 61, 64, 130, 205
Ghazâlî, al- 249
Goldingay, John 70, 166, 242
Gospel 40, 64–65, 117–124, 127, 134, 137–138, 140–141, 166–171, 203, 205–206, 208, 210, 213–215, 235, 242, 243, 247
Graham, Billy 29–30, 193–195
Great Trek xx
Greek xxvii, 25, 109, 111–112, 116, 118, 123, 127, 129–134, 140, 158, 210, 246, 247, 248
Gregory of Nazianzus 126

ḥadîth 9–10, 13–14, 44, 46–49, 51–57, 213, 246, 247, 248, 249, 250, 251
Ḥafṣa 144–146, 148
Hagar 179
Halliday, Fred 224–225
Halsell, Grace 30–31, 196
Ḥanbal 6, 248–250
Harris, Joanne 197, 242
Ḥasan al-Basrî 158
Hassan, Riffat 192
Hebrew xvii, 109–113, 115–116, 119, 127, 129–134, 165, 196, 218, 248
hermeneutic ix, xiii, xv–xvi, xix, xxii, xxiv, xxvi, xxviii, 3, 15, 17, 19, 26, 33, 49, 51, 55, 120, 151–153, 171 178, 180–181, 183, 187–190, 192, 195, 200, 202–203, 206, 216–218, 223, 232, 244
Hibri, Azizah al- 192
hijra 8, 49, 72, 93, 107, 177, 247
Holy Fools 197, 242
Holy Spirit 37, 64, 68–69, 107, 134, 140–141, 156, 166, 199, 203–204, 210–211, 214, 236
holy war xvii, xix, xxv, 3, 6, 14, 17, 76
homosexuality 23–24, 63, 201
House Resolution 28

Iblîs 104
Ibn ʿAbbas 48, 56, 79, 148, 250
Ibn al-ʿArabî 181, 249
Ibn Ḥazm al-Andalusi 12, 53, 56–57, 250
Ibn Ishâq 48–49, 242
Ibn Kathîr 11–14, 79, 98, 100, 107–108, 156–157, 250
Ibn Taymîyya 4, 8, 10–11, 15, 76, 228, 250, 251
ijtihâd xv, 4–6, 15, 17, 185, 247
inerrancy xviii, 212, 232

Injîl *See* Gospel
International Christian Embassy 30
Iran 21, 175–178, 224, 227, 250
Isaiah 111, 115, 126, 130–131, 196
Ishmael 171
Islam ix, xiv–xvii, xxv, xxviii–xxix, 3–6, 11, 13–19, 21–22, 32–33, 37, 40, 48–49, 52, 56–59, 72–73, 75–76, 78, 97, 128, 142, 146, 148, 151–154, 157, 159–160, 163, 168, 171–172, 176–185, 187, 190, 192, 201, 205–206, 213, 215, 221, 223–225, 230–231, 233–234, 241, 242, 243, 244, 246, 247, 248, 249, 250, 251, 252
islâm xv, 72, 247
Islamism xvii, 7, 16, 33, 177
Islamist xiii–xiv, xvi–xvii, xxv–xxviii, 3–8, 10, 14–19, 21, 32–33, 37, 56–57, 59, 72, 75, 161, 171–172, 175, 183–184, 190–191, 219–223, 227, 231, 242, 252
Islamophobia ix, 225
isrâ' 98
Israel xviii–xx, xxii, 17, 20–21, 27–31, 58, 62, 67, 98–99, 101, 107–108, 110, 133, 141, 167, 169, 181, 219, 221–222, 227, 242, 246

Jabotinsky Centennial Medal 30
Jacob 79–81, 83, 85–88, 91–92, 121, 164–165
Jenkins, David xxvii
Jeremiah 111, 130–131, 133, 166
Jerome 109, 132, 139–140, 248
Jerusalem xxii, 20, 30–31, 39, 65, 98, 100–101, 112, 118, 124, 129, 148, 196
Jesus ix, xviii, xxii, xxv, xxviii, 20, 25–26, 32, 60–62, 64–69, 109, 117–124, 126–127, 129–130, 138, 151–152, 156, 164–171, 186–187, 196, 200, 204–205, 207–208, 211–215, 217, 234–235, 241, 242, 247, 248
jihâd ix, xxv, 4–9, 13–15, 17–18, 39, 56–57, 72–73, 76, 188, 190–191, 221, 224, 227, 241, 247, 251
Job ix, 111, 131
Joseph 61, 78–93, 154, 165, 243
Josephus 128, 131, 196
Joshua xix, 130
Judah 113–116, 166, 170, 235
Judaism 21, 33, 109, 128, 150, 154, 181, 184, 243

ka'ba 94, 247
Kepel, Gilles 21–22, 24, 32
Khalafallah, Muhammad 180
Kharijî xxviii, 4, 33, 249
Khomeini: Imam 19, 21, 178, 234, 250
Kilo 151
Kureishi, Hanif 230–231, 243

Larry King Live 32
Late Great Planet Earth: *The* 25, 31, 197, 243
Law: the ix, xxvi, 60–61, 64, 67, 69, 103, 128, 130
Lebanon xix, xxi, 113, 221
Leiden University 183
Letter to the Corinthians 60, 110, 129, 135, 137–139
liberation ix, 187–191, 241, 242
Life of Muhammad: *The* 48, 242
Likud 21, 29
Lindsey, Hal xxiii, 25, 27, 31, 243
Littell, Franklin 28
logos 117, 210–211, 232, 247
London xiii–xxix, 17, 33, 198, 221, 223, 230–231
Luke ix, 65–67, 118, 120–121, 124, 126–127, 134–135, 140–141, 164–171, 196, 205

Madrid xvii, 221
Mahound 97
Manât: *al-* 95–96, 247
Manji, Irshad 18, 243
mansûkh 12, 38–39, 42, 56–57, 247
Maps for Lost Lovers 229–230, 241
Mark ix, xxii, 62, 64, 66–67, 70, 117–124, 126–127, 135, 140, 167–169, 196, 205, 210, 215
marriage 10, 30, 39, 54
Marsden, George ix, xxiii, 22, 25, 27, 193–195, 243
Mary: Virgin 138, 156, 164–166
Masoretic Text ix, 109–112, 115–116
Materials for the History of the Text of the Quran 148, 243
Matthew ix, 26, 61–62, 64, 66–69, 111, 117, 120–121, 123–124, 134–135, 138, 140, 164–169, 171, 196, 199, 205, 242
Mawdûdî 5, 19, 96, 251
Mecca 37, 39, 73–74, 76, 80, 94, 107, 175, 179, 246, 247, 248, 250
Medes 61, 116
Medina xvii, 16, 37, 43, 46, 48–52, 72–74, 76, 80, 89, 144, 146–147, 175, 187, 228, 245, 246, 247, 249, 252
Messiah 20, 65–66, 70, 120–121, 123, 129, 166–167, 169–171
Middle East xvii–xviii, xx, xxii, 27, 198–199, 207, 211, 227
Mishkât al-Masâbîh 247
Mongol 10, 11
Moral Majority 22–23, 28
Moses 43, 61–62, 68, 101, 106–108, 128–129, 151, 161, 169–170, 187, 190, 211, 245, 248

Muḥammad: *See* Prophet Muḥammad
Muḥammad ʿAli: Maulana 37, 40
Muslim xiii–xvii, xxii–xxvii, xxix, 3–11, 14–20, 22, 31–33, 37, 40, 43, 45–47, 50–57, 72–78, 80, 88, 91, 93, 95–97, 107, 121–122, 142, 144–153, 158–159, 163, 171–172, 175, 177, 179, 181–192, 197, 201, 205–207, 209, 215, 219–231, 233, 239, 247, 248, 249, 250, 251, 252
Muslim Association of Britain 223
Muslim Brotherhood 5, 7, 221, 245, 249, 251, 252
Muslim Council for Religious and Racial Harmony UK xvi
Muslim Council of Britain xvi, 33, 223
Muslim Institute xvii
Muʿtazila 158–159, 180, 250

Nahum 113, 115–116, 127, 130–131
Najm: *al-* 94, 96
nâsikh 38–39, 41–42, 247
Nâsikh w'al-Mansûkh: *al-* 12, 56–57
Nathan: son of David 164–167, 170–171
National Council of Churches 29
Nawawî, al- 9–10, 251
Neglected Duty: *The* 7–8, 242
New Testament ix, xx–xxi, xxvi, 60, 62, 67, 71–72, 109–110, 112, 117, 123, 126, 129–130, 134–140, 152–153, 199, 205, 210, 215, 217, 235, 246
New York xvii, 25, 29–31
Newbigin, Lesslie 206–209, 212, 232, 243
Night of Power 160
Nimeiri: President 75
Nineveh 113–116

Old Testament ix, xix–xxi, xxvi, 28, 60–61, 63–68, 71–72, 109, 112, 115, 127–134, 170, 199, 205, 217
Omar Abdul Rahman 15–16
Origen 126
Orthodox xxi–xxii, 120, 134, 205

Packer, J.I. 141, 243
Paul: apostle xxi, xxvi, 60, 62, 65, 69–70, 123, 129, 137–140, 203, 215
Pentateuch ix, 109–110, 112, 128, 130
Peshitta 109, 112
Pharaoh 61, 83, 107, 116, 190
Pharisees 62, 64–65, 67, 69, 169
Philemon xxi, 135
Philips, Bilal 52–53
Pre-Islamic Literature 179
Pre-Islamic Poetry 179
Prescription Against Heretics: *The* 135–136
Prophecy and Politics 30
Prophet Muḥammad xv, 3–4, 9, 16–17, 37–38, 40, 43, 46–54, 57, 72–74, 76, 78–80, 92–101, 105–108, 142–144, 146–147, 149–152, 157–163, 171, 175, 177, 179, 181, 185–187, 189, 213, 233, 246, 247, 248, 249, 250
Protestant ix, xxii, 22, 25, 28, 60, 130–133, 193–195, 212, 234

Qumran 112
Qur'ân ix, xiv–xvii, xxii, xxv–xxviii, 3–7, 9–12, 14–15, 17–19, 32–33, 37–40, 42–44, 46–59, 72–80, 89–98, 101, 103–104, 106–108, 122, 142–161, 163–164, 171–172, 175–192, 201, 205, 213–214, 220, 222, 228–229, 231, 239, 241, 242, 243, 244, 245, 246, 247, 248, 249, 250, 251, 252
Quraysh 73, 78, 92–95, 100, 146–147, 182, 246, 247, 250
Qutb, Sayyid 5, 19, 251

Rahman, Fazlur 18, 184–188, 243
Ramadan, Tariq 161, 163, 171–172, 214, 244
ransom 13, 50, 110, 122–126, 218
Râzî, Fakhr al-Dîn al- 79, 89–91, 93, 249
Reagan: President Ronald 21–22, 27–28, 32
Reed, Ralph 23
religion xvi, xxvii, 5, 17, 21, 31, 37, 40, 56, 58, 74–75, 83, 92, 128, 154, 181–182, 201–202, 206, 209, 223, 226–227, 234, 241, 243, 244, 246
religious Other 187–188, 190–191
Rescuing the Bible from Fundamentalism 200, 244
Resolution 3379: UN 28
revelation ix, xiv–xvi, xxiv–xxvii, 3, 7, 37–38, 40, 42–43, 45–46, 49, 59, 72–73, 78, 80, 92–97, 108, 128–129, 145–146, 150, 152–153, 155, 157–162, 171, 179, 181–186, 204, 207, 211, 213–214, 228, 248
Revenge of God: *The* 21
Robertson, Pat xxiii, 23, 27–28, 195
Roman Catholic ix, xviii, xxi, 25, 32, 130–134
Rushdie, Salman 96–97, 231

Sabbath 60–61, 64–71, 117, 122
Sadât: President Anwar al- 6, 11, 15
Saddam Hussein xxviii, 223
Safavid Shîʿism 178
Sajid, Abdul Jalil xvi–xvii
Samaritan text of the Pentateuch ix, 109–110, 112
Sanneh, Lamin 208

Sardar, Ziauddin xvi, 5, 33, 223–224, 228, 233, 244
Sarwar, Ghulam xiv, 151
Satan ix, 32, 45, 78, 80, 83, 88, 94–97, 104, 154–155, 215, 231
Satanic Verses: The ix, 96–97, 231
Scofield Reference Bible 25
scripture xiii–xiv, xviii, xxiv–xxv, xxvii, 6, 11, 33, 48, 58, 66–67, 70, 128–137, 139–142, 148, 153, 157–158, 198–200, 205, 211–214, 216–217, 232, 242, 243, 244, 248
Second Treatise of the Great Seth 168
Sennacherib 116
Septuagint ix, 109–112, 129–130, 132–134, 248
sermo 210
Seventh Day Adventist 71
Shâh Walî Allâh ix, 40–41, 43, 55, 251
sharî'a 5, 49, 73–75, 182, 248, 251, 252
Shari'ati, 'Alî 175–178
Sheikh al-Sha'râwî 8
Shî'a 52–55, 159, 178, 221, 247, 248, 250
Siddiqui, Ghayasuddin xvii
Sinai 61, 65–66, 68–69, 72, 246
Six Days War xix, 28–29
slavery xxi, 72
Smith, John 115
Son of Man 64–65, 122–126
South Africa xx, 187, 190–191
Spong, John Shelby· xxvii, 200–201, 204–206, 244
Stop the War Coalition 223
Ṣûfî 73, 181, 249
sunna 9, 49, 172, 182, 185, 248
Sunnî 52–55, 159, 247, 248, 249, 250, 251
Suyûtî, al- ix, 39–40, 51, 79, 152, 250, 251

Ṭabarî, al- 79, 94, 101, 251
tafsîr 11, 12, 78–79, 90–91, 93, 157, 213, 248, 249, 250
Tâhâ, Maḥmûd ix, 72–77, 175
Tâhâ Ḥusayn 179
taḥrîf 53–54, 264
Talibân 4
Tanakh 109
tanzîl ix, 12, 37–38, 72–75, 79, 97, 151, 154, 158–160, 163–164, 175, 213, 248, 252
taqwâ 186, 188–189, 191
Taurât See Torah
tawḥîd 159, 177, 188–190, 248
Tel Aviv xvi, 30
ten commandments *See* Decalogue
Tertullian 125, 135–136, 251
Tiller, John 203
Time magazine 29
Torah 51, 62, 66, 69–70, 128–129, 161, 246, 248
Trend of Rational Exegesis of the Qur'an: The 180
Trouble with Islam: The 18, 243
Twelfth Imam 178

Ubaî ibn Ka'b 51, 147, 149
Uhud: battle of 45–46
'Umar 47–50, 53–54, 57, 142–144, 147, 252
umm al-kitâb 156
uncertainty xxviii–xxix, 144, 172, 193, 196, 198, 203, 206, 209, 234–235
United Kingdom xvi, 17, 198, 207, 220, 222
United States of America xxiii, xxvi, xxix, 18, 21, 24–27, 29, 31, 59, 185, 193, 195, 200, 222–224
University of Cairo 6, 180, 182
Unthought in Contemporary Islamic Thought: The 184
USSR xviii
usury ix, 162–163
'Uthmân 44, 49, 53, 144–149, 181, 241, 252
'Uzzâ: al- 95–96, 165, 248

Verse of Stoning 47–54
Verse of the Sword ix, 11–12, 18, 57, 76
Vulgate 112, 132, 140, 210, 248

Wadud, Amina 192
Wahhâbî 4, 76, 224, 233, 251, 252
Wansbrough, John 152–153, 244
Warsh 90
Washington Post 28
Westminster Confession 61
White House xxiii, 23, 223

Yabneh 128
Yahweh xix–xx, 113, 115–116, 141, 248

Zaid ibn Thâbit xiv, 143–145, 147–148, 252
Zamakhsharî, al- 38, 79, 159–160, 252
Zionism 28
Zulaykha 82, 91